Language Assessment
of Hearing-Impaired School Age Children

Contributors

W. Gary Allinger	– Teacher
Cathy L. Berg	– *Communication Disorders Specialist
Kathleen Black	– Teacher
Carolyn Burns	– *Communication Disorders Specialist
Pam Forbush	– Teacher
Kerry Harder	– *Communication Disorders Specialist
Connie Jorgensen	– Teacher
Rosanne McCall	– *Communication Disorders Specialist
Kathy Oliver	– *Communication Disorders Specialist
Kay Opfer	– Teacher
Courtney Reed	– Teacher
Stan Serafin	– Teacher
Joclyn Stedman	– Teacher
Laura Stedwick	– *Communication Disorders Specialist
Elaine Talbot	– Teacher
Karen Taylor	– Teacher
Joe Whalen	– *Communication Disorders Specialist

*In Washington State, Speech-Language Pathologists and Audiologists who work for the schools are referred to as Communication Disorders Specialists, or CDS.

Language Assessment
of Hearing-Impaired School Age Children

Marie Thompson
Patricia Biro
Susan Vethivelu
Constance Pious
Nancy Hatfield

UNIVERSITY OF WASHINGTON PRESS
Seattle and London

Copyright © 1987 by the University of Washington Press
Manufactured in the United States of America

All rights reserved. No part of this publication may be reproduced or transmitted in any form or by any means, electronic or mechanical, including photocopy, recording, or any information storage or retrieval system, without permission in writing from the publisher.

Library of Congress Cataloging-in-Publication Data
Language assessment of hearing-imparied school age
    children.

    Bibliography: p.
    Includes index.
    1. Hearing impaired children—Language—Ability testing. I. Thompson, Marie
HV2391.L35   1987   371.91'2   87-13345
ISBN 0-295-96544-4

CONTENTS

	Page
ACKNOWLEDGMENTS	ix
PREFACE	xi

LANGUAGE ASSESSMENT: INTRODUCTION 3
   Purpose 3
   Organization of This Book 6

SECTION I: OVERVIEW OF LANGUAGE DEVELOPMENT 7
   The Major Components of Language. 8
   Overview of Language Development in
      Hearing-Impaired Children 21

SECTION II: EVALUATING TESTS. 27
   Purpose of a Language Assessment. 27
   Preliminary Issues. 32

SECTION III: SELECTING A TEST BATTERY 52
   What is a Test Battery? 52
   Considerations for Compiling a Test Battery 65
   Examples of Language Test Batteries 69
   Test Modification Techniques. 82

SECTION IV: ADMINISTERING THE TEST BATTERY. 84
   Testing the Hearing-Impaired Child:
      Special Considerations. 84
   General Considerations for Administering Tests. 89
   The Test Environment. 91
   Using Resource Personnel in Test Administration 93

Contents

SECTION V: OBTAINING AND USING LANGUAGE SAMPLES 96
    Introduction. 96
    Ways to Obtain a Language Sample. 97
    Guidelines for Obtaining Informal Language Samples. . . 103
    Recording and Analyzing Spontaneous Language. 106
    Examples of Using Expressive Language Recording
        and Analysis Forms. 146
    Summary 165

SECTION VI: TEST DESCRIPTIONS 166
    Introduction. . . . . 166 –178
    Test Descriptions 179

REFERENCES 277

TESTS DESCRIBED IN SECTION VI, LISTED ALPHABETICALLY
BY AUTHORS . . . . 284 – 286

GLOSSARY . . . . 287 – 290

INDEX 291

TABLES

		Page
Table 1:	Pragmatic Behaviors in Young Children	11
Table 2:	First Fourteen Morphemes	15
Table 3:	Examples of Syntactical Development Based on MLU	17
Table 4:	First Words Understood by Hearing Children 8 to 18 Months Old	19
Table 5:	Summary of Nelson's Analysis of First 50 Words Produced by 18 Children	20
Table 6:	Examples of the Language of Deaf Children	24
Table 7:	Language Assessment of Hearing-Impaired School Age Children: Reasons for Testing	30
Table 8:	Checklist for Evaluating Language Tests	42
Table 9:	Example of Completed Checklist	44
Table 10:	Example of Completed Checklist	48
Table 11:	Kendall Communicative Proficiency Scale Worksheet	56
Table 12:	Test Battery Summary Chart	70
Table 13:	Sample Test Battery: 3-Year-Old Hearing-Impaired Child Entering School	76
Table 14:	Sample Test Battery for Age Category: 3 to 5 Years Old	79
Table 15:	Sample Test Battery for Functional Age Level: 6 to 10 Years Old	80
Table 16:	Sample Test Battery for Functional Age Level: 11+ Years Old	81
Table 17:	Environmental Checklist	92
Table 18:	Language Sample and Analysis	108
Table 19:	TAGS Recording Form	111
Table 20:	Language Sample Recording Form	113
Table 21:	Language Analysis Form: Phase 1	115
Table 22:	Language Analysis Form: Phase 2	117
Table 23:	Language Analysis Form: Phase 3	121
Table 24:	Language Analysis Form: Phase 4	126
Table 25:	Language Analysis Form: Phase 5	131

Tables

Table 26:	Language Analysis Form: Phase 6.	136
Table 27:	Language Sample Recording Form: Larry.	148
Table 28:	Language Analysis Form, Phase 5: Larry	151
Table 29:	Language Sample Recording Form: Kate	158
Table 30:	Language Analysis Forms: Kate.	162
Table 31:	Alphabetical List of Tests.	168
Table 32:	Summary Chart by Test Characteristics	169
Table 33:	Test Battery Summary Chart (Repeat of Table 12) .	174

ACKNOWLEDGMENTS

We wish to thank the many people who have made this book possible. Much of the work was supported by Grant No. G008200501 from the United States Department of Education, Office of Special Education and Rehabilitative Services, to Marie Thompson, the senior author. The opinions expressed are those of the authors and do not necessarily reflect the position or policy of the U.S. Department of Education, and no official endorsement should be inferred. We deeply appreciate the work of the contributors to this volume, who met many times over 2 years to make the book comprehensive and relevant. At the University of Washington, the authors and contributors received generous assistance from Jana Ewing, Jacquolynn Roberts, Marge Bleifuss, Margaret Nissing, Jane Purtee, and Nancie Smith. Our excellent word processors, Susan Isoshima, Jeanne Inouye, Valerie Curnow, and Bonita Lenk, have patiently worked with the manuscript from rough draft to its final form. At the University of Washington Press, Juanita Pike and Veronica Seyd have been enthusiastic friends of the project. To all, we extend our gratitude.

PREFACE

This book is the product of a collaborative effort between public school speech-language pathologists and teachers and university educators, all of whom are professionally involved in the education of hearing-impaired students and others with problems in learning language. The book was developed in a series of work sessions over the course of 2 years. The role of the public school teachers of the hearing impaired, speech-language pathologists, and others was to bring to this project, based on their own experience, a strong sense of what is needed in the public school setting to help children who have a hearing loss, and who are learning English, to develop language as competently as possible, and to keep the work realistic in terms of what can be done in the schools. Throughout the work sessions, the authors, contributors, and consultants focused on the realities and constraints operating in schools and on suggesting ways that school personnel with responsibilities for hearing-impaired and other language delayed children can work together to make language assessments and intervention productive rather than overwhelming tasks. In this sense, the book is not concerned with abstractions or "ideal" but infeasible procedures. Rather, it acknowledges that language deficits are severe educational and social consequences of hearing impairment, that these problems are present in many hearing children, and that teachers and ancillary specialists face a challenging task in helping to remediate these deficits. The book does not approach teachers and speech-language pathologists as though they were linguists or psycholinguists. Expectations cannot be the same for both groups. Teachers and clinicians must perform as carefully as possible but efficiently. They must function under constraints of time and mandated requirements of their school districts and are not always free to function as researchers. It is preferable that they assess each student's language—even if it means using only commercial tests—than not assessing language at all, which happens all too often. The book was written because of the authors' strong belief that "...language, through communication and reading, forms the foundation of the educational career for all students" (Hasenstab & Horner, 1982, p. 140) and that hearing-impaired children and others with language delays <u>can</u> achieve language levels more like those of their nonhandicapped peers. In order to do this, however, they must first receive appropriate assessment, which is the first step toward developmentally sound programming. The book is designed for those who are required to evaluate the language of their students, but who may not be sophisticated in all areas of language nor have readily available all of the information they need about assessment. Professionals using this book will find that, although the emphasis is placed upon hearing-impaired children, the skills discussed and tests reviewed will be helpful in evaluating the language of other students with communicative delays. The work was supported by a Program Assistance Grant from the United States Department of Education, Office of Special Education and Rehabilitative Services, of which Marie Thompson, the senior author, was the principal investigator.

Language Assessment
of Hearing-Impaired School Age Children

LANGUAGE ASSESSMENT: INTRODUCTION

Purpose

The greatest deficit sustained by hearing-impaired persons occurs in language development and use. Research reports are full of results illustrating how severely language delayed most hearing-impaired students are, and these students rarely gain full use of the English language as do their hearing peers. One way to begin to attack this problem is for speech-language pathologists and teachers of the hearing impaired to work together as a team in order to assess language, develop intervention goals and objectives, and monitor progress of the hearing-impaired child's language. In order to facilitate such a plan, these professionals must be knowledgeable about both normal language and the language of the hearing impaired and know how to assess language.

We recognize that many teachers of the hearing impaired do not have a strong background in normal language development theory and assessment. Likewise, many speech-language pathologists are trained in language development and assessment procedures, but are unfamiliar with the special problems inherent in evaluating the language skills of hearing-impaired children. One result is that there are all too few professionals who are equipped to evaluate the language of hearing-impaired students. A second result is that hearing-impaired students are being taught language out of the normal sequence of development and at levels that are too difficult for them to absorb, and that the students' use of language or ability to communicate what they mean is being ignored. The consequence is a language system full of holes and groups of students who are totally frustrated. An additional problem occurs because many professionals believe that the language of hearing-impaired children cannot be evaluated unless all of the assessment tools are specifically developed for this group. Whether or not this view is accurate depends upon how the professional wishes to use the results. Adequate assessment is essential for developing appropriate intervention

Language Development

plans or strategies for individual students and ensuring that they make progress. Our intention is to provide speech-language pathologists and teachers of the hearing impaired who are responsible for assessing the language of hearing-impaired students within the school program with information that will assist them in working together to perform this important task within the educational program.

The purpose of this book is to provide teachers of the hearing impaired and speech-language pathologists with the information necessary to assess the English language skills of their hearing-impaired students reasonably and within the constraints imposed by time and school district regulations. The goal is to help professionals develop skills that will increase their flexibility, creativity, and effectiveness in meeting the language needs of these students. These skills include:

1) evaluating language tests
2) formulating goals for assessment
3) planning individualized test batteries
4) administering language tests appropriately
5) compiling and interpreting test results.

At the outset, it is important to recognize that assessment is only one part of the total management process for hearing-impaired children, and that language assessment is only one subset, albeit an important one, of the total assessment process. Under ordinary circumstances, language is global and intrinsic to all aspects of life, academic or otherwise. Assessment of parts of language, or language only under contrived conditions, is obviously less than ideal but may be the most efficient way to obtain information in the school setting. The teacher and clinician must remember this and analyze all results together, relating them as much as possible to the total language environment.

The objectives of language assessment will be: 1) to plan an appropriate placement, and, in that placement, 2) to obtain baseline measures of a student's strengths and weaknesses in language; 3) to plan intervention strategies based upon baseline measures; and 4) to monitor a student's progress to determine whether the intervention is effective. The focus of this book is to help speech-language pathologists and teachers of the hearing impaired develop the tools needed to do an effective job of language assessment of hearing-impaired children who are learning English, either through an oral or manually coded approach, because the largest group (approximately 96%) of children with a hearing loss are born to hearing parents and English is the primary language both at home and at school. Children from homes in which English is not the primary language are learning English at school.

Next, we must define the word "language" as used in this book; that is, what do you measure when you assess a student's language performance? Language in normally hearing children is commonly understood to mean the understanding (reception, comprehension) and use (expression, production) of a formal system in spoken form, as well as knowledge about rules that govern how language is used for communication, which include communicative intentions, presupposition, and social organization of discourse (Roth & Spekman, 1984). When language development follows a different course, as in the case of hearing-impaired children, the term "language" is not as clear-cut. In assessing the language of a hearing-impaired child, we could conceivably be measuring any or all of the following skills: speechreading, speech, use of residual hearing, reading, writing, or signing. To further complicate matters, there may be more than one language involved: English, American Sign Language, Spanish (in a Spanish-speaking home), and so on.

This book emphasizes assessment of receptive and expressive <u>English in simultaneously signed/spoken form</u> as well as the communicative/social framework of language. In selecting this emphasis, we do not imply that the other language skills listed above are not important or need not be assessed. These skills are certainly crucial to a child's success in academics and in communicating with others, and should be assessed. Likewise, we realize that a child's ability to use residual hearing, speech, and speechreading affects his or her skills in receiving and using English in any form. Because these skills are so important, we believe they need special attention and should be addressed separately. It is our contention, however, that a hearing-impaired child's development of

Language Development

the ability to receive and use English in spoken/signed form, although delayed, most closely parallels the case of the hearing child developing receptive and expressive skills in spoken English.

Obviously, a working knowledge of normal language development is necessary for assessing language skills effectively. Although a brief review of normal language development is provided below, extensive background knowledge is essential and should be acquired through appropriate coursework and training. Numerous references about language and language development are provided for the reader in the reference section at the end of the book.

Organization of This Book

Following a brief overview of language development, the book is organized into sections which constitute "steps" in the assessment process. The final section, <u>Section VI</u>, contains descriptions and critiques of available language tests. The "steps" in the assessment process are:

>Evaluating Tests
>Selecting a Test Battery
>Administering the Test Battery
>Obtaining and Using Language Samples

By becoming skilled in each of these areas, teachers and speech-language pathologists will be able to effectively obtain the baseline measures upon which to build appropriate intervention strategies and to use these same techniques for later monitoring of progress.

SECTION I: OVERVIEW OF LANGUAGE DEVELOPMENT

Language includes both knowledge about and appropriate use of rules that enable us, as humans, to communicate with each other in our society. As adults, we may not be able to describe these rules, but we use them every day when we read, write, or talk to others. Children must eventually learn these adult rules but cannot and do not learn the adult forms of expressing them immediately. Normal hearing infants begin to learn about their language during the first few months of life. They attend to adults talking and smiling and begin the process of turn-taking even though it may be limited to a returned smile or gurgle (Snow, 1977). They listen, watch, and learn more about the entire communication process and begin to use their first words at about the same time they begin to walk (Berko Gleason, 1985). Sometime during the second year, they begin to combine their single words into two-word combinations without the grammatical modifications required in adult language (Brown, 1973). By the time they reach kindergarten age, normally developing children have a vocabulary of approximately 8,000 words and most of the basic grammatical forms of their language (Berko Gleason, 1985). This type of cumulative learning suggests that normal hearing children begin to understand the language system as infants and gradually, systematically begin to use it expressively. They <u>comprehend</u> certain language constructs (receptive skills) before actually <u>producing</u> them (expressive skills). For example, a child will be able to point to or pick up a shoe or ball on command before producing the word shoe or ball. As a child develops better understanding about her language, she begins to attain linguistic competence or inner understanding about the rules, including those that control social discourse as well as the grammar, of her community. The use of these rules on a daily basis is known as performance.

Language Development

The Major Components of Language

When children are learning their language system, they must learn about a variety of parts or subsystems such as phonology, morphology, lexicon, semantics, and syntax. They must learn not only how to combine these components into a comprehensible language system, but also how to use this language system in appropriate ways on different occasions with different individuals or groups of people.

Use (pragmatics)

Pragmatics is the framework within which other subsystems of language operate. It is the nonlinguistic part of language that assists the listener in interpreting the speaker's intent, because understanding a communication depends upon more than decoding grammar alone (Dore, 1976; Kramer, 1977). According to Roth and Spekman (1984), there are three major aspects of the use of language: a) the functions of language or why people speak, b) the way in which people make decisions about the language form they will use in order to reach the communication goal they have in mind, and c) the social organization of discourse. Muma (1978) sums it up by stating that pragmatics is concerned with the rules that most people know and use to determine "...who says what to whom, how, why, when and in what situation" (p. 137).

(a) The functions of language or communicative intentions have, in the past, been identified as asking a question (interrogative), making a statement (declarative), making a strong statement or demand (imperative), or expressing excitement or surprise (exclamative). More recently, functions of language have been identified in more social terms that refer to interaction and personal control (Halliday, 1975; Dore, 1975; Lucas, 1980). The social use of language provides a basis for discussing language in terms of the "speaker's" goals or communicative intentions. These intentions are identified as separate from grammatical structure (Dore, 1975) and therefore can be observed and discussed either with or without linguistic corollaries. Recent studies have suggested that very young children are successful in expressing a variety of intentions when only at the one-word stage (Halliday, 1975; Dore, 1975; Bates, 1976). They are simultaneously learning a grammatical system and the ways they must modify this system according to the social demands of the situation. Examples of communicative intentions of young children are presented in Table 1. Although they are presented separately in terms of linguistic and nonlinguistic behaviors, it is important to recognize that a linguistic communication is often accompanied by a gesture.

(b) <u>The second aspect of use</u>, <u>language form</u>, or <u>presupposition</u>, refers to the entire situational context: who is being spoken to, how much information is known and unknown by the listener, whether the objects or persons discussed are present or absent, and whether the speaker's action is initiated or is made in response to someone else's message. New information is obligatory whereas given information is optional. There is a tendency, in the "typical" English sentence, to start off with information which is shared by speaker and hearer—called given information—and to move to "new" information. Given information may have been supplied by previous conversation, or by the context (non-verbal).

For example, if two people are going for a walk, and they see some houses built by one person's grandfather, there are two possibilities. If they are already having a conversation about the person's grandfather, the comment would be "He (My grandfather) built those houses." "He" (Grandfather) is the given information, "houses" the new information. If the two people see the houses, without previous reference to the grandfather, the comment might be "They (Those houses) were built by my grandfather." "They" (houses) is given by context, and "grandfather" is new information. The new information is signaled by stress and, often as in this case, by using the passive voice. Thus, even if the sentence is organized differently, as in "My <u>grandfather</u> built those houses," the stress indicates which information is new.

You can view the passive voice as a way of keeping the given information to the left of the verb. Thus, if you have the sentence "The President stepped off the airplane," the next sentence would probably not be "Newspapermen immediately surrounded him," but rather "He was immediately surrounded by newspapermen." The speaker or writer assumes that the listener can recover the information, and so the given information may be pronominalized, as in the above sentence, where "he" is substituted for "president." A speaker may also delete given or old information, as in this dialogue: "What's your name?" "Tommy." The second person has deleted the unnecessary information, "My name is."

Hearing-impaired children often do not understand the relations between sentences and that only given (or old) information can be deleted. They delete new information, which produces communication that is difficult or impossible to interpret. Or their writing may contain no given information to link sentences together so that the sentences are not cohesive but appear to be random observations. This may be inadvertently fostered by teaching. The class goes on an outing together, then comes back and writes about it. The teacher asks "What happened first?" "What happened next?" If only facts are written down, without sentence connection, the story may come out as an unrelated list. The students get the impression that each sentence is independent, that one does not shape the next or that one could be embedded in another.

The abbreviated language and slang we use with peers is not used in more formal circumstances. Lakoff (1977) refers to this as a social signaling function, a formal register used with superiors and strangers and an informal register with close friends or those believed to be socially inferior. A person must consider all factors about the contextual situation and his listeners in order to determine the appropriate "use" of language. "Social signaling" is learned intuitively by normal hearing children who begin to hear these differences from birth, but it must be assessed and often taught to hearing-impaired children.

(c) The third aspect of language use, the social organization of discourse, refers to social interaction and communication. This social organization refers to "discourse mechanisms" (McGinnis, 1985, p. 108) that assist people in structuring a variety of communications. Such mechanisms include greetings, topic continuity or topic change, beginning and ending a conversation, repairing communication when it breaks down or is interrupted, and turn-taking, which is learned at a very early age. Pragmatic aspects of communication must be considered at all age levels, especially when one is assessing and developing intervention plans for those who are not developing language normally, such as students who are hearing impaired.

Table 1

PRAGMATIC BEHAVIORS IN YOUNG CHILDREN

Category	Definition	Examples Non-linguistic	Linguistic
Requesting	Solicitation of a service from a listener:		
Object requests	Gestures or utterances that direct the listener to provide some object for the child.	C holds out hand toward car mother is playing with and vocalizes loudly.	C reaches for bottle on table, says "milk."
Action requests	Gestures or utterances that direct the listener to act upon some object in order to make it move. The action, rather than the object, is the focus of the child's interest.	C, unable to push a peg through hole, utters "uh uh" while looking at mother.	C sitting on swing says "push."
Information requests	Gestures or utterances that direct the listener to provide information about an object, action, or location.	C brings a worm to mother, looks up inquisitively.	C picks up book, looks at mother, and says "book?" with rising terminal contour. Mother answers, "Right, it's a book."

			Examples	
Category	Definition		Non-linguistic	Linguistic
Greeting	Gestures or utterances subsequent to a person's entrance that express recognition.		C sees mailman through the window and waves.	C says "hi" when teacher enters room.
Transferring	Gestures intended to place an object in another person's possession. (May be accompanied by an utterance.)		C hands father a book, nods, and says "da."	C hands mother her key, says "here."
Showing off	Gestures or utterances that appear to be used to attract attention.		C repeatedly sticks tongue out at mother, laughing.	C says "lookit" before turning somersault.
Acknowledging	Gestures or utterances that provide notice that the listener's previous utterances were received.		Mother asks, "See the doggy?" and C nods.	Father asks "Want a spanking?" C shakes head and says "uh-uh."
Answering	Gestures or utterances from the child in response to a request for information from the listener.		Mother asks, "Show mommy your nose?" C points to nose.	Mother points to a picture of a dog and asks, "What's that?" C answers "bow-wow."

Labeling	Word utterance from child while attending to object or event. Child does not address adult or wait for a response.	C touches a doll's eyes and says "eyes."
Repeating	Repetition of part or all of previous adult utterance. Child does not wait for a response.	C overhears mother's utterance of "doctor" and says "doctor"
Practicing	Use of word or prosodic pattern in absence of any specific object or event. Child does not address adult. Does not await response.	C utters "Daddy" when he is not present. C vocalizes while playing with telephone as if having a conversation.
Calling or attention getting	Calling adult's name loudly and awaiting response, or child waves to or taps adult in order to gain attention.	C taps adult while standing beside her, looking up. C shouts "mama" to his mother across the room.
Negating	Denial, resistance to, or rejection by child of adult statement, request, or question.	C shakes head (no) when mother says, "O.K., time to go." C shakes head (no) when mom asks, "Did you push baby?" C, when his mother attempts to put on his shoe, repeatedly pushes it away. C says "no! no!" and runs away. C says "no" or "no push." Mother attempts to feed C a bite of vegetable; C loudly says "No-no-no."

Language Development

Form: Phonology, Morphology, and Syntax

Phonology: Each language is composed of a variety of speech sounds that, when combined in specific, ordered ways, form the basic words or lexicon of a given language. Speech sounds that are specific to a given language are referred to as phonemes because they are the smallest unit of sound that can signal a difference in what is being said, such as the difference between b_ed and b_id. Phonemes are families of sounds that are very similar (Owens, 1984), and the study of phonology includes a review of these phonemes, their distribution and sequencing, and the different ways in which they are produced. Young children's understanding of the phonological system is usually expressed through speech production. Because speech production in hearing-impaired children is usually considered to be of such importance that it is treated separately, it will not be addressed in this book. For an excellent treatment of this subject, the reader is referred to Ling, 1976.

Morphology: The smallest meaningful unit of language is a morpheme. The rules for forming words by combining morphemes is called morphology. There are two types of morphemes: free and bound. A free morpheme carries its own meaning and can stand alone; e.g., bird, girl, run. A bound morpheme does not carry meaning by itself and therefore cannot stand alone; e.g., -ly, -ness, -s. Bound and free morphemes are combined in order to develop the variety of words in our language; e.g., walk, walk_ed; girl, girl_s; great, great_est. Brown (1973) reported on young children's acquisition of their first 14 morphemes as evidenced by use in the language of three children he studied extensively. He observed a reliable order of acquisition by using a criterion of 90% correct usage. Table 2 suggests the developmental stage and approximate age range during which specific morphologic structures are acquired by young children and reflects the findings of several researchers.

Syntax: Within the English language, there is a certain word order or syntax that is standard; for example, it is appropriate to say "The girl is wearing the red sweater," not *"The is girl wearing is the sweater red." Developmentally, somewhere around 18 months of age, young children begin to

Table 2

FIRST FOURTEEN MORPHEMES

*Developmental Stage	Approx. Age	Morpheme	Example	Meaning
II	27-30 months	-ing	me play<u>ing</u>	ongoing activity, presently occurring
		plural	that book<u>s</u>	number agreement
		in	cookie monster <u>in</u> there	containment
III	31-34 months	on	doggie <u>on</u> car	support
		possessive	mommy'<u>s</u> shoe	possession
V	41-46 months	regular past	He walk<u>ed</u>.	earlier in time relative to time of occurrence
		irregular past	She <u>came</u>. We <u>went</u>.	
		regular third person singular	It jump<u>s</u>. She play<u>s</u>.	occurs with regularity
		articles: "a"	That's <u>a</u> puppy.	indefinite
		"the"	Here is <u>the</u> paper.	definite
		contractable copula "be"	Here'<u>s</u> my coat. There'<u>s</u> Johnny.	number agreement
V+	47+ months	contractable auxiliary "be"	They'<u>re</u> playing. I'<u>m</u> coming.	ongoing activity, presently occurring
		uncontractable copula "be"	(Who's here?) I <u>am</u>. Are they the boys?	number agreement
			<u>Was</u> that a dog?	earlier in time
		uncontractable auxiliary "be"	<u>Is</u> he running?	number agreement; ongoing activity, presently occurring
			<u>Were</u> they at home?	earlier in time
		irregular third person singular	<u>Does</u> the dog bite?	number agreement

Adapted from: Brown (1973), deVilliers and deVilliers (1973), and Clark and Clark (1977)

* Included are only those developmental stages when morphemes reportedly are acquired.

Language Development

produce two-word utterances that are stated in the appropriate word order that an adult would use in order to convey a specific semantic relation such as:

agent + action:	boy run	N+V
action + object:	push wagon	V+N
agent + object:	mommy truck	N+N
patient + action:	doll broke	N+V
action + locative:	sit chair	V+N
entity + locative:	cup table	N+N
possessor + possessed:	mommy sock	N+N
entity + attribute:	coat blue	N+M
demonstrative + entity:	that ball	M+N

N = noun
V = verb
M = modifier

As children mature and their knowledge about the world increases, the length and complexity of their sentences gradually increase, always following the general rules of their native language. As sentences increase in length, the complexity of the language within the sentences increases also (see Table 3). As the child's language complexity increases, the number of nouns, verbs, and modifiers expands, thus increasing the richness of his or her language. Normal hearing children, with constant auditory input, are able to use appropriate word order and, at the same time, are able to generate a variety of sentences they have never heard because they have learned the rules of syntax and the correct semantic-syntactic relationships.

Language Development

Table 3

EXAMPLES OF SYNTACTICAL DEVELOPMENT BASED ON MLU*

MLU	APPROX. AGE	TYPE OF UTTERANCE	PRIMARY SYNTACTICAL FEATURES
1.7 - 2.2	18 - 24 months	"boy chair" "boy walk"	Uninflected forms; 2-word semantic relations
2.2 - 2.7	24 - 30 months	"boy on chair" "boy walking"	Emergence of grammatical morphemes such as preposition or "ing" form
2.7 - 3.5	30 - 36 months	"boy sitting on chair" "he walking"	More consistent use of grammatical forms, wider variety. Primarily active, declarative sentences.
3.5 - 4.0	36 - 42 months	"He sat on my chair." "They are not walking." "Where are they walking?" "Make them walk!"	Transformation of basic sentence into: negative sentence, question form, imperative.
4.0 - 5.2	42 - 50 months	"They are walking up the hill." "He doesn't want to walk."	More consistent use of auxiliaries and obligatory "do," use of subordinate clauses and phrases.
5.2 - 6.0	52 - 60 months	"When it's raining the boys don't walk." "They walk fast because they'll get wet."	More complex sentence structures, use of dependent and independent clauses.

*Mean Length of Utterance

Language Development

Content: (semantics and lexicon)

Content refers to both the words (lexicon or vocabulary) known and used by an individual and the semantic component, or the rules that govern the meanings conveyed by words within a given syntactic structure. "A word does not contain a unitary, unalterable, or static meaning" (Wiig & Semel, 1980); rather, meanings change as words are combined or as new words, such as slang, are added. For instance, the meaning of the word "glasses" changes: "I can read better when I wear my glasses." "The dirty glasses are in the sink." "The glass in the window is broken." "John hit the ball so hard, his bat was broken." "John was a big hit at the party." Consider the following list of words and identify the "verbs."

        hit   walk   bat   name   leave

This is really an impossible task when words are presented in isolation because each of the above words changes meaning and grammatical identification when placed in a different relationship with other words. The meaning of relational terms such as yesterday, today, and tomorrow is difficult to learn because these words have no single referent. Instead, each time the word is used, its meaning changes depending upon the specific time it refers to. "You know what, Mommy? Yesterday today was tomorrow."*

Children's first words relate very much to themselves and their immediate environment. Consequently, the very young child will first learn to understand the names of mother, father, siblings, family dog or cat, clothing, and favorite food and toys, as illustrated in Table 4, and to produce these same categories of words when he or she first starts to talk, as reflected in Table 5. As children mature and gain greater cognitive skills, both their knowledge about the various meanings of words as well as their actual lexicon or vocabulary increase.

---

*Elizabeth, age 3-1/2 years, from deVilliers and deVilliers, 1978.

Language Development

Table 4

FIRST WORDS UNDERSTOOD BY HEARING CHILDREN 8 TO 18 MONTHS OLD

First Words Understood: 8 to 12 Months

mommy	shoe
daddy	ball
names of family members and pets (often known idiosyncratically)	cookie
	juice
bye-bye	no-no
baby	wave bye-bye

First Words Understood: 12 to 14 Months

hi	hair	chair (highchair)
kitty (cat)	come here	book
dog (doggy)	sit down	socks
cup	stand up	dance
cracker	get up	patty-cake
care	stop that	peek-a-boo
eyes	hug	kiss
ears	water	bring
feet	drink	give mommy, me...
kiss me	throw the ball	brush your hair

First Words Understood: 14 to 18 Months

milk	bed	coat (jacket, sweater)
spoon	cereal	apple
telephone	bottle	teeth
keys	horse	brush your hair, teeth
blanket	hat	where is, are...
go get...	show me	don't touch
let's go...	do you want...	open, close the door
find	go get...	

From the book THE FIRST THREE YEARS OF LIFE by Burton L. White. © 1975. Reprinted by permission of the publisher, Prentice-Hall, Inc. Englewood Cliffs, New Jersey.

Table 5

SUMMARY OF NELSON'S ANALYSIS OF FIRST 50 WORDS PRODUCED BY 18 CHILDREN

	Word Category	Example	% of 1st 10 words	% of 1st 50 words
I.	Nominals—Specific (total)		24	14
	People	"mommy"		
	Animals	"Dizzy" (name of pet)		
	Objects	"car"		
II.	Nominals—General (total)		41	51
	Objects	"ball"		
	Substances	"milk," "snow"		
	Animals & people	"doggie," "girl"		
	Letters & numbers	"e," "two"		
	Abstractions	"good," "birthday"		
	Pronouns	"he," "that"		
III.	Action Words (total)		16	13
	Demand-descriptive	"go," "bye-bye," "up"		
	Notice	"look," "hi"		
IV.	Modifiers (total)		8	9
	Attributes	"big," "red," "pretty"		
	States	"hot," "dirty," "all gone,"		
	Locatives	"there," "outside"		
	Possessives	"mine"		
V.	Personal-Social (total)		5	8
	Assertions	"no," "yes," "want"		
	Social-expressive	"please," "ouch"		
VI.	Function words (total)		6	4
	Questions	"what," "where"		
	Miscellaneous	"is," "to," "for"		

Note: Data from "Structure and Strategy in Learning to Talk" by K. Nelson, *Monographs of the Society for Research in Child Development*, 1973, 38, No. 149. Reprinted by permission of the Society for Research in Child Development.

Language Development

Summary of Language Acquisition

The following summary of language acquisition offered by Hasenstab and Horner (1982) must be considered whenever any form of language evaluation is to occur.

- Language acquisition is developmental.
- Hearing-impaired children and most language delayed children are more similar to than they are different from normal children in the acquisition process.
- Hearing-impaired children and most language delayed children have the potential for acquiring language and its various communicative functions in speaking/signing, reading, writing and thinking.
- Language systems are rule-governed and observations of instances of these rules can assist the diagnostician in formulating a hypothesis regarding a child's language system.
- Language acquisition is a hypothesis testing process.
- The sequence of language acquisition is fairly stable while the rate is variable.
- Pragmatic, semantic, syntactic [morphologic] and phonologic components are interactive in language/communicative acquisition. [p. 140]

Overview of Language Development in Hearing-Impaired Children

The acquisition of signed language, American Sign Language (ASL), by young deaf children of deaf parents follows the same general course as that of hearing children in comparable language-learning contexts. Like hearing children, deaf children in a signing environment babble at approximately 6 months of age - but with their hands. At about 1 year, they begin to produce single signs. Two-word signed utterances are formed at about 18 to 24 months of age. The rate of deaf children's increase in mean length of utterance (MLU) in signed language parallels that of hearing children acquiring English as a native language, and the acquisition of certain syntactic mechanisms, e.g., negation, follows a course similar to that for English (Siple, 1978). By early childhood, deaf children of deaf parents are native "speakers" of the signed language in which they were immersed from birth.

For the hearing-impaired child of hearing parents, language development is quite a different matter. Because the use of the auditory system is implicit in acquiring spoken language, the defective hearing of congenitally hearing-impaired children (or those who acquire a loss at an early age) often presents an insurmountable obstacle to their

Language Development

learning language as do their normal hearing peers. Even if parents continue to provide verbal input, the language message may be terribly distorted before it reaches the point where the child processes it. For normal hearing parents, the addition of signs is usually a difficult task, and they often learn and use signs imperfectly (Swisher & Thompson, 1985). In either case the language input to the child is severely restricted.

The acquisition of English skills by both groups of deaf children, those with deaf parents and those with hearing parents, lags far behind that of their hearing peers. In a study of reading achievement, Furth (1966) found that by age 11, only 1% of deaf children were functionally literate (having reading scores of Grade 4.9 or better), and that even by age 16, only 12% of deaf children reached this level. Similar findings were described in the 1969 Annual Survey of Hearing-Impaired Children and Youth: by age 15-1/2 to 16-1/2, the mean reading achievement grade equivalent was 3.5 (Brooks, 1978). Later studies have concurred in the conclusion that deafness from an early age is universally associated with serious problems in reading English (e.g., Conrad, 1977; Hammermeister, 1971; Berko Gleason, 1985). The Winter, 1985 issue of the Gallaudet Research Institute Newsletter states that the median achievement level of 14-year-old deaf children is third grade in reading comprehension and sixth grade in math computation; no figures are given for math problem-solving, which involves language comprehension (Harkins, 1985). Although tests of reading achievement do not measure language ability, they do reflect the reader's knowledge about and understanding of the language system.

Typically, hearing-impaired people also perform poorly in the expression of English, producing written and spoken language that is simpler and more stereotyped than that of normally hearing people. Reviews of the kinds of errors made and their prevalence may be found in Quigley and Paul (1984) and Swisher (1976). In her review article, Swisher concluded that: 1) Compared to hearing persons, deaf people use shorter sentences for spoken and written language and they overuse nouns and articles, with frequent errors of omission, substitution, addition, and word order. 2) Functors (small words such as a, the, an) are especially difficult for the deaf, leading to spoken and written output which is frequently referred to as "telegraphic." 3) Deaf children use phrases or sentences in a stereotyped manner (see Table 6).

Cooper (1967) noted the superiority of hearing subjects, compared to a group of hearing-impaired students, in the ability to apply morphological rules, pointing out that the average 19-year-old deaf student could not compare to the average 9- to 10-year-old hearing student. Quigley, Smith, and Wilbur (1974) found similar retardation in hearing-impaired children's understanding of all aspects of relative clauses, and Power and Quigley (1973) found that at 17 and 18 years of age, nearly 40 percent of their hearing-impaired population failed to understand the passive voice. Additional studies of hearing-impaired students provide similar information. However, although available research results suggest that hearing-impaired children's language development is similar to but slower than that of normal hearing children, no complete developmental sequence of language in hearing-impaired children has been established.

It must be emphasized that an overriding characteristic of the hearing-impaired population is its diversity. The actual language performance of deaf children varies greatly from child to child, according to factors such as: age at onset, type, degree, and etiology of the hearing impairment; the child's age at identification of the hearing loss; type of language input the child receives; education; parental acceptance of deafness; parental hearing status; and hearing aid use. In fact, as Meadow (1978) points out, variations within groups of deaf subjects are often greater than variations between deaf subjects and hearing control groups.

Pragmatics

Little research has been done in the area of pragmatics with the hearing-impaired population. Curtis, Prutting, and Lowell (1979) and Schirmer (1985) examined very young hearing-impaired children and found that these children used the same range of nonverbal pragmatic strategies as normal hearing children but that they were delayed compared to hearing peers of the same chronological age. Although extensive research

Table 6

EXAMPLES OF THE LANGUAGE OF DEAF CHILDREN

Structural Environment in Which Construction Occurs	Description of Construction	Example Sentences
Verb system	Verb deletion	The cat under the table.
	Be or have deletion	John sick. The girl a ball.
	Be-have confusion	Jim have sick.
	Incorrect pairing of auxiliary with verb markers	Tom has pushing the wagon.
	By deletion (passive voice)	The boy was pushed the girl.
Negation	Negative outside the sentence	Beth made candy no.
Conjunction	Marking only first verb	Beth threw the ball and Jean catch it.
	Conjunction deletion	Joe bought ate the apple.
Complementation	Extra for	For to play baseball is fun.
	Extra to in POSS-ing complement	John goes to fishing.
	Infinitive in place of gerund	John goes to fish.
	Incorrectly inflected infinitive	Bill likes to played baseball.
	Unmarked infinitive without to	Jim wanted go.
Relativization	NPs where whose is required	I helped the boy's mother was sick.
	Copying of referent	John saw the boy who the boy kicked the ball.
Question formation	Copying	Who a boy gave you ball?
	Failure to apply subject auxiliary	Who the baby did love?
	Incorrect inversion	Who TV watched?
Question formation, Negation	Overgeneralization of contraction rule	I amn't tired. Bill willn't go.
Relativization, Conjunction	Object-object deletion	John chased the girl and he scared. (John chased the girl. He scared the girl.)
	Object-subject deletion	The dog chased the girl had on a red dress. (The dog chased the girl. The girl had on a red dress.)
All types of sentences	Forced subject-verb-object pattern	The boy pushed the girl. (The boy was pushed by the girl.)

Source: Quigley, Wilbur, Power, Montanelli, & Steinkamp (1976)

still needs to be accomplished in the area of pragmatics and the school-age hearing-impaired population, many teachers recognize and discuss their students' inappro- priate use of language. Specific examples of these problems have been provided by Kolzak (1983):

Turn-taking. Hearing-impaired children, especially those with severe losses, do not initiate a communication. If, on occasion, they do initiate, they do not have the skills to take turns in order to maintain the interaction. Very often, they do not understand the social use of language and therefore do not exchange greetings or use "please," "thank you," and "you're welcome" as required in certain situations.

Sustaining or repairing conversations. Beyond turn-taking, hearing-impaired children often are unable to carry on an extended conversation considering the original communicator's frame of reference and interests and using a variety of appropriate structures: questions, statements, exclamations. They have great difficulty asking the other speaker/communicator for clarification, repetition, or confirmation; e.g., "Please repeat that," "What did you say?" "Could you write that [number, page, name] down for me?" "Did you say the report was due tomorrow or Wednesday?" [Kolzak, 1983, pp. 134-135].

Conclusion

As noted earlier, language deficits are the most serious consequences of hearing impairment: they affect a child's educational progress and social development. From what we know, based on research and the cumulative experience of professionals who work with this population, hearing-impaired children can develop language in the same sequence experienced by their hearing peers, although often at a slower rate of acquisition (e.g., Schirmer, 1985), and that "improving language skills" is the most often chosen goal of deaf students attending college (Ouellette, 1985, cited in Report on Education Research). Therefore, it is their right to be provided with adequate evaluation of their language in reference to normal language development in order that appropriate developmental language plans for remediation can be established and monitored. This is important because, as Luetke-Stahlman

Language Development

(1982) points out, the goal of those educating hearing-impaired children is to teach English literacy skills that will lead to a job and social skills equal to the student's intellectual potential. This goal has implications for the child's lifelong adjustment.

SECTION II: EVALUATING TESTS

Purpose of A Language Assessment

A well formulated language assessment plan is essential for gathering relevant information and to assist you in making decisions about an individual student's goals and objectives. It can assist you in determining whether or not a student's language is deviant or delayed and in what particular area(s) problems are present. An accurate picture of the child's abilities and deficits should lead to an appropriate language program and monitoring process for each student. Making a language assessment plan is not a once-only procedure, however. Language assessment must be an ongoing process, and is not "finished" after a single instance. Each time you intend to assess a child's language, you will need to consider all of the factors that are included in the initial plan.

Although, as Bates has observed, "...language is acquired and used in a social context" (1976, p. 412), "...the other psycholinguistic components should not be ignored" (Hasenstab, 1983, p. 96). What is needed then is an approach that, as much as possible, allows language to be studied or assessed within a variety of contexts and uses communicative interaction as the framework within which grammatical competency is analyzed. As Hasenstab states, "The pragmatic base fosters an understanding of the purpose, function and interactive nature of each of the components" (1983, p. 96).

The most obvious technique to use in order to evaluate the variety of ways in which language is used within different contexts is to obtain the spontaneous language sample, which is "...the centerpiece of child language assessment" (Gallagher, 1983, p. 2) and is discussed in detail in Section V of this book. Using the language sample, however, presupposes that each and every child is able to use all of the subcomponents of language in an expressive fashion. Such a supposition is not necessarily accurate. For example, the very young hearing-impaired child may be able to demonstrate certain pragmatic intentions, such as requesting or greeting, only through gestural communication or gesture and vocalization;

Selecting A Battery

an orthopedically impaired student may not be able to speak or sign. However, it is essential to obtain information about what these students comprehend when a communication is transmitted _to_ them from another person using a conventional language system and before intervention strategies are developed. For children from whom an expressive language sample can be obtained, it is important to determine how much language they understand beyond that which they are using. For example, a hearing-impaired student may not use the plural form in a sample of expressive language. Is this because the student does not understand the concept of plurality, because he understands it and chooses not to use it, or because he has not been encouraged to use the plural form on a regular basis? An initial step in attempting to analyze what these various students understand is to evaluate their receptive language skills. Thus, tools to assess receptive language need to be part of every teacher's and clinician's repertoire.

Knowledge about a variety of expressive language assessment tools (in addition to the language sample) may assist the teacher or clinician in obtaining information about selective language subcomponents. For example, information from an expressive language test may demonstrate that within a structured situation, with contextual cues, a student can correctly use tense markers but does not do so during unstructured communicative interactions. Such information provides valuable clues for developing intervention strategies. For, if this student is to be completely communicatively effective, adding tense markers during normal discourse will assist in clarifying the student's information to the listener.

Knowledge about a variety of tests and what they can and cannot help with is critical for all teachers and clinicians because tests that are appropriate for one child may be totally inappropriate for another. A thorough evaluation of a spontaneous language sample may provide all of the information necessary to develop intervention plans for one student but may provide only partial information about another.

Language Tests

Language tests are those tests that have been specifically designed to analyze the various areas of language--form, content, and use--both receptively and expressively. They may be commercially developed or written by teachers and/or speech-language pathologists. They can be formal or informal, such as an expressive language sample. The main point is that they were designed to evaluate some aspect of language. Before you select tests to use in language assessment, there are several steps that will assist you in selecting them.

Review your reasons for testing. It is important to determine why you are testing the student before compiling a test battery (see Table 7). If you are testing in order to provide numerical results to your school district or state office, it is important to select standardized tests that are normed on a similar hearing-impaired population; if they are not, be prepared to justify your interpretation of the results. It also means that you must follow the test protocol exactly because any deviation from the protocol will diminish the validity of the quoted norms. However, if you are interested in obtaining baseline data for a particular student so that you can establish his or her developmental level and provide intervention plans, as well as measure progress, you may want to modify existing tests, use parts of many tests, and include tests you or other teachers/clinicians have developed. Make the tests your own and make them useful.

Review many tests. Before you can assemble an appropriate test battery, you must be familiar with a wide range of language tests that are available and select for yourself a variety of "good" tests to have on hand.

Once you have a number of tests on hand and have established why you are testing, there is only one way to determine, to your own satisfaction, if a test is appropriate. READ THE MANUAL. This may not always be a pleasant task, but it is the only way to evaluate a test's strengths and weaknesses. The test descriptions in this book will help guide you in choosing a test to examine, but you cannot avoid the task of reading that test's manual. If upon reading the manual you are satisfied that the test is appropriate for your purposes, then you must practice giving it and become skilled at using it. (See Section IV: Administering the Test Battery.)

Table 7

LANGUAGE ASSESSMENT OF HEARING-IMPAIRED SCHOOL AGE CHILDREN: REASONS FOR TESTING

WHY: To compare the hearing-impaired student's language to:
  (1) the language of those who have normal hearing and/or
  (2) the language of those who have a hearing loss or
  (3) his own past record

- To provide numerical scores to school districts or state offices
- To identify a developmental language level and specific language targets for remediation purposes
- To measure efficacy of intervention based upon change in language behavior

---

WHAT: Content: Lexicon and semantics

Form: Phonology (units of sound)
Morphology (units of meaning)
Syntax (ways in which units are combined)

Use: The different ways language is used

Receptive Language: How well units of language or combined units of language are understood

Expressive Language: How well and in what form language is produced

---

HOW: Standardized Tests
Used strictly, adhering to all stated rules in order to obtain scores.
Used informally in order to gain more information about an individual student

Non-standardized Tests
Teacher made; Criterion referenced

Developmental Scales

Observation of the student in different situations

Obtain tests. It may be difficult to obtain a variety of language tests to examine, but there are several ways to do so: 1) consult with other professionals in your district (school psychologists, speech-language pathologists, and/or teachers) to determine which language tests they have access to; 2) contact your local speech and hearing clinic (private or university); or 3) write to publishers of specific tests, who are sometimes willing to send a sample of the test and the manual for review.

Evaluate tests. At this point you need more information about how to evaluate the "goodness" of a test. As you read the test manual, keep in mind seven basic questions:

- Why do I want to test?
- For whom was the test designed? (Who is the norm group?)
- What does the test claim to measure? (Does it measure receptive or expressive skills, morphology, syntax, semantics, or pragmatics?)
- Does the test truly measure what it claims to measure? (Is it valid?)
- Are the test results consistent? (Is the test reliable?)
- How usable is the test? (Evaluate factors such as cost, length of time to administer and score, group vs. individual testing, etc.)
- Will a portion of it provide additional information 1) not found elsewhere or 2) to supplement information found through informal means?

Several of these questions contain statistical/testing terms you may not be familiar with, e.g., norm group, validity, reliability. A working knowledge of these terms is essential as you read and evaluate tests. Each term will be discussed, with examples, as it appears in this section.

Evaluating Tests

Preliminary Issues

For Whom Was the Test Designed? (Who is the norm group?)
  1) <u>Norm Group</u>

A NORM GROUP is simply a large, well defined group of individuals who were given this test, and whose raw scores are then compiled in various ways and presented as numbers (NORMS) against which you can compare your students' scores. It is essential that the test developers inform the user how they chose their norm group--that is, what criteria they used to select individuals ("subjects") tested. If the test was designed for hearing individuals, then you must be aware that you will be comparing your deaf students to hearing children. This does not mean that the test may not be used -- only that you must be aware of how the norm group selection affects your interpretation of a student's performance on that test.

Likewise, be cautious in evaluating tests designed for use with hearing-impaired subjects. What criteria were used to choose the norm group? It is extremely difficult to obtain data on large numbers of hearing-impaired students, all of whom have the same background such as: age, sex, age at onset of hearing loss, amount of time in an educational program, degree and extent of hearing loss, amplification, communication methods used by the subjects' parents and/or school, socioeconomic status, IQ, etc. Was the test designed to be administered using speech alone, written English, or simultaneously signed/spoken English? For example, the <u>Maryland Syntax Evaluation Instrument (MSEI)</u> was normed on students attending residential schools. Therefore the scores may not be valid to use with students attending public or private day schools because the populations may not be the same. <u>The Test of Auditory Comprehension-Revised (TACL-R)</u> was normed on normal hearing children and therefore its norms cannot be compared to students' scores when the test is administered in sign unless there is interest in determining type and amount of delay. The <u>TACL-R</u> might, however, be an appropriate test to administer orally before mainstreaming a hearing-impaired child into a hearing classroom; or you could administer it, using total communication, to identify problem language areas of an individual student for whom a management plan will be developed.

Evaluating Tests

Further, how many subjects constitute the norm group and how many are in the various age categories within the norm group? There is no magic number that is "right," but numbers of subjects vary greatly and you can judge for yourself whether a particular norm group contains "enough" subjects. Generally, the more subjects, the more you can trust the normative data, provided these subjects were selected carefully and meet the defined criteria. To give you an example, the Maryland Syntax Evaluation Instrument has 220 students in the total norm group and as few as 15 in some age categories, as compared to 4,000+ norm subjects in the Peabody Picture Vocabulary Test, and 200 subjects in each of the 21 age categories. Obviously, the Peabody is the stronger test because of the larger overall number of subjects and the larger number within each age category. However, obtaining such a large number of matched deaf students for one test would be impossible because this is such a low-incidence population.

2) Norm-Referenced vs. Criterion-Referenced Measurement

One last distinction must be made here: norm-referenced versus criterion-referenced measurement. Assessment that uses normative data is called NORM-REFERENCED MEASUREMENT. This type of test is concerned with how a student performs relative to the members of a well defined norm group, or how the behavior of one child compares with the behavior of other children. Virtually all standardized tests are norm-referenced. If you intend to compare your students' performance to a test's norms, you must follow carefully the instructions for administering and scoring the test. (See Section IV: Administering the Test Battery.) However, if you simply wish to obtain information about an individual student's language, you may use the test or part of it and not compare the results to the test's norms. What you are doing is changing the test to meet your and the student's needs. The test, in this case, is no longer "standardized" nor norm-referenced.

By comparison, CRITERION-REFERENCED MEASUREMENT is concerned with whether or not a particular performance measure achieved by your student exceeds or falls below a predetermined cutting point. It determines whether or not a child has established a particular behavior, rather than indicating how he or she compares with others. Any normed test may be used as a criterion-referenced test. Or you may choose to use the results of a test for both purposes: comparing your students to a specific population and determining whether a specific behavior or behaviors are present. One example of these dual purposes would be using the results of the Boehm Test of Basic Concepts, which was normed on hearing children in Grades K, 1, and 2. The results of this test might be used to compare hearing-impaired students' use of these concepts to that of their hearing peers (the norm group) in order to determine whether there is a delay and, if so, how extensive it is (e.g., Davis, 1974); or it may be used as a criterion-referenced measurement for hearing-impaired students of any age to determine whether or not they know certain concepts, and to monitor individual progress in learning these concepts.

To summarize, in evaluating a test, you must know who the norm group is, and whether or not you can or want to compare the performance of a particular student with that of the norm group or whether you would prefer to modify the test and use it differently.

Validity: Does the Test Measure What it Claims to Measure?

Validity or "truthfulness" of the results is a major consideration when you choose a test. A test is said to be VALID if it is an accurate way of measuring what it sets out to measure. For example, if you tried to measure the weight of one of your students with a ruler, you could not obtain accurate results. If, however, you measured the length and width of the student's desk with a ruler, you would be measuring units the ruler was designed for and your results would be valid. Validity is the single most important property of a test. Look in the test manual for information on how the test's validity was established. There are many ways to determine the validity of a test, the four principal means being: content validity, face validity, criterionrelated validity, and construct validity. Recognize that face validity is not acknowledged by all psychologists as an acceptable method for reviewing the validity of tests and may be combined within the discussion of content validity in some test manuals. Ideally,

Evaluating Tests

either three or four types of validity should be discussed in the test manual; at worst, the test's validity may not be mentioned. If the latter is the case, peruse the test items yourself to get an idea of the test's face validity, but recognize that you will be the sole judge as to whether or not the test is appropriate.

CONTENT VALIDITY: The test is contructed so that it assesses the content area you are interested in measuring. The test items must be both content- and age-appropriate. For example, if you want to measure a student's knowledge of American history, you would not select a test that had questions primarily about German, African, and Japanese history because its content validity would be poor. If so-called language tests contain items primarily relating to history or require mathematical computation, they are not really testing the basic elements of language but are confounded by the intrusion of other content areas; their content validity would be low. If a test developed for third graders uses vocabulary normally assigned to twelfth graders, content validity would be low. It is likely that a student will be able to respond quite differently to a language test presented in sign versus one he must read. To determine content validity requires careful analysis of the test to ensure that it is both representative of and suitable for the area it presumes to test.

FACE VALIDITY: This type of validity is often referred to as content validity because it also evaluates the content of the test. However, strictly speaking, face validity is less stringent than content validity, and usually implies that a single individual has perused the material to see if the test appears to contain content-appropriate questions. Establishing content validity, on the other hand, requires careful analysis by many "experts." However, if:

- the test is based upon recent theory and research,
- the items are specific to the content area identified,
- there are sufficient numbers of items to measure each specific area, and
- new appropriate items could easily be added by the user

it is likely that the content is valid.

CRITERION-RELATED VALIDITY: Establishing criterion-related validity involves determining the degree of relationship between the scores on a particular test and measures on some external criterion variable with which the test scores should have something in common. For example, a test of music aptitude should have a high correlation with a criterion measure of music achievement.

CONSTRUCT VALIDITY: Construct validity is often difficult to establish and therefore is usually the least reported (Taylor, 1984). Construct validity is often established through carefully designed empirical studies "...in which the constructs are defined operationally and used as independent variables" (p. 65). Another way of viewing construct validity is to compare one test with others that have long been recognized as appropriate tests. If scores on the test of concern have a very high correlation with scores on other tests designed to measure the _same_ trait, and have a low correlation with scores on other tests which are designed to measure some _other_ trait, then the test possesses a high degree of construct validity. For example, if you were developing a receptive test of vocabulary, you would want your scores to have a high correlation with the Peabody Picture Vocabulary Test scores for the same groups of subjects, and a low correlation with a test of math aptitude. If both conditions occurred, you could be reasonably sure that your measure indeed assessed receptive vocabulary, and was not confounded by tapping unrelated skills.

CORRELATION is a summary of the strength of the relationship between two factors or "variables." A high correlation indicates that the variables "go together" or have common elements, whereas a low correlation suggests that the variables are relatively independent of one another. In reading the test manuals, you will notice that symbols such as r, R, or the Greek p are used to indicate correlation coefficients. A perfect relationship between two variables would yield an "r" of 1.00; if the two variables were not related at all, the correlation coefficient would equal zero. If one variable is inversely related to another, the correlation is "negative." Whether a particular correlation coefficient is "high enough" (statistically significant) depends on many factors such as

Evaluating Tests

the number of subjects involved in determining the correlation, but generally speaking, the higher the coefficient, the more closely the variables go together. For example, r = .90 is a very high correlation coefficient, while r = .10 is very low.

Guilford (1956), cited in Williams (1979), offers the following rough guide:

```
   < .20   slight; almost negligible relationship
 .20-.40   low correlation; definite but small relationship
 .40-.70   moderate correlation; substantial relationship
 .70-.90   high correlation; marked relationship
   > .90   very high correlation; very dependable
           relationship
```
[p. 128, Williams]

Reliability: Are the Test Results Consistent?

RELIABILITY is concerned with the dependability or consistency of the measures obtained. If a test is not reliable, it is not stable, dependable, or accurate (Kerlinger, 1973). A test with high reliability will yield the same relative magnitude of test scores for a group of people under differing conditions or situations. Test scores are never perfectly reliable, and test reliability can never be determined directly. Instead, reliability is estimated by one or more statistical techniques. The four most commonly used procedures for estimating the reliablity coefficient of a test are: the test-retest method, the parallel forms method, the split-halves method, and the Kuder-Richardson method.

TEST-RETEST METHOD: This is probably the form most evaluated and reported. If authors report a reliability coefficient without specifying type of reliability, it is usually a test-retest coefficient (Taylor, 1984). It is a measure of the stability of the test scores over time. Thus, one finds the correlation coefficient by comparing the test scores of the first test of a group of individuals with the scores of the second test of the same group of individuals. Usually, the time between tests is 2 weeks.

PARALLEL FORMS METHOD: Here, in cases where a test has two forms, both forms of a test are administered to the same groups of subjects, with the order of administration counterbalanced. The correlation between the scores on Form A and Form B is obtained.

Evaluating Tests

SPLIT-HALF TECHNIQUE: This involves a single administration of the test, scoring each subject on two equivalent halves of the test (e.g., oddand even-numbered items), determining the correlation between the halves, and estimating the reliability of the whole test through the use of a special formula (usually the "Spearman-Brown" formula).

KUDER-RICHARDSON METHOD: The Kuder-Richardson (K-R) formulas are equations (derived by psychologists Kuder and Richardson) for estimating the reliability coefficient of a test. These formulas are used mainly in the situation where an investigator would like to get an estimate of the homogeneity, or internal consistency, of a set of test items.

A test can be reliable but not valid; however, it is more difficult to find a valid test that is not reliable. Obviously, both qualities are important. If a test manual makes no mention of how its authors established test reliability, be wary! If the test appears to have good content validity, you might want to get an idea of its reliability yourself by administering it to several students once, then again after a reasonable -- but not too lengthy -- period of time (e.g., 2 weeks). Or give a student both forms if these are available and determine the stability of the scores for both forms.

For further reading, see Sowell and Casey (1982), Popham (1981), and Kazden (1980).

Is it a Screening Tool or a Diagnostic Test?

In examining test reliability it is important to identify whether the test is a screening instrument or a diagnostic test. Screening tests are designed to quickly assess a student's language abilities in a gross manner before diagnostic testing or intervention. Because they frequently contain only a few items, or focus on the developmental highlights at a particular stage, their reported reliability may be lower than that of a diagnostic test (perhaps .60 to .80). This is not a reflection of the test itself, but rather an acceptable characteristic of the type of test.

Screening tests are used primarily for identification purposes. In language assessment they can help to identify a) students who require further assessment and b) specific areas

Evaluating Tests

of a student's language which need further diagnostic assessment. The Early Language Milestone Screening Test and the Northwestern Syntax Screening Tool are examples of screening tests which attempt to identify children who require further assessment. The screening test of the Test of Syntactic Abilities helps the examiner to pinpoint specific syntactic structures which require an in-depth assessment.

Screening tests do not diagnose students' language problems. They are not intended to be, or substitute for, a complete diagnostic evaluation. They are most appropriately used before a complete language assessment. In some cases it may be appropriate to readminister a screening test periodically during intervention.

A diagnostic test attempts to examine in depth the range of a student's skill in a particular language area--for example, receptive vocabulary. In order to achieve this, it should contain a large number of items. In general, diagnostic tests have a narrower focus than the screening test and require more time to administer. The outcome of a diagnostic test is a score that leads to a "diagnosis." Diagnostic tests are best used for program placement and intervention programming. Diagnostic tests or parts of diagnostic tests are often useful in developing a test battery.

The majority of tests referred to in this book are diagnostic tests. Some tests contain both a screening version and a diagnostic test, such as the Miller-Yoder Test of Grammatical Comprehension (M-Y), and the Test of Syntactic Abilities (TSA). It is important to clarify for yourself the objective of the test and what your intended purpose is.

Guidelines for Evaluating Language Tests (How usable is the test?)

New language tests are published daily. You must ask yourself if a particular new test is better or different than the tests you are presently using, or will provide you with information that is different than what they yield. Just because a test is new or "in" does not mean that it will provide you with additional information about your student.

Evaluating Tests

If you plan to use a test <u>formally</u>, including normative data, you should use it only if it meets the following conditions:

a) The norms were obtained from a population demographically similar to your student,
b) test-retest reliability is high,
c) interexaminer reliability is high,
d) variability data are reported (mean, percentile rank, standard deviation), and
e) the test really tests what it purports to test.
[Launer & Lahey, 1981, p. 13]

Before you order a test, find out how "usable" it is and how expensive is it. Determine how long it takes to administer and score the test and whether it must be given to groups or can be given to individual students or <u>modified</u> to be given to individuals. Be sure you know how many sheets of paper or objects must be manipulated at once in administering the test. If all other factors are equal regarding the reliability, validity, and norms of two similar tests, then the usability factor may be the deciding issue in your selection of a test. Some tests, designed specifically for the hearing impaired, may superficially appear to be "better" tests. However, you may be able to achieve the same results, i.e., identifying specific problem areas in language, with assessment tools you already have.

In Table 8, there are guidelines, incorporated into a checklist, which were developed to help the examiner evaluate unfamiliar test materials for possible inclusion in a test battery. The guidelines cover four important facets of a test: 1) test content, 2) test administration and scoring, 3) test norms, reliability, and validity, and 4) the test materials. Each of the 37 questions is written to produce a "yes" score for each positive aspect of a test. Thus, a score close to 37 may indicate that a test is suitable for your needs. The score form also contains room for comments and additional questions. Tables 9 and 10 provide examples of how the Checklist might be used.

<u>Reminder</u>--your major goal is to identify the specific language problems of your students so that you can develop an appropriate program for remediation and monitoring.

Begin by examining the manual. Much of the information needed to answer the guideline questions is found there.

Evaluating Tests

Examination of the scoreforms or record books is also important. If the test includes pictures, objects, or other separate items, these also should be carefully examined. Pictures, in particular, can be very deceiving and misrepresent the language item to be evaluated. Depending upon the experiences of the hearing-impaired child, the pictures may represent items or activities not within the student's conceptual knowledge or lexicon. If you plan to administer the test in total communication, you must determine if there is a sign equivalent for each picture or decide what you will do if signs are not available. If there are many objects, you may wish to see if they may be individually replaced or if you must purchase the entire set to replace items, if they really contribute to obtaining the information you need, and if the individual hearing-impaired students know what each of the objects represents.

The information obtained from the guidelines can be used for a variety of purposes:

1) To aid in selection of tests in order to develop an appropriate test battery.
2) To select test materials for future purchase.
3) To validate the appropriateness of a test you are currently using.
4) To validate the use of a test instrument for IEP purposes.

The guidelines give the examiner a brief overview of the salient features of a test. However, they should never be considered a replacement for adequate preparation for administering the test.

Refer to <u>Section VI</u> for test descriptions and reviews of a variety of language tests. These will assist you in evaluating tests, but cannot substitute for actually examining a test and reading the manual.

After you have examined and evaluated a variety of language tests, you should know for whom the tests were designed, what they claim to measure, how valid and reliable they are, and how usable they are. Now you are prepared to move on to <u>Section III: Selecting a Test Battery</u>.

Table 8

CHECKLIST FOR EVALUATING LANGUAGE TESTS

The Content   Yes   No

1. Is the test geared to the <u>ability level or developmental level</u> of the child you are going to assess?
2. Are the objectives of the test clearly stated? (e.g., "This is a test of receptive vocabulary.")
3. Is the material arranged in developmental sequence, or levels of increasing difficulty?
4. Are there sufficient numbers of items for each area (vocabulary, morphology, syntax) tested if more than one area is evaluated?
5. Are the test items appropriate for the hearing-impaired population (for example, not too dependent on auditory discrimination or auditory memory)?
6. Are there "practice" test items to ensure that the task and the required response are understood by the child?
7. Is it a screening instrument?
8. Is it a diagnostic instrument?
9. Will it aid in programming/remediation plan development?
10. Would this test enhance your diagnostic/screening effectiveness?
11. Will the test increase your knowledge about the language of your student?
12. Are there parts of this test not available in other tests that could improve a test battery?

Administration - Scoring   Yes   No

1. Can the test be given, scored, and interpreted in a reasonable amount of time?
2. Can the test be given without extensive training in administration and scoring?
3. Can the test be easily administered in total communication (e.g., are there signs for all of the words)?
4. Are the directions/manual written clearly?
5. Can you locate information within the manual quickly?
6. Are there samples of scoring techniques in the manual?
7. Can the test be administered over a period of time to allow for rest breaks?

Norms - Validity - Reliability: Yes   No

1. Are there normative data on hearing-impaired children?

2. If hearing-impaired children are included in the norms, are they similar to your students, i.e., are deaf, all from residential schools, oral, hard of hearing and deaf, etc.?

3. How many children were included in the norm group?
    a. how many hearing impaired?
    b. how many normal hearing?

4. Are there reasonable numbers of norm group subjects for each age level (e.g., at least 25 within each group)?

5. Are there different norms for boys and girls?

6. Are there different norms based on socio-economic status?

7. Are the norms arranged at 6-month intervals or less for younger children (5 years and below); 1-year intervals or less for older children (5 years and above)?

8. Is the test-retest reliability good?

9. Has the validity of the test been demonstrated?

The Materials: Yes   No

1. Are the pictures or visual materials clear and unambiguous?

2. Are the materials an appropriate size for young children or others with visual problems?

3. Are the pictorial items arranged in such a way that they do not appear "crowded?"

4. Are the materials easy to manipulate?

5. Are the test materials not so stimulating that they cause distraction?

6. Are the required materials easily transportable?

7. Is the price reasonable for the materials provided?

8. If the test materials are lost or destroyed can they be easily replaced?

9. Are the pictures geared to the age and interest level of the student?

Other:

10.

11.

TOTALS
Comments:

Evaluating Tests

Table 9

EXAMPLE OF COMPLETED CHECKLIST

Test Name : __Northwestern Syntax Screening Test (NSST)__

CHECKLIST FOR EVALUATING LANGUAGE TESTS

The Content:

		Yes	No	Comments
1.	Is the test geared to the ability level or developmental level of the child you are going to assess?	x		
2.	Are the objectives of the test clearly stated? (e.g., "This is a test of receptive vocabulary.")	x		
3.	Is the material arranged in developmental sequence, or levels of increasing difficulty?	x		
4.	Are there sufficient numbers of items for each area (vocabulary, morphology, syntax) tested, if more than one area is evaluated?	x		Screening tool for syntax
5.	Are the test items appropriate for the hearing-impaired population (for example, not too dependent on auditory discrimination or auditory memory)?	x		
6.	Are there "practice" test items to ensure that the task and the required response are understood by the child?	x		
7.	Is it a screening instrument?	x		Screening use only
8.	Is it a diagnostic instrument?		x	
9.	Will it aid in programming/remediation plan development?	x		Identifies those who require additional assessment
10.	Would this test enhance your diagnostic/screening effectiveness?	x		
11.	Will the test increase your knowledge about the language of your student?	x		
12.	Are there parts of this test not available in other tests that could improve a test battery?		x	

Evaluating Tests

Administration – Scoring:	Yes	No	Comments
1. Can the test be given, scored, and interpreted in a reasonable amount of time?	x		
2. Can the test be given without extensive training in administration and scoring?	x		
3. Can the test be easily administered in total communication (e.g., are there signs for all words)?	x		
4. Are the directions/manual written clearly?	x		
5. Can you locate information within the manual quickly?		x	No table of contents for manual
6. Are there samples of scoring techniques in the manual?		x	
7. Can the test be administered over a period of time to allow for rest breaks?		x	Manual recommends giving entire test at one time

Norms – Validity – Reliability:	Yes	No	Comments
1. Are there normative data on hearing-impaired children?		x	
2. If hearing-impaired children are included in the norms, are they similar to your students; i.e., all deaf, all from residential schools, oral, hard of hearing and deaf, etc.?	n/a		

3. How many children were included in the norm group?
   a. how many hearing impaired?
   b. how many normal hearing?
			0 h.i.
			344 hearing

4. Are there reasonable numbers of norm group subjects for each age level (e.g., at least 25 within each group)?		x	
5. Are there different norms for boys and girls?		x	
6. Are there different norms based on socio-economic status?		x	

Evaluating Tests

7. Are the norms arranged at 6-month intervals or less for younger children (5 years and below); 1-year intervals or less for older children (5 years and above)?	x		1 yr age level for 3-8 years. No information provided
8. Is the test-retest reliability good?		?	No information provided
9. Has the validity of the test been demonstrated?		?	No information provided

The Materials:	Yes	No	Comments
1. Are the pictures or visual materials clear and unambiguous?	x		
2. Are the materials an appropriate size for young children or others with visual problems?	x		
3. Are the pictoral items arranged in such a way that they do not appear "crowded?"	x		Expressive section has 2 pictures per page/Receptive, 4 to a page
4. Are the materials easy to manipulate?	x		
5. Are the test materials not so stimulating that they cause distraction?	x		
6. Are the required materials easily transportable?		x	
7. Is the price reasonable for the materials provided?	x		
8. If the test materials are lost or destroyed can they be easily replaced?	x		
9. Are the pictures geared to the age and interest level of the student?	x		

Other:

10.

11.

TOTALS

Evaluating Tests

Comments:

The repetitive format can become overtiring for younger children. Pages containing four stimuli are sometimes distracting.

The absence of reliability and validity information makes it difficult to evaluate the quality of the test construction.

This test may be preferable for _receptive_ screening. Have the student identify one item (receptively) all the way through test, then repeat entire test using second item. This strategy reduces the possibility of selecting the correct answer by chance.

Use a different method for reviewing expressive language.

Evaluating Tests

Table 10

EXAMPLE OF COMPLETED CHECKLIST

Test Name : Test of Expressive Language Ability (TEXLA)

CHECKLIST FOR EVALUATING LANGUAGE TESTS

The Content:

		Yes	No	Comments
1.	Is the test geared to the ability level or developmental level of the child you are going to assess?	x		
2.	Are the objectives of the test clearly stated? (e.g., "This is a test of receptive vocabulary.")	x		
3.	Is the material arranged in developmental sequence, or levels of increasing difficulty?		x	
4.	Are there sufficient numbers of items for each area (vocabulary, morphology, syntax) tested, if more than one area is evaluated?			Only syntax is evaluated
5.	Are the test items appropriate for the hearing-impaired population (for example, not too dependent on auditory discrimination or auditory memory)?	x		
6.	Are there "practice" test items to ensure that the task and the required response are understood by the child?	x		
7.	Is it a screening instrument?	x		Use short form as screening test OR long version
8.	Is it a diagnostic instrument?	x		
9.	Will it aid in programming/remediation plan development?	x		
10.	Would this test enhance your diagnostic/screening effectiveness?	?	?	Response: read, write in missing word is different from other tests, may be too difficult for some h.i. students

49
Evaluating Tests

11. Will the test increase your knowledge about the language of your student?	x		If they can follow prescribed format of reading and writing in missing word, results would have litte relationship to signed-oral language in context.
12. Are there parts of this test not available in other tests that could improve a test battery?		x	

Administration - Scoring: Yes   No   Comments

1. Can the test be given, scored, and interpreted in a reasonable amount of time?   x

2. Can the test be given without extensive training in administration and scoring?   x

3. Can the test be easily administered in total communication (e.g., are there signs for all words)?   n/a   n/a   Response: read and write in missing word

4. Are the directions/manual written clearly?   x

5. Can you locate information within the manual quickly?   x

6. Are there samples of scoring techniques in the manual?   x

7. Can the test be administered over a period of time to allow for rest breaks?   x

Norms - Validity - Reliability: Yes   No   Comments

1. Are there normative data on hearing-impaired children?   x

2. If hearing-impaired children are included in the norms, are they similar to your students; i.e., all deaf, all from residential schools, oral, hard of hearing and deaf, etc?   x   Residential schools in Canada

Evaluating Tests

3. How many children were included in
   the norm group?
   a. how many hearing impaired?   82 total
   b. how many normal hearing?   65 h.i.
                                          17 hearing

4. Are there reasonable numbers of norm   x
   group subjects for each age level
   (e.g., at least 25 within each
   group)?

5. Are there different norms for boys   x
   and girls?

6. Are there different norms based on   x
   socio-economic status?

7. Are the norms arranged at 6-month   x
   intervals or less for younger children (5 years and below); 1-year
   intervals or less for older
   children (5 years and above)?

8. Is the test-retest reliability good?   No infor-
                                             mation

9. Has the validity of the test been   x
   demonstrated?

The Materials: Yes   No   Comments

1. Are the pictures or visual materials   x   most, but
   clear and unambiguous?   not all

2. Are the materials an appropri-   x
   ate size for young children or
   others with visual problems?

3. Are the pictoral items arranged in   x
   such a way that they do not appear
   "crowded?"

4. Are the materials easy to manipulate? x

5. Are the test materials not so stimu-   x
   lating that they cause distraction?

6. Are the required materials easily   x
   transportable?

7. Is the price reasonable for the   x
   materials provided?

8. If the test materials are lost or   x
   destroyed can they be easily
   replaced?

9. Are the pictures geared to the age   x
   and interest level of the student?

Other:

10.

11.

TOTALS

Comments:

A number of items have multiple answers which could be correct. Specific information to determine an acceptable answer is not provided. Further, no breakdown of specific test item numbers and the structure tested is provided. For example, the manual and score form report 5 items to test plurals, but no test item numbers are given.

Could modify test and <u>sign</u> it to students so they could "fill in" missing word. More students would understand how to "take" test.

Several pictures are ambiguous and therefore misleading as to actual language knowledge.

SECTION III: SELECTING A TEST BATTERY

What Is a Test Battery?

"Because language is profoundly complex, language evaluation must also be complex if it is to provide a total description of the child's facility with the process" (Hasenstab & Horner, 1982, p. 139). It is for this reason that language data should be obtained, as much as possible, within meaningful contexts such as snack time, show-and-tell, group art activities, field trips, etc. It is not always possible to obtain information about both receptive and expressive language for all students in this manner. This is particularly true when you are attempting to gather information about receptive language. During this part of the assessment process, it may be necessary to use a combination of a formal-informal approach, such as recording some data within a classroom situation and supplementing this informal activity with formal tests or parts of formal tests, or using teacher/clinician made tests. Whatever approach is selected for assessing receptive language, a single test will not suffice. Instead, a test battery comprising many tests or parts of tests must be developed in order to evaluate all aspects of the child's language system.

A test battery is a compilation of several tests, parts of tests, or teacher/clinician made tests that will measure various aspects of language both receptively and expressively for an individual child. It may include formal and/or informal methods of assessing both receptive and expressive language as well as parts of formal tests or modified tests. The selection of the various tests or parts of tests to be included in an individual battery is based upon why you are testing, or how you wish to use the results, and on the child's functional age. The functional age reflects the age at which a child is operating, rather than his or her chronological age. For example, it is very likely that a 3-year-old hearing-impaired child just entering a public school program will be functioning more like an 18-month or 2-year-old hearing child. Therefore tests would be included in the test battery that were designed for children under 3 years, _especially_ if these tests had been developed for hearing children. Neither tests nor programs should _ever_ reflect the chronological age alone.

Receptive-Expressive Language

When you measure a child's receptive language, you are attempting to learn about what a child _understands_. In order to learn about what children understand, you can have them follow directions or point to pictures. You do not expect them to speak and/or sign or write. You expect them to follow the direction or point to an object or picture. When you assess expressive language, you want to review what a student is able to _produce_ and how he or she uses the language being produced. Therefore, you would expect the response from the child to be speech and/or sign or writing.

Formal-Informal Testing

An assessment battery may include both formal and informal assessments or informal assessments only.

Formal assessment. It is our view that formal assessment may include:

1) Administration of a commercially available test, following the protocol for administration, scoring as outlined in the manual, and utilizing the normative data as provided in the test. Information from this assessment might provide information: a) to assist in placement, b) to document delay, c) to measure ability in using total communication or oral mode, or d) to compare the hearing-impaired student's language to that of hearing or hearing-impaired peers. Results of such testing might help in determining the appropriateness of mainstreaming, changing placement, and so forth.

2) Administration of a commercially available test, following the protocol described in the manual, and using all test materials as described, **but not using the norms provided**, thereby changing the test from "normed" to criterion referenced. Valuable information can be obtained from actually scoring the test and abstracting the information you want about an individual child from those scores. One example would be to administer the _Bankson Language Screening Test_ to an older student whose chronological age is beyond the age of the children in the test norms but who still has language

Selecting A Battery

deficits in areas evaluated by the <u>Bankson</u>. This procedure allows the examiner to measure the student's performance against himself or a predetermined standard or criterion.

   <u>Informal assessments</u>. Informal assessments are frequently used for evaluating hearing-impaired students. They can provide valuable information not obtained in other assessments. They are most commonly used for ongoing assessment and monitoring rather than for diagnoses or placement decisions. Examples of informal assessment include:

   1) <u>Informal use of formal tests</u>: Many formal tests provide excellent materials which can be used for other purposes. For example, a teacher could use the objects provided in the <u>Grammatical Analysis of Elicited Language</u>, but she would develop her own "script" for administration, and use her own recording and scoring method; or she could use the pictures in the <u>Test of Expressive Language Ability</u> but sign the sentences instead of having the student read them.

   2) <u>Teacher/Clinician-made tests</u>: These tests are commonly used to measure a student's knowledge based on what the teacher believes he should know or what has been taught. These are helpful for ongoing assessment and monitoring as well as for obtaining baseline measures. Teacher-made tests are very subjective and are likely to vary a great deal in quality based on the training and expertise of the teacher. However, if the same test is given for both pre- and posttest results, these results can provide helpful information about the child's progress. Also, parts of normed tests can be adapted and made into teacher made tests. An example of a teacher/clinician developed checklist is found in Table 11. This particular checklist provides an effective and easy way to measure language <u>use</u> over time.

   3) <u>Language/Communication scales</u>: Scales are generally checklists of language skills or behaviors arranged in a developmental progression. Both the <u>SKI-HI Language Development Scale</u> and the <u>Kendall Communicative Proficiency Scale Worksheet</u> (Table 11) are examples of different types of checklists. Scales can be administered in question and answer format, or through observation, or a combination of approaches. Language scales are widely used in the assessment of very young children. Because scales generally do not use a basal

Selecting A Battery

or ceiling cut-off score, children may demonstrate a wide range of skills. However, because the scales are developmental, the results provide important information about how close a specific child is to others his age, how solid his skills are at a given age, or whether they are splintered and scattered below and above the target age.

4) <u>Observation</u>: Informal observation can provide extremely valuable information regarding a student's language, especially production and <u>use</u> of language. Observation and data collection in natural contexts are particularly important for obtaining information about expressive language of the hearing-impaired student. Many different types of information can be obtained from watching the student throughout his day. For example:

- Does the student use language voluntarily in class? On the playground? In other settings?
- Is his language different with peers than with teachers?
- Does the student initiate conversation or is he usually the responder?
- Does he respond at all? Appropriately?
- Does he use good eye contact, facial expression, or other non-verbal communication?
- Is he able to respond to and ask questions?

These are just a few of the many language and communication skills which can be identified through observation. Observation is an appropriate informal technique for all age levels and is most often used when one is obtaining an expressive language sample (see <u>Section V</u> for a complete discussion).

Selecting A Battery

Table 11

KENDALL COMMUNICATIVE PROFICIENCY SCALE WORKSHEET

Kendall Demonstration School, Gallaudet University

Student: _____

Year:	Teacher:	Current Proficiency Level: (P-Level)	Language Proficiency Goal: (P-Level)
1985-86	_____	_____	_____
1986-87	_____	_____	_____
1987-88	_____	_____	_____
1988-89	_____	_____	_____
1989-90	_____	_____	_____

Used by permission of Outreach Pre-College Programs, Gallaudet University.

Selecting A Battery

LEVEL 0+ CRITERIA

CIRCLE ONE

0.1. Does the child determine what another person is talking about by looking in the same direction as the other person?   yes   no

0.2. a. Does the child communicate about his or her own comfort, pleasure, and distress (non-verbally)?   yes   no

   b. Does the child communicate about clothing or other things associated with his or her person?   yes   no

0.3. a. Does the child usually respond attentively to turn-taking activities, such as peek-a-boo (but does not usually initiate the activity)?   yes   no

   b. Does the child request objects by reaching for them and sometimes opening and closing his or her fists?   yes   no

   c. Does he or she call attention to novel things in the environment by holding them for others to see or by pointing?   yes   no

0.4. Does the child use non-verbal signals, such as following another's gaze or looking in the direction that someone is pointing, to achieve cohesion?   yes   no

0.5. Does the child communicate by stretching and holding gestures, facial expressions, and differentiated cries?   yes   no

Selecting A Battery

LEVEL ONE CRITERIA

CIRCLE ONE

1.1. Does the child refer to objects by holding them, looking at them, pointing, and touching?   yes   no

1.2. Does the child communicate about toys, lights, animals, and particular foods (or (or other things he or she can control)?   yes   no

1.3. a. Does the child initiate peek-a-boo and other turn-taking activities?   yes   no

  b. Does the child imitate the movements of others although not necessarily to bring about action?   yes   no

1.4. Does the child use non-verbal means to

  a. call attention to physical needs?   yes   no

  b. express personal reaction?   yes   no

  c. request help by shifting his or her gaze back and forth between the object and the person whose help he or she wants in getting the object?   yes   no

1.5. Does the child sometimes imitate the signs produced by others, although with imperfect hand configurations and movements?   yes   no

LEVEL TWO CRITERIA

CIRCLE ONE

2.1. Does the student often use conventional signs or words to refer to the immediate physical context?   yes   no

2.2. Does the student identify objects upon request?   yes   no

2.3. Does the student sometimes repeat what was just said?   yes   no

2.4. Does the student often use the language to

    a. request a few objects and simple services?   yes   no

    b. get the attention of others or to call them to his or her location?   yes   no

    c. greet others?   yes   no

    d. protest other peoples' actions that he or she wishes to avert?   yes   no

    e. label objects (without cueing)?   yes   no

    f. note the presence of objects?   yes   no

    g. note or call for the disappearance (or removal) of objects?   yes   no

2.5. Does the student leave it to others to figure out what he or she leaves unsaid? Does the student use non-verbal signals to extend meaning?   yes   no

Selecting A Battery

LEVEL THREE CRITERIA*

<u>CIRCLE ONE</u>

3.1. Does the student refer primarily to things that are of interest to him or her? yes no

3.2. Does the student communicate about

    a. a substantial number of objects and actions affecting him or her (that is, too many to keep track of readily)? yes no

    b. the location of objects? yes no

    c. the destination of objects when they are moving or being moved? yes no

    d. both temporary as well as more or less permanent characteristics of people and objects? yes no

    e. who owns what and what belongs to whom? yes no

3.3. Does the student link in any way what he or she says to what others say? yes no

3.4. Does the student use the language to

    a. represent a broad range of his or her actions? yes no

    b. affirm the presence of a substantial number of objects, (note or call for) their absence, disappearance, or removal, and note (or try to bring about) their return or recurrence? yes no

    c. request a broad range of objects and services? yes no

    d. identify objects and actions in pictures? yes no

3.5. a. Does the student usually use utterances consisting of at least two syntactically related components? yes no

    b. Does the student rely often on others to figure out what has been left unsaid? yes no

*See Bloom, L. (Ed.). (1978). <u>Readings in language development</u>. New York: John Wiley and Sons, for definitions of referential/semantic categories.

Selecting A Battery

LEVEL FOUR CRITERIA

<u>CIRCLE ONE</u>

4.1. Does the student

    a. refer to actions he or she is about to take, and does he or she express the intention to take action?   yes   no

    b. refer to actions (taken by others) that do not affect him or her?   yes   no

4.2. Does the student

    a. use a broad variety of combinations of semantic categories of meaning in a single utterance? (See Bloom, 1978, for more information.)   yes   no

    b. talk about several coordinated but independent events and states at the same time?   yes   no

4.3. Does the student achieve cohesion in conversation by using elements (words or phrases) from the prior utterances of his or her conversational partners?   yes   no

4.4. Does the student use the language to

    a. establish the identity of things and people?   yes   no

    b. create and maintain worlds of make-believe (as opposed to simply participating in make-believe worlds created by others)?   yes   no

4.5. Does the student

    a. usually express most of what he or she means to say, rarely leaving unsaid things that should be expressed?   yes   no

    b. usually understand friends and familiar adults, and can they understand him?   yes   no

Selecting A Battery

LEVEL FIVE CRITERIA

<u>CIRCLE ONE</u>

5.1. Does the student communicate confidently and intelligibly on topics that go entirely beyond the immediate physical context and that require him or her to interrelate objects, states, and events located outside present time and space?   yes   no

5.2. Does the student express explicitly a variety of relationships between events (or states): relationships involving time, causality, contradiction, states of knowledge?   yes   no

5.3. Does the student carry on a conversation contributing details or comments relevant to his or her partner's theme without changing the subject?   yes   no

5.4. Does the student use the language to find out

    a. what is happening?   yes   no

    b. who is taking what action?   yes   no

    c. what state things are in?   yes   no

    d. why people are doing what they are doing?   yes   no

5.5. Does the student

    a. usually tell stories or provide descriptions with clear overall meaning and structure? (Hazy details are <u>readily</u> clarified by questioning the student.)   yes   no

    b. communicate with ready intelligibility on a one-to-one basis with strangers accustomed to deaf children?   yes   no

Selecting A Battery

LEVEL SIX CRITERIA

<u>CIRCLE ONE</u>

6.1. Does the student

    a. refer to objects, actions, events, and states in a hypothetical mode (that is, without regard to their reality or truth) and consider the implications? yes no

    b. refer expressly to nonroutine and complex actions and feelings of a more or less perceptible sort? yes no

6.2. Does the student communicate successfully on any topic within his or her experience? yes no

6.3. Does the student

    a. engage in sustained dialogue and narrative with strangers with a high degree of intelligibility and comprehension? yes no

    b. follow with accuracy (but not necessarily full detail) the general meaning of multi-cornered conversations even though they do not bear on closely familiar topics? yes no

6.4. Does the student use the language explicitly to influence opinion and attitudes as well as actions? yes no

6.5. Does the student

    a. maintain a steady flow of accurate and fully intelligible expression only occasionally having to circle around it or use un-idiomatic language? yes no

    b. provide sufficient contextual background to enable conversational partners to interpret messages containing a considerable amount of new information? yes no

    c. communicate with sufficient clarity so that only occasional clarifying questioning by his or her conversational partner is required? yes no

Selecting A Battery

LEVEL SEVEN CRITERIA

CIRCLE ONE

7.1. Does the student build referential contexts sufficiently rich to allow him or her to explain the details of moderately elaborate systems, such as the rules of a game or how something works, to others who are unfamiliar with what is being explained?   yes   no

7.2. Does the student communicate with strangers in one-on-one situations and multi-cornered conversations with a high degree of intelligibility?   yes   no

7.3. Does the student

    a. paraphrase and amplify his or her own comments to accommodate the needs of his or her conversational partner?   yes   no

    b. pinpoint the information he or she needs to clarify an ambiguous message?   yes   no

7.4. Does the student use the language to express <u>general principles</u> for the purpose of influencing opinions, attitudes, and actions of others?   yes   no

7.5. Does the student usually maintain a steady flow of fully idiomatic expression free of circumlocution?   yes   no

Selecting A Battery

Considerations for Compiling a Test Battery

No single test can be used alone to provide a comprehensive language assessment. After considering your information needs, you can select tests which may become part of your test battery. The development of a test battery is an important step. Give yourself ample time to review available tests. Also consider the test and its performance requirements in relation to the student you are going to assess. For example, small test pictures may not be suitable for a very young or visually impaired student. When you have selected a group of tests that suit your needs you can then familiarize yourself with these tests, decide which ones to use intact, which to modify, and what parts (if any) you will develop. Select those tests, parts, etc. that will measure the different language areas and put them together to form your test battery. Practice giving each of the tests many times before using it with a student. If you modify the test to make it more practical by writing a new script or using objects from the test in a different manner than the one prescribed, you must still practice. This will permit you to feel confident when administering the test and will avoid disruption during the evaluation. Remember, if you plan to use the test as a norm-referenced measurement, which may be more appropriate for your testing needs, any modification of the administration, stimuli, or response invalidates the test as it was developed and normed.

When you are reviewing a test for possible inclusion in a test battery, maintain a flexible attitude. For instance, you may find that a portion of the test appears to be superior to the rest of the test, or may contain some diagnostic information not found elsewhere. Examples of this would be the <u>Categories</u> and <u>Functions</u> sub-tests of the receptive portion of the <u>Bankson Language Screening Test</u>. You might want to remove these from the test, add a few other ones, and make this a part of your test battery. Another example of functions is found in the <u>Sequenced Inventory of Communication Development</u> where the child is required to follow directions such as pointing in response to "What do you wear on your feet?" It may be far more appropriate to use only the portion of the

Selecting A Battery

test that assesses receptive language and not use the expressive portion at all. Or you might choose to use selected expressive items from various commercial tests to supplement an expressive language sample. The administration of a test in its present form may not be appropriate for your student. For example, although the receptive <u>One Word Picture Vocabulary Test</u> and the <u>Peabody Picture Vocabulary Test</u> are designed to be given orally, you may want to administer either one in total communication to a particular student. These factors should not deter you from including the test or portions of the test in your final test battery.

1) <u>Attempt to Match your Information Needs to Students' Performance Abilities</u>

A test battery can be compiled after careful review of available test materials. It is important to consider the individual student to be evaluated when you select items for your battery. A good test battery reflects both the examiner's information needs and the student's functional level and performance abilities. For example, a test of expressive vocabulary could be administered through identification and labeling of either pictures or real objects. A visually impaired or very young child may be able to perform better using real objects. Both methods would provide similar diagnostic information.

2) <u>Consider: Normal Language Development</u>

The professional who attempts to evaluate the language development of a hearing-impaired student must be well prepared in order for her efforts to be successful. An important part of this preparation must be a thorough understanding of normal language development. Current research findings have important implications for the assessment and remediation of language disorders related to deafness. It is imperative that both teachers and speech-language pathologists remain current in information about both normal language and language of the hearing impaired in order to select and use the most appropriate language tests and to be able to use the results for remediation.

3) <u>Consider: Developmental Age</u>

When one has a firm understanding of normal language acquisition, the task of determining a student's developmental

Selecting A Battery

age is made easier. Developmental or functional age and chronological age are not necessarily the same. <u>Chronological age</u> (CA) refers to the child's physical age in years and months, based on his birthdate. If the child was born prematurely, this should be considered in calculating his chronological age, which is then often referred to as a <u>corrected age</u>. <u>Developmental age</u> (DA) or <u>functional age</u> (FA) refers to the level of development of a student's skills and can be used as a composite statement of the student's functional level in a specific area. For example, a child's chronological age (CA) may be 5 years but his developmental age (DA) or functional age (FA) for language may be 2-1/2 years. Knowing the child's developmental age is critical for selecting language tests and for planning intervention because tests, activities, and materials selected should reflect the child's DA and not necessarily his CA.

4) <u>Consider: Reasons for Assessment</u>

As discussed previously, the examiner must identify his reason(s) for testing in order to select appropriate test materials. Most evaluation materials state clearly their intended purpose. There should be a match between the examiner's need for information and the selected assessment tool. Failure to consider the reason for testing could result in a waste of valuable time and produce information that is of limited value. Misleading test results may also hinder the child's progress or placement.

5) <u>Consider: Biases</u>

Objective assessment should be the goal of the examiner. Personal biases toward the student or his family must not be allowed to interfere with the assessment. Especially dangerous is permitting your biases about what the student "should" know to color your assessment. If you "expect" either failure or success from a student, your results may not be objective.

Biases towards evaluation materials abound. Selection of specific tests should not be based solely on the recommendation of a supervisor, colleague, or school district. Their information needs may differ from yours. The inclusion of a test in a battery should be based only on the merits of the test, the child's abilities, and your information needs.

Selecting A Battery

6) **Consider: Form, Content, and Use**
As you will note in *Examples of Language Test Batteries* later in this section, tests have been selected in consideration of the major language components. Because no one test can provide all the information needed, a well planned battery will be composed of a number of tests, parts of tests, or made-up tests which can provide information regarding the student's receptive and expressive language in all areas of language.

7) **Include Informal and Formal Assessment**
While this book does discuss the use and interpretation of formal assessment tools, the major emphasis for language assessment of hearing-impaired children should concern the social use of language and, therefore, informal assessment or informal use of formal assessment tools may provide the most and best information. Observation is an outstanding means of viewing a child's language within the social context. One way to observe and record your observations is found in Table 11. Observing the student in class, on the playground, or with various people can provide information regarding her comprehension of directions and vocabulary or her ability to use language in a variety of situations. Non-linguistic factors such as eye contact, body language, and gesture can also be observed in this way. Informal observations can provide valuable diagnostic information and should be a) shared with others working with the student and b) documented as part of the final report or IEP. Careful selection and use of a well rounded test battery will yield assessment data that best reflect the student's overall language ability and will assist teachers and speech-language pathologists in implementing an appropriate educational program for each student.

8) **Consider: Developing a Screening Test of Your Own**
Put together a variety of grammatical skill items from other tests or your own with which you can easily and quickly screen each student's receptive skills. Once you have screened quickly and have found what appear to be grammatical errors, you can use your test battery to test those specific areas.

Selecting A Battery

Summary

Consideration of the points discussed above can help to make assessment an activity that produces valuable information for all those who work with the student. Assessment does not have to be an annual or ongoing drudgery! Although the eight considerations discussed may seem like a large array of issues to cope with before you even begin to assess each student, they are based on common sense and dovetail with the ideas that are emphasized throughout this book. They can be considered a checklist of the most important factors to consider in compiling a test battery, and, with practice, should become easily integrated into the testing process.

Examples of Language Test Batteries

To illustrate how you might go about putting together a language test battery, we have provided a summary chart and four sample batteries for four age categories of hearing-impaired children: the 3-year-old child just entering school, 3 to 5-year-olds, 6 to 10-year-olds, and 11+-year-olds. These are <u>only</u> <u>samples</u>. Your choice of tests or parts of tests will depend upon your student's characteristics, your testing objectives, and the various tests and parts of tests that you prefer and have available.

On the Test Battery Summary Chart (Table 12), language tests are categorized by three main parameters: <u>Age Group</u> that the test is designed for (0-5 years, 6-12 years, 13-18+ years); <u>Language Component</u> to be tested (morphology, syntax, semantics, other); and <u>Communication Mode</u> tested (receptive, expressive, or both). This chart can help you select tests that are appropriate for a particular child. For example, if you are putting together a test battery for an initial evaluation of a 10-year-old hearing-impaired child, you can select several tests from the 6-12 year column that will help tap the child's receptive and expressive ability in various areas of language.

Table 12

TEST BATTERY SUMMARY CHART

Communication Mode:
E = Expressive
R = Receptive
* = Designed for Hearing Impaired Children

Language Component

Age Groups

Morphology (Form)

0 to 5 Years

Test	R/E	Years
BLST	R/E	4 to 8
CELI	E	3 to 8
SPELT-II	E	4 to 9.5
TACL-R	R	3 to 10
*TAGS Pre-sentence	R/E	0 to 5
TEEM	E	3 to 8
VANE-L	R/E	2.6 to 6

6 to 12 Years

Test	R/E	Years
BLST	R/E	4 to 8
CELI	E	3 to 8
SPELT-II	E	4 to 9.5
TACL-R	R	3 to 10
*TAGS Simple Complex	R/E	5 to 9 9+
TEEM	E	3 to 8
*TERLA	E	3 to 8
*TEXLA	E	7 to 12
VANE-L	R/E	2.6 to 6

13 to 18 Years

Test	R/E	Years
*TAGS Complex	R/E	9+

Language Component

Age Groups

Lexicon/Vocabulary (Content)

0 to 5 Years			6 to 12 Years			13 to 18 Years		
Test	R/E	Years	Test	R/E	Years	Test	R/E	Years
ACLC	R	3 to 6	ACLC	R	3 to 6	EOWPVT-UE	E	12 to 16
BEAR-CAPS	R	1.6 to 5.9	BTBC	R	5 to 8	PPVT-R	R	2.6 to 40
BTBC	R	5 to 8	BBCS	R	2.6 to 8			
BBCS	R	2.6 to 8	CPVT	R	4 to 11.6			
CPVT	R	4 to 11.6	EOWPVT	E	2 to 12			
EOWPVT	E	2 to 12	EOWPVT-UE	E	12 to 16			
PPVT-R	R	2.6 to 40	PPVT-R	R	2.6 to 40			
ROWPVT	R	2 to 12	ROWPVT	R	2 to 12			
*SECS	R/E	2 to 8	*SECS	R/E	2 to 8			
*SKI-HI RLT	R	3 to 6.6	*SKI-HI RLT	E	3 to 6.6			
TACL-R	R	3 to 10	TACL-R	R	3 to 10			
*TCRVT	R	3 to 12	*TCRVT	R	3 to 12			
VANE-L	R/E	2.6 to 6	TWT	E	7 to 12			
			VANE-L	R/E	2.6 to 6			

Language Component

Age Groups

0 to 5 Years

Test	R/E	Years
ACLC	R	3 to 6
BLST	R/E	4 to 8
BEAR-CAPS	R	1.6 to 5.9
BTBC	R	5 to 8
BBCS	R	2.6 to 8
ELM	R/E	0 to 3
PLAI	R/E	3 to 6
*RITLS	E	5 to 17+
*SECS	R/R	2 to 8
*SKI-HI RLT	E	3 to 6.6
*TAGS Presentence	R/E	0 to 5
VANE-L	R/E	2.6 to 6

6 to 12 Years

Test	R/E	Years
ACLC	R	3 to 6
BLST	R/E	4 to 8
BTBC	R	5 to 8
BBCS	R	2.6 to 8
BLST	E	4 to 8
PLAI	R/E	3 to 6
*RITLS	R	5 to 17+
*SECS	R/E	2 to 8
*SKI-HI RLT	R	3 to 6.6
*TAGS Simple Complex	R/E	5 to 9 9+
TWT	E	7 to 12
VANE-L	R/E	2.6 to 6

13 to 18 Years

Test	R/E	Years
*RITLS	R	5 to 17+
*TAGS Complex	R/E	9+

Semantic Relation-
ships/Semantic
Knowledge
(content)

Language Component

Age Groups

0 to 5 Years

Test	R/E	Years
CII	E	.7 to 2
PLAI	R/E	3 to 6
BLST	R/E	4 to 8
BEAR-CAPS	R	1.6 to 5.9
BTBC	R	5 to 8
ITPA	R/E	2.7 to 10
RIDES	R/E	0 to 4
SICD	R/E	.4 to 4
*SKI-HI LDS	R/E	0 to 5
VANE-L	R/E	2.6 to 6

6 to 12 Years

Test	R/E	Years
ILSA	E	8 to 14
PLAI	R/E	3 to 6
BLST	R/E	4 to 8
BTBC	R	5 to 8
ITPA	R/E	2.7 to 10
VANE-L	R/E	2.6 to 6

13 to 18 Years

Test	R/E	Years
ILSA	E	8 to 14

Pragmatics (Use)

Other

Language Component

Age Groups

Syntax

0 to 5 Years

Test	R/E	Years
BLST	R/E	4 to 8
CELI	E	3 to 8
ELM	R/E	0 to 3
*GAEL	E	5 to 9
M-Y	R	4 to 8
NSST	R/E	3 to 8
*RITLS	R	5 to 17+
*SECS	R/E	2 to 8
SPELT-II	E	4 to 9.5
TACL-R	R	3 to 10
*TAGS Pre-sentence	R/E	0 to 5
VANE-L	R/E	2.6 to 6

6 to 12 Years

Test	R/E	Years
BLST	R/E	4 to 8
CELI	E	3 to 8
*GAEL	E	5 to 9
M-Y	R	4 to 8
*MSEI	E	6 to 12
NSST	R/E	3 to 8
*RITLS	R	5 to 17+
*SECS	R/E	2 to 8
SPELT-II	E	4 to 9.5
TACL-R	R	3 to 10
*TAGS Simple Complex	R/E	5 to 9 9+
*TERLA	R	7 to 12
*TEXLA	E	7 to 12
*TSA	R	10 to 19
VANE-L	R/E	2.6 to 6

13 to 18 Years

Test	R/E	Years
*RITLS	R	5 to 17+
*TAGS Complex	R/E	9+
*TSA	R	10 to 19

Test Battery for A Hearing-Impaired Child: Functional Age, Pragmatics, Cognition, and Vocabulary

When developing a test battery for hearing-impaired students, it is important that you evaluate the tests, as described previously. There are several other issues you must consider. First, it is essential that you pay close attention to the functional age of the child because that will often differ from his or her chronological age; the ages identified on many of the tests often refer to a chronological age and functional age that are the same. Because hearing-impaired students are usually delayed in language compared to their hearing peers, you will often have to use a test designed for younger hearing children. Table 13 provides an example of a battery developed for the hearing-impaired child at C.A. (chronological age) of 3 years who has just entered school and is functioning as a much younger child. This child may have little or no language. The child's language may be so limited that the usual tests designed for 3-year-olds are not appropriate. In addition, 3-year-old hearing-impaired children have not usually acquired test-taking skills such as making a correct response to "show me..." or "point to the..." Therefore, a hearing-impaired child who is chronologically 3 years old is often functioning well below 3 years and must be tested differently or test results will either be inaccurate or unobtainable.

Because of the differences in C.A. and F.A., we need to use diferent means of assessing this hearing-impaired child. Although not everything in this battery is truly "linguistic," much of it relates to communication and all of it will assist in developing intervention and monitoring plans. We feel that you will need some sort of developmental checklist or developmental profile (such as the Rockford Infant Developmental Evaluation Scales) which will provide information about gross motor, fine motor, adaptive, and school readiness ability as well as a screen of receptive and expressive language. The "normal" hearing-impaired child should be functioning within normal range in areas other than language. Thus you will obtain general information about how the child is functioning and how you might expect the child to perform. This information will also assist you in establishing a functional age.

Selecting A Battery

Table 13
SAMPLE TEST BATTERY:
3-YEAR-OLD HEARING-IMPAIRED CHILD ENTERING SCHOOL

ASSESSMENT TOOL	INFORMATION PROVIDED
Developmental Scale/Checklist; e.g., Rockford Infant Developmental Evaluation Scales (RIDES)	Gross motor; fine motor, social/adaptive, school readiness, overview of receptive-expressive communication
Language Scale; e.g., SKI-HI Language Development Scale (LDS)	Receptive-Expressive language
Checklist of Pragmatic Behaviors (Observations accomplished over time within a meaningful context)	Non-linguistic and beginning linguistic _use_ of language
Charts of First Words; e.g., Burton White (receptive) Katherine Nelson (expressive)	Receptive and expressive vocabulary of normal hearing children within categories
Plus list of words used by individual student obtained in class and from parents	Expressive vocabulary of each individual student
BEAR-CAPS Bare Essentials in Assessing Really Little Kids; Concept Analysis Profile	Comprehension of conceptual relationships that contribute to language development
Cognitive Developmental Checklist: e.g., Uzgiris Hunt or modification	Cognitive skills/levels
Observation	Summary of above that will reinforce, add to, or modify your previous results

Selecting A Battery

Because the very young hearing-impaired child just entering school may not be using sign or voice to express language, it is even more important to look at how this child does communicate and what the range of communicative behaviors is. Tools you could use to evaluate these behaviors, in addition to the developmental checklist, would be a checklist of pragmatic behaviors (Table 1), and portions of the Kendall Communicative Proficiency Scale, Level 0+, Table 11. The young hearing-impaired child may or may not have some of these pragmatic behaviors but because they are part of the communicative/language process, it is important to determine which, if any, are present and which are absent in order to be able to include these in your intervention plans.

Another nonverbal area to explore would be that of cognitive development. A checklist of cognitive skills can be developed and a complete inventory of concept development such as BEAR-CAPS (Hasenstab & Horner, 1985) can be used. It is important to know the cognitive levels of the hearing-impaired child in order to modify the environment accordingly and, if necessary, provide a more cognitively enriched environment.

After using procedures to assess the child's developmental levels, pragmatic behaviors, and cognitive status, a fourth procedure would provide you with a simple method of evaluating vocabulary and comparing this vocabulary to the "first words" of normal hearing children. You can make a list for each student that will include both vocabulary that is understood and that which is expressed. Information can be obtained from parents, staff of programs the child previously attended, or through direct interaction and observation. For example, vocabulary that the child comprehends might be compared to White's "First Words Understood" (Table 4) or the expressive vocabulary might be compared to Nelson's "First Fifty Words Produced" (Table 5). If the hearing-impaired child understands or uses only a limited category of vocabulary, this information will assist you in formulating intervention plans. For example, it is very common for some young hearing-impaired children to be limited to understanding and using only a naming vocabulary and therefore not use action words, modifiers, function words, and so on. It is also often true that the child's naming vocabulary itself is more restricted than that

Selecting A Battery

of normal hearing peers and needs to be expanded. It is essential that the teacher and speech-language pathologist identify such omissions immediately in order to develop appropriate intervention plans for each child that will facilitate qualitative as well as quantitative growth.

Tables 14 through 16 provide examples of test batteries that might be used with older children. A team including the teacher and speech-language pathologist might have their favorites that could overlap several age levels, such as the TACL-R and the Rhode Island Test of Receptive Language, or they may have a sequence of directions using toy figures that they have laid out developmentally and that will provide them with knowledge about receptive vocabulary, semantics, and syntax over a broad age span. There is no "best" set of tests but all areas of language must be evaluated.

Table 14

SAMPLE TEST BATTERY FOR AGE CATEGORY: 3 TO 5 YEARS OLD

	RECEPTIVE	EXPRESSIVE
MORPHOLOGY	Test for Auditory Comprehension of Language-Revised (TACL-R)	Language Sample recorded within meaningful contexts Test for Examining Expressive Morphology (TEEM)
SYNTAX	TACL-R	Language Sample
SEMANTICS	SKI-HI Receptive Language Test (SKI-HI RLT) Made-up phrases using objects and vocabulary known to the child and used naturally in the classroom; e.g., "push the ball," "big truck"	Language Sample Parts of the SICD; e.g., "What do you wear on your feet?"
LEXICON	Total Communication Test of Receptive Vocabulary SKI-HI Receptive Language Test (SKI-HI RLT) Parts from the SICD; e.g., following simple directions ("Give me the ___"), function of vocabulary ("What does mom cook on")	Expressive One-Word Picture Vocabulary Test (EOWPVT) Language Sample
PRAGMATICS	Informal Observation of Child	Communicative Intentions Inventory (CII) The Kendall Communicative Proficiency Scale

Table 15

SAMPLE TEST BATTERY
FOR FUNCTIONAL AGE LEVEL: 6 TO 10 YEARS OLD

	RECEPTIVE	EXPRESSIVE
MORPHOLOGY	Test of Receptive Language (TERLA)	Language Sample recorded within meaningful contexts
		Structured Photographic Expressive Language Test-II (SPELT-II) (supplemental)
		Test for Examining Expressive Morphology (TEEM)
SYNTAX	Rhode Island Test of Receptive Language Structure (RITLS)	Teacher Assessment of Grammatical Structures (TAGS)
		Language Sample recorded within meaningful contexts
SEMANTICS	Boehm Test of Basic Concepts (BTBC)	Language Sample recorded within meaningful contexts
	Parts of the Bankson; e.g., function and categories	
	Rhode Island Test of Receptive Language Structure (RITLS)	
LEXICON	Total Communication Receptive Vocabulary Test (TCRVT)	Expressive One-Word Vocabulary Test (EOWPVT) or The Word Test (TWT)
PRAGMATICS (USE)		Informal Observations/ Recording
		Kendall Communicative Proficiency Scale
OTHER		Visual and Auditory Perception Subtests of the ITPA

Table 16

SAMPLE TEST BATTERY
FOR FUNCTIONAL AGE LEVEL: 11+ YEARS OLD

	RECEPTIVE	EXPRESSIVE
MORPHOLOGY	Test for Auditory Comprehension of Language (TACL-R)	Language Sample recorded within meaningful contexts Teacher Assessment of Grammatical Structures (TAGS)
SYNTAX	Test of Syntactic Ability (TSA)* Test for Auditory Comprehension of Language (TACL-R)	Language Sample recorded within meaningful contexts
SEMANTICS	Rhode Island Test of Receptive Language Structure (RITLS)	Language Sample recorded within meaningful contexts
LEXICON	Peabody Picture Vocabulary Test (PPVT) Rhode Island Test of Language Structure (RITLS) or Teacher-made test of vocabulary used in social studies and science	Expressive One-Word Picture Vocabulary Test (EOWPVT) or Expressive One-Word Picture Vocabulary Test Upper Extension
PRAGMATICS		Language sample recorded within meaningful contexts Interpersonal Language Skills Assessment (ILSA) Subtests of the Detroit Tests of Learning Aptitude** (1967); e.g., pictorial and verbal absurdities, pictorial and verbal opposites, visual attention span for objects.

* The <u>TSA</u> requires that the student be able to read.
** Note that this refers to the 1967 edition (Baker & Leland, 1967). These subtests are not included in the newer (1984) edition but the types of subtests can be very helpful. This test is not described in <u>Section VI</u> because the older edition may no longer be available.

Selecting A Battery

Test Modification Techniques

When you are reviewing assessment materials for possible inclusion in a test battery, maintain a flexible attitude. For instance, you may find that a portion of a test appears to be superior to the rest of the test, or may eventually yield some diagnostic information not found elsewhere. The administration of the test in its present form may not be appropriate for your student. These factors should not deter you from including portions of the test in your final battery or using them as a model in order to develop your own materials. While any modification in the administration, required response, or scoring of the test invalidates the norms as they were developed, it is far more important to gain information about language status for planning intervention or monitoring rather than to simply obtain scores. Therefore, modifying tests and using parts of tests may be highly desirable in order to enhance the match between examiner needs and the student's needs, abilities, and performance.

Below are three examples of test modifications that you might make: modification of test administration, required response, and scoring techniques.

1) <u>Modification of Test Administration</u>

One of the most common test modifications is to administer a group test such as the <u>Boehm Test of Basic Concepts</u> to an individual child. This is essential when one administers the test to hearing-impaired students. The examiner may also wish to administer such a test, which was developed for normally hearing students, to a student whose primary communication mode is simultaneous communication. This change represents another form of test modification.

Or the examiner may wish to give Form A of the <u>Boehm</u> orally to the student to assess his understanding of concepts through the auditory mode alone. The test may be repeated, with Form B, and administered in simultaneous communication, or sign only. These modifications may provide valuable information about a child who is being considered for "mainstreaming" into the regular classroom or simply provide more information to the teacher about signed vs. oral input.

Selecting A Battery

In the case where a specific test contributes information not found in other evaluation tools, the examiner may wish to administer only certain subtests or specific items. An example is found in the Bankson Language Screening Test. The subtests for Categories or Functions, which are generally not found in other language tests, may be administered independently of the other subtests as part of the total language battery.

2) Modification of Required Response

Where a test protocol requires an oral response, allowing the student a change to simultaneous communication is a common modification. For a student with limited motor or expressive skills, a possible modification from an oral or signed response to a pointing response may permit more extensive and profitable testing to occur.

3) Modification of Scoring Techniques

It is sometimes important to know how a hearing-impaired student compares in language development to her hearing peers; for example, when she is being placed in a mainstream classroom. In this case, you might use part of the test and results exactly as developed and part modified to incorporate the use of total communication. A comparison against a) norms and b) use of total communication may provide important predictions about the child's success in the regular classroom. At other times, you will not want to make this comparison, but you will want to obtain baseline data on a student before intervention. It is still possible to use the same test with hearing norms but use it as a criterion- referenced test rather than as a norm-referenced test.

REMEMBER: There are no "perfect" tests. Don't eliminate a test from a possible test battery without considering using portions of it or making modifications which may improve its usability. When considering test modifications, think creatively and be flexible.

SECTION IV:

ADMINISTERING THE TEST BATTERY

Testing the Hearing-Impaired Child: Special Considerations

Hearing loss is not a "simple" impairment, nor is it usually a single one. For this reason, as mentioned previously, hearing-impaired students exhibit great variability; each student is very different from another. Their learning styles, behavior, academic achievement, and use of residual hearing are all dependent on a number of variables which help to create the extreme dissimilarities among them. Variables that contribute to these differences are the child's age at onset of the hearing loss, age at the time of first intervention, degree of loss, impact of hearing loss on auditory discrimination, parental support and effectiveness of communication in the home, length of time that hearing aids have been used, effectiveness of past school programming, and additional handicaps.

The differences among students caused by these variables will also contribute to the students' ability to take tests, especially standardized, commercial tests that do not usually relate directly to their environment and often limited body of knowledge. Therefore, the process of assessing the language of the hearing-impaired student is more complex than one might expect, largely because of the complexity of the factors noted above that, in various combinations, affect each hearing-impaired child. The following section identifies numerous issues that you must consider when assessing the language of hearing-impaired students.

Natural Context vs. Use of Commercial Tests

Receptive language. The ideal method for obtaining the most information when you are assessing language is to conduct the assessment within the daily contextual environment. Thus, to obtain information about receptive language, you might "test" to see if all students in a given classroom understand 1) all of the vocabulary being used socially and academically, 2) different types of directions being given, and 3) a variety of grammatical constructions. This type of assessment of receptive language is not impossible, but could be very time-consuming. It might be more appropriate to use these techniques for individual students in order to obtain baseline data and to monitor their progress after you have identified areas of strength and weakness using a more formal approach. It is far less time-consuming to put together a battery of tests or parts of tests in order to make the initial observations and identify problems within the different areas of receptive language. Once problem areas have been identified, you could test them further using a natural context if desired.

Using commercial tests that relate to everyday activities, vocabulary, and concepts will obviously provide more meaningful information than any others. An example is the <u>Boehm Test of Basic Concepts</u>, which includes vocabulary and concepts used daily in the school experience. However, when you select commercial tests or teacher-made tests designed for other groups, you must take precautions when using them with hearing-impaired students. (See below.)

<u>Expressive language</u>. The preferred method for evaluating language production of hearing-impaired children is to take a language sample from each student, within the student's normal setting. It is the only meaningful way to obtain information about how an individual hearing-impaired student uses language. Hearing-impaired students often use language inappropriately, even when they produce sentences that are syntactically correct. The language sample may be supplemented by standardized testing (Klee, 1985) or by more structured evocation procedures (Roth & Spekman, 1984). One example of this would be to supplement the language sample with a more formal test of expressive vocabulary. Although the language sample would enable you to observe the student producing some vocabulary and would show whether or not he used the words appropriately in context, you might wish additional information about the breadth of his vocabulary and whether he was using the same word over and over again when a different word would provide variety and improve the style of the message he is communicating. The more formal test might provide this additional information.

Test Administration

Vocabulary. The vocabulary understood and used by hearing-impaired students is often more limited than that of their hearing peers. Therefore, whenever instructions or directions are given in preparation for testing and for explaining what is expected of the student, it is imperative that you use vocabulary that the student understands. This applies both to commercial and teacher/clinician-made tests. It is also essential to use vocabulary known to the individual student when you are checking his or her comprehension of grammatical structures. If you use vocabulary that the student does not understand, the test results are confounded and you will not obtain accurate information about the grammatical structures.

If you use commercial tests of vocabulary, be sure that the pictures depicting the object or event are conceptually understood by the child. Hearing-impaired children often do not have as rich and varied experiences as their normal hearing counterparts and, therefore, their vocabulary may be more limited. For example, if a test picture shows children jumping over waves in the ocean, and the student has never seen the ocean or pictures of it, an erroneous answer might reflect lack of knowledge about the picture of the ocean rather than of a particular language structure.

Many hearing-impaired children have difficulty "clozing" or "filling in" one word in a sentence, especially if they have never been exposed to this technique. You are most likely testing a student's ability to learn a new technique rather than a particular language form if you use the cloze procedure in a test situation unless the student has used the procedure previously.

Practice items. Not all tests include practice items. If the ones you are considering do not, develop some yourself. Hearing-impaired students often do not understand instructions and you want to be sure your hearing-impaired student understands what he or she is expected to do before testing begins.

Functional Age vs. Chronological Age

It is important to at least estimate the age level at which a student is functioning. Language tests are most often designed for normal hearing children of certain chronological ages, and hearing-impaired students are usually language

Test Administration

delayed. Therefore, it is not appropriate to give a test or test items that are beyond the hearing-impaired student's functional age.

Hearing Aids

If the student wears a hearing aid or aids on a daily basis, the aids must be worn during testing; they must also be in good operating condition, with good batteries. If the student is not usually aided, amplification should not suddenly be introduced for the testing situation.

Health

Because of colds and allergies, hearing-impaired students can also have a conductive hearing loss superimposed on their sensorineural hearing loss. For those who rely on auditory input for all or part of the incoming message, the addition of a conductive loss can severely reduce the ability to understand. If there is any doubt about the health of the student's ears, do not test until until the problem is remediated.

Comfort and Attention Span

Many writers have noted that hearing-impaired children tend to have a shorter attention span than their hearing peers, and that they are more distractible. Don't be afraid to take a break; get a drink of water, stretch, walk around the room. This is especially important when you are testing younger children, and will increase the comfort of all hearing-impaired children you test as well as increase the validity of the test results.

Lighting

Because most hearing-impaired students rely upon their ability to read lips and/or signing and fingerspelling, light must be adequate and never be located so that it shines in the student's eyes.

Mean Length of Utterance

Mean length of utterance (MLU) has been identified as a simple index of grammatical development because, as the child's knowledge about new grammatical structures increases,

Test Administration

so does the length of his or her utterances (Brown, 1973). MLU has often been used clinically to measure the effects of intervention with language disordered children, but recently has been shown not to be reliable or sensitive to grammatical changes in normal children beyond Brown's Stage II (approximately 2 years of age), and does not seem to be useful in matching normal to language disordered children (Klee, 1985). It may not be useful in comparing the hearing-impaired student's language to that of his or her hearing peers either, because when the hearing-impaired child's utterance increases in length, the complexity of the utterance may not be greater than it was previously. Rather, it may simply be a longer string of utterances that are grammatically incorrect.

Communication Modes

The preferred communication mode of the student to be tested -- e.g., simultaneous communication, American Sign Language, spoken English -- should be identified before the evaluation. If the preferred mode involves sign language, the examiner should be proficient in the form of sign language the child uses in order to administer the test. If not, resource personnel who are proficient in the student's preferred mode may facilitate assessment. An interpreter, teacher's aide, or parent may serve in this way. A caution must be noted here: If your goal is to assess a student's comprehension of English in signed/spoken form (simultaneous communication) and you are using a resource person to help administer a test to a student whose preferred mode is ASL, make sure that the resource person clearly understands your testing objectives. In this situation, all instructions should be given in ASL to ensure that the student understands the task, but the test itself would be presented in signed/spoken English. Reasons for testing in this manner might be to determine how much assistance this student will need in understanding reading assignments (which are written in English), just how much the student really does understand of English communication so that he or she might enjoy greater success in a mainstream situation, or whether it is preferable for this student to be educated using ASL only. When a resource person is called in to help, you must have a conference with that person before the

Test Adminstration

testing in order to clarify the test objectives, administration, reinforcement, and signs to be used. Practicing together will help you to deliver a smooth presentation. (See Using Resource Personnel in Test Administration, below, for further discussion.)

Total Communication
When you are testing students who are in a total communication program and usually speak and sign simultaneously, it is helpful to obtain information about how much they understand using 1) the auditory system, 2) sign alone, and 3) a combination of the two. Therefore, part of the testing of receptive language would be performed orally, part in sign only, and part using total communication. When you record a sample of language, it is important to note the same information regarding language production.

General Considerations for Administering Tests

In addition to the special considerations just discussed, we recommend that you also consider the following general issues, which affect test administration.
1) Consider: Reinforcement
The test manual may delineate a specific reinforcement schedule as part of the test administration. If so, follow it; if not, decide what type of reinforcer you may use and what the schedule of reinforcement will be. Consider also your own behavior when scoring the test or reinforcing the student. Unconsciously you may be unfairly helping the child to answer through your body language or facial expression. Consider whether your reinforcement is effective. These factors may influence the child's performance. Each individual has different requirements for reinforcement -- consider each child's unique needs. Many students become anxious when the examiner scores items during a test. Scoring or writing something for each item, not just those items that are wrong, or covering your score form may help modify this reaction.
2) Consider: Organization
The testing environment, materials, and scheduling should all be organized before the assessment begins. Multiple ses-

Test Administration

sions are often very important for hearing-impaired students and therefore testing may need to be scheduled over a period of several days. Specific environmental factors to be considered are found below. The examiner should also prepare the student before the test. An explanation of the test procedure and what is expected may reduce a great deal of "test anxiety." For the speech-language pathologist, getting to know the student through classroom observation will help. Talking with parents, teachers, and others who work with the child will give the examiner valuable background material. For the teacher, reviewing files, talking to parents, allowing time for a new child to become comfortable in the classroom, and sharing information with the speech-language pathologist will assist in establishing appropriate test conditions and obtaining better test results.

3) <u>Consider: Behavior During Testing</u>

Be aware of the student's behavior during testing: is he upset, anxious, sleepy, or hyperactive? The student's behavior during the assessment can provide useful information. If the child appears to be tiring, stop rather than continuing to test. If the child is new to the school situation and appears uneasy, he or she may need more reinforcement or need to have the test continued at a later date. Tuning in to the emotional state of the child can make assessment easier and the results more accurate.

4) <u>Consider: Coordinating Administration of the Tests</u>

Once the speech-language pathologist and teacher have decided upon the battery of tests to be used, consider dividing the actual administration of the tests or parts of tests between you. For example, the teacher and her aide might obtain the expressive language sample, while the speech-language pathologist might administer the tests for receptive language. Scoring and interpretation might be done together. Such an approach lessens the burden of testing while encouraging a team effort which results in better intervention for the student.

5) <u>Consider: Integration of Results</u>

Group staffings, teacher consultations, and parent interviews can provide a means of integrating and evaluating assessment data. If the speech-language pathologist and teacher

Test Adminstration

of the hearing impaired work together as a team, they can split the various tasks involved in obtaining the language data, then share their results, plan intervention together, provide information to the parents, and suggest ways for them to reinforce your intervention plans at home. The hearing-impaired student will benefit greatly from this teamwork.

The Test Environment

Before attempting a formal evaluation of the language skills of any child, the examiner should create a good testing environment; however, the environment may be even more critical when one is testing a hearing-impaired child. Many hearing-impaired children have problems with maintaining attention and are easily bothered by extraneous visual and auditory distractions. Thus other students wandering around the classroom could interfere with testing. It would be preferable for you to develop a quiet area, possibly using room dividers so that the student is removed from the general traffic flow and visual distractions. If sign plus voice are to be used, it will be important for the examiner to wear a sweater, blouse, or shirt that contrasts with his or her hands. If the student must rely upon lipreading, it will help if female examiners wear lipstick; _all_ examiners should make sure that they are not sitting with the light behind them. What you are striving for is an environment conducive to obtaining the best results. Creating a good test environment is the first step in a successful formal evaluation. Before testing the student, consider the factors noted in Table 17, An Environmental Checklist (some apply to the speech-language pathologist, some to the teacher, some to both):

Table 17

ENVIRONMENTAL CHECKLIST

1. **The Location**   Yes   No

    a. Are auditory and visual distractions eliminated or reduced?

    b. Is the temperature controllable?

    c. Does the space provide adequate ventilation?

    d. Can you sit so that you are at eye level with the child?

    e. Is the lighting adequate for lip-reading and other visual input?

    f. Will you, the examiner, be placed appropriately for the best use of lighting?

    g. Is the testing location away from the traffic flow of other adults/children?

2. **The Examiner**   Yes   No

    a. Is your appearance distraction-free?

    b. Have you arranged all necessary materials close by?

    c. Have you familiarized yourself with the test procedures?

    d. Have you scheduled several short test blocks rather than one long one?

    e. Have you considered the child's optimum test time in planning your schedule?

    f. Have you acquainted yourself with the child and prepared her for the assessment and what is expected?

3. **The Student**

    a. Does the student use an oral approach?

    b. Does the student use a total communication approach?

    c. If necessary, have you arranged for and discussed testing with an interpreter?

    d. Does the student use amplification?

    e. Have the aids been checked to ensure that they are in good working condition?

    f. If necessary, have you made the appropriate modifications for other handicapping conditions?

Using Resource Personnel in Test Administration

Integrating resource personnel into a language assessment plan is a practice that can be extremely productive when appropriately managed and planned beforehand. The decision to use a resource person in your language assessment will vary with the needs of the student, your skills, and the skills of the resource person.

Throughout this book, the speech-language pathologist and teacher of the hearing impaired are encouraged to act as a team. In fact, each can serve as a resource person for the other. For example, when working as a team they might divide the work so that the teacher signs the information and the speech-language pathologist records and interprets the results; or the teacher may act as interpreter for part of the testing and complete other parts of the testing herself, in the classroom. Be flexible in thinking about who else may serve as a resource in your assessment: an interpreter, a parent, an aide, or other school personnel may serve a variety of functions in assessing language effectively. For example, they may serve: 1) to put the young or difficult-to-test child at ease; 2) to supplement the examiner's signing skills; or 3) to obtain extra information during the assessment. Each of these functions is discussed below.

1) To Put the Young or Difficult-to-Test Child at Ease

If you are the speech-language pathologist, you may want to include a parent, the teacher, or the aide when assessing a very young child. The presence of a parent or other primary caretaker may reduce the child's anxiety and permit you to obtain a better indication of his language skills. By permitting the parent or the teacher to accompany the child and perhaps aid in the administration of the test, you are more likely to obtain the child's optimal performance and have an opportunity to observe him in spontaneous communication with a person he is close to. This might be an opportue time to obtain a meaningful language sample. The presence of a parent or teacher may also effectively mollify the difficult-to-test child, one who is new to the system, or one who has other behavioral problems.

Test Administration

2) <u>To Supplement the Examiner's Signing Skills</u>
   a) <u>Assessment of simultaneous communication</u>: If the examiner's skill in simultaneous communication is not adequate to ensure smooth administration of the test items without error or confusion, the services of an interpreter, teacher, or classroom aide who knows the student and is fluent in that communication mode should be obtained. This resource person would sign the test items and verbalize the student's responses to the examiner.
   b) <u>Assessment of American Sign Language (ASL)</u>: For the examiner who is not fluent in ASL, there are several situations in which a resource person may provide needed services. A resource person who is fluent in ASL may help in assessing a student who is more fluent in ASL than in signed English by presenting instructions for a test and asking and answering questions to ensure that the student understands the task. If the purpose of the test is to assess receptive or expressive skills in signed English, however, it is essential that the test items themselves be presented in the target communication mode. Thus, a resource person skilled in both ASL and signed English may present instructions in ASL and test items in signed English, or may only give instructions in ASL and have the examiner (if she is fluent in signed English) administer the test items. Whatever the child's mode of communication -- Pidgen, ASL, or other modifications -- it is critical that he or she be given <u>INSTRUCTIONS</u> in that mode. The testing should then proceed with the child using the mode being examined.

3) <u>To Obtain Added Data During Assessment</u>.
   During most assessments, the examiner has little time to record information other than the student's responses. In this situation a resource person could be used effectively to record spontaneous language, or to tape record or videotape the child during the assessment. A great deal of valuable information can be obtained from this type of recording. Additionally, when the examiner wishes to obtain information regarding a student's pragmatic use of language, the resource person can record a number of behaviors, such as eye contact with the examiner, non-verbal communication, and turn-taking. If the use of a resource person is not possible, talking into a tape recorder will provide you with additional information.

Obviously, the greatest amount of information will be obtained by videotaping, because the tape can be reviewed many times, each time the examiner looking for and scoring a different aspect of the communicative process.

<u>Suggestions</u>

If you decide to ask a resource person to participate in your assessment procedures, we recommend the following steps:
1) Before assessment, meet with the resource person to discuss your test objectives, what you hope to accomplish, and what his or her role will be in the assessment.
2) Familiarize the resource person with the assessment materials.
3) Schedule time to practice together in a "dry run" situation.

SECTION V:

OBTAINING AND USING LANGUAGE SAMPLES

Introduction

Previous discussion in this book has covered procedures for using published tests or parts of tests in order to assess language. The use of a test battery has been emphasized because no single test can address all aspects of language knowledge. Although a careful evaluation of a spontaneous language sample may provide all the information needed for some students, it is always a critical part of any test battery for <u>all</u> students.

There are three basic ways to obtain a language sample: 1) Students review pictures and write about the pictures, e.g., when assessed with the <u>Maryland Syntax Evaluation Instrument</u> (<u>MSEI</u>). 2) Students imitate what the tester has said/signed, e.g., from such instruments as the <u>Carrow Elicited Language Inventory (CELI)</u>, and the <u>Grammatical Analysis of Elicited Language (GAEL)</u>. Here the tester elicits the response to be imitated by using a specific stimulus. 3) Students talk about pictures, activities, or "happenings," and all responses are recorded in written form and on audio- or videotape. This is referred to as a spontaneous language sample because there is no specific sentence to be repeated and therefore children are able to talk about pictures or objects as they choose. Both Lee (1974) and Tyack and Gottsleben (1974) provide standardized techniques for obtaining the language sample and for scoring it which have been very popular with speech-language clinicians. These techniques were developed for clinicians who assess the language of hundreds of children suspected of language delay or language disorder and who wish to establish procedures that will allow them to systematically review data across all children.

Ways to Obtain a Language Sample

Written Language Samples

Students' written language samples are important academically and are usually gathered readily from the students' work in social studies, language arts, and reading. One may make a formal analysis by using a test such as the Written Language Syntax Test (Berry, 1981) or make an informal analysis using samples of writing. However, such tests do not provide information about a student's everyday use of language when they are communicating with peers, teachers, parents, or others in spoken/signed exchange. Analysis of written language samples will not be discussed in this book.

Elicited Language Samples

Elicited language samples (obtained through such tests as CELI and GAEL) are often popular because they are compact and self-contained, and specific scores can be obtained in a restricted period of time. Measures eliciting language samples are relatively easy to administer and always follow the same format. Elicited language samples are designed to bypass the problems inherent in obtaining a spontaneous language sample in that the stimuli are provided for the child and therefore specific grammatical structures may be tested. Although this type of sampling does ensure that specific grammatical constructions are assessed, the number of examples given to "test" each structure are limited and the format is somewhat restrictive: no new knowledge is gained about the child's use of language in the everyday environment and the grammatical constructions used are limited to those within a given test. Prutting, Gallagher, and Mulac (1975) suggest that a language sample obtained from a structured test does not provide the same information as one obtained in a more informal, natural, and relaxed environment. Longhurst and Grubb (1974) found that less structured, more natural settings elicited more language and more complex language than did the structured, prescribed tasks or talking about pictures. In addition, concerns have been raised that the results of elicited language sampling are not the same as results obtained during spontaneous discourse (McDade, Simpson, & Lamb, 1982). During

Language Samples

spontaneous speech, the speaker has a specific communicative intent (Schlesinger, 1971) and applies rules to produce the appropriate vocabulary, syntax, and meaning. When one requires a response through elicitation there is no communicative intent on the part of the speaker. Rather, the speaker must memorize what the other person is saying in order to repeat it back. Without the speaker's interest and need to comment, this approach may merely test short-term memory; a high score may simply imply that the speaker has rote memorized surface structure (Miller, 1973; Slobin & Welsh, 1973). Or the material to be repeated may exceed the memory of the child and he or she may rephrase the sentence in order to more evenly match current memory span (Miller & Chapman, 1975). Two studies have shown spontaneous language samples to be better than imitated ones (Menyuk, 1969; Slobin & Welsh, 1973).

Spontaneous Language Samples

Spontaneous language samples provide information about the speaker's use of language as well as appropriate production of form and content. This type of sampling can provide information about all aspects of language depending upon how the sample is obtained.

Formal approach to obtaining language samples. The quality and quantity of the child's spontaneous utterances will depend partly upon the examiner's skill and partly upon the environment in which the sample is obtained. Variables that affect the language output include the topic of a conversation, the tasks and toys provided the child, the child's familiarity with the examiner, and the type of questions asked (Cazden, 1970). For example, "why," "how," and "how come" appear to elicit more elaborate answers than do other question forms (Turnure, Buium, & Thurlow, 1976). Unfortunately, these particular question forms are often the most difficult for hearing-impaired children to answer. An additional problem is that the sample may not contain all structures the child is capable of using and may include stereotyped utterances.

A formal approach to obtaining a language sample involves following certain procedures both for eliciting production and for scoring the results. Descriptions of these procedures may be found in Lee (1974), Brown (1973), and Tyack and Gottsleben (1974). These procedures, developed for use in clinics, were designed to assist clinicians in obtaining the most accurate language samples and results that could be scored consistently across children. Developers make recommendations regarding use of materials that are both age- and interest-appropriate, taping all productions of each child, and eliciting complete sentences. For example, Tyack and Gottsleben suggest using the same visual stimuli (pictures), in the same order, and with the same verbal stimuli (such as "Tell me about this" and "What else do you see?") so that comparisons between samples will be meaningful. The corpus to be evaluated must contain 50 or 100 complete sentences which are in consecutive order. There are specific rules for what constitutes a complete sentence, what utterances must be eliminated, and how to score the results.

Lee's <u>Developmental Sentence Analysis</u> (1974) analyzes eight categories of grammatical forms. The examiner derives scores by giving weighted points for forms that meet all requirements for adult standard English. Thus a child may receive a point for correct use of indefinite or personal pronouns, main verbs, secondary verbs, negatives, conjunctions, interrogative reversals, and wh- questions, plus an additional point for a complete sentence. The total of these points is divided by the total number of sentences, providing the Developmental Sentence Score (DSS). The child's DSS can then be compared with a table of language norms for normally developing children of the same chronological age. The evaluator can see, for instance, whether or not an individual child falls below the 10th percentile and, if so, how much.

In the Tyack and Gottsleben (1974) approach, the evaluator finds a mean of words and morphemes, assigns a linguistic level, and analyzes all forms and constructions; goals selected for training are based upon this analysis. Such an approach can be useful when you analyze grammatical structures, although sentences may be somewhat stilted, as suggested from the following example of a 9-year-old deaf student talking about a picture:

Language Samples

> The man and the boy is petting the dog.
> The man is older than the boy and the dog.
> The man is bigger than the boy. The boy is bigger than the dog.
> The man and boy has a little machine.

It is also time-consuming and may not be the appropriate approach for the classroom teacher who has eight or so students to evaluate within the first 2 or 3 weeks of school and who does not necessarily want to standardize all procedures for comparison across children, but is more interested in developing and monitoring appropriate individual intervention targets. Additionally, neither the Lee nor the Gottsleben and Tyack approach makes provision for describing or analyzing the individual student's skill level in the areas of semantics and pragmatics.

Informal approach to obtaining language samples.
(1) What it is. An informal approach to obtaining a language sample is less constrained than the formal procedures, and would yield no formal scores that would result in percentiles, scaled scores, and so forth. However, this procedure can provide easily acquired language information about each student that, combined with the results of other testing and compared to normal developmental stages in language acquisition, can lead to appropriate goals and objectives. In order to obtain information about all aspects of the student's expressive language, it is essential that the language sample be obtained in contexts that are meaningful, varied, and a part of the student's daily experience. The more contrived the assessment situation, the less likely it is that the language sample represents the child's communicative ability and that the information can be generalized to other situations (Roth & Spekman, 1984). Recording language utterances in natural environments is a sampling procedure. Therefore, it is very likely that certain features may not appear within the time(s) of the sampling. If specific features are missing, the teacher/clinician may want to use a part of an expressive language test or establish a more structured situation in order to elicit the desired response. If the particular language feature is produced in a more restricted manner, this should be noted and

the feature should be looked for within a more natural context at a later date.

2) <u>Information needed</u>. It is important to obtain information about pragmatics and discourse as well as grammatical structure, although analysis will be difficult because taxonomies have not yet been completed in the area of <u>use</u>. Although these three areas are inseparable within the context of normal language, it may be necessary to attempt to artificially separate them for assessment purposes. This is especially true considering the difficulties that arise when one is recording the language output of a hearing-impaired child who uses total communication. It will be important to record and analyze breadth of vocabulary and semantic appropriateness, grammatical completeness, communicative intent, discourse strategies, as well as if and how sign and verbal production differ. Kolzak (1983) identifies a number of language skills necessary for hearing-impaired students if they are to be mainstreamed in regular classrooms successfully. However, these same skills contribute to successful interactions with English users both in and out of school and will lay the groundwork for eventual job success. You should consider these same language skills when analyzing the expressive language of any hearing-impaired student.

  a) What are the child's syntactic competencies? As the child matures, he or she should be able to use simple sentences, a wide range of transformations, and complex structures and be able to generate new structures with an expanded vocabulary.
  b) Can the student use language for a variety of communicative purposes? Structures that are grammatically correct will not suffice unless the student can understand and use directions, statements, questions, and explanations and be able to discuss events sequentially.
  c) Does the child show turn-taking skill in verbal communication? This skill requires that the student be able to communicate about experiences, wait, and understand that the communication will gain a response. It also requires that the student reciprocate with appropriate greetings and understand that requests for information require a response.
  d) How skillfull is the student at sustaining or using adaptive dialogues? The student must learn to carry on extended conversations, asking and answering questions, making statements, and understand and respond to the emotional content of the topic [Kolzak, 1983, pp. 133 - 134].

Language Samples

Simon (1981) points out that syntactic skills are only one component of a comprehensive communication system. Those with competent communication skills can "...use language effectively for any purpose, in any context, and in any role that arises" (p. 38).

Simon lists some specific components of an __ineffective__ communicative style which would interfere with development of appropriate pragmatic skills.

> - There is an egocentric communication style due to referents that are not clear. The perspective of the listener is not taken into consideration when information or instructions are related...
> - Messages are characterized by static, uncreative structural patterns...
> - There is very little planning of the message prior to its delivery...
> - Carrying on a dialogue is a difficult task...
> - The language system has not been molded to flexibly adapt to varying communication needs...
> [Simon, 1981, pp 38-39]

Simon elucidates these components by mentioning such factors as the speaker's failure to consider the listener's age and background or ability to comprehend the message; the speaker's use of simple sentences lacking details or nuances; the lack of sequence in the speaker's messages, "false starts," and revisions mid-message. Dialogue may be difficult because of "difficulty maintaining the 'flow of meaning'...a cluttering of words, or sometimes slurred speech..." The listener may hear only the surface structure of "tactfully devious" messages without understanding their underlying meaning. Simon cites the example of the teacher who says "Peanut butter all over the lunch table annoys me," when what he means is "Next time, clean up the table after you have finished your lunch." The listener may not infer the underlying message. Finally, Simon discusses the person's failure to understand that what may be an adequate language for social situations is not acceptable in more formal or intellectual circumstances. All of these communicative components must be considered when you evaluate the hearing-impaired student's use of language.

Guidelines for Obtaining Informal Language Samples

Guidelines for obtaining informal language samples follow and should be modified as needed. The team of the teacher and speech-language pathologist could easily share the responsibility for obtaining these language samples, compare their results, and plan intervention together. Such a team effort will result in more appropriate targets and a more cohesive language intervention plan for the hearing-impaired student.

Specific Suggestions

1) Obtain a sample of each student's language at least two times per year, at the beginning and end of the year.
2) Obtain eight to ten utterances of each student's language for 5 days, for a total of 40 to 50 utterances. Make every effort to obtain samples of running discourse. Otherwise you will not be able to fully assess <u>use</u> of language. You do not have to sample all students during the same week. For example, if you have eight students, sample four during one week and four the next.
3) Each day obtain the eight to ten utterances at different times when the student is communicating with different people in different circumstances so that you sample <u>use</u> of language in different contexts. For example, on Monday you might write down four or five utterances when the student arrives for class and four or five at recess. On Tuesday, you might choose different times and places such as lunch time in the lunch room or when the student is in the school office talking to the secretary or principal, and so forth. Or you might obtain eight utterances on one day when the student arrives and eight the next day at recess, etc. Part of the decision will be based upon how much communicating an individual student does at any given time. This provides an opportunity to evaluate, for example, if a student knows how to use appropriate language with the principal or another teacher and different language (incomplete sentences, slang) with peers, how to take turns, and how to provide additional information at the appropriate time.

Language Samples

4) Always record some continuous dialogue because this will help you to evaluate discourse strategies the student is using. An effective way to accomplish this is to ask a student to describe a favorite T.V. show or movie or talk about a recent trip or experience.

5) Record the setting (environment) and the gist of the other person's comments. For example, if you are recording a language sample early in the morning and talking to the student about what he did last night, identify that situation. If you have to ask questions in order to obtain language from the student, record that also. Including these elements will provide the examiner information about turn-taking, approriateness of initiation and response, and intended meaning. A recording sheet might look like the following:

Context	Antecedent Event or Stimulus	Response	Other Behaviors/ Comments	Use
Bob arriving for class in a.m.	T."What did you do last night?" T."Tell me about what you saw."	"Saw T.V."	Maintained eye contact. Needed constant prompting to continue.	

6) Don't talk too much yourself. The goal is to get the student to do the talking.

7) Avoid using questions that elicit a yes/no answer such as "Did you like it?" "Was it good?"

8) Use questions like "What happened next?" "What do you think will happen?" or "That's interesting. What else can you tell me?"

9) Write (or ask an aide or someone else to write) what the student says or speak it into a mike to record it on audiotape. Videotaping may catch all the signing and gesturing but it may be expensive, it may not always elicit the most spontaneous language, and the equipment is not always readily transportable when you are recording spontaneous language within different environments.

Language Samples

10) Keep a clipboard handy or use a wall chart in order to be able to record language utterances quickly and at any time for each student.
11) After you have identified the student's grammatical error patterns, identify his functional language level by comparing the results of your sampling to normal language development norms. You can do this by using information about normal language development such as that found in Limber (1973), Appendix A in Miller (1981), and the charts that follow in this section.*
12) If all grammatical elements do not appear within the informal approach, supplement with "formal" tests, parts of formal tests, or teacher/clinician tests.
13) Be sure to use the Pragmatic Checklist, the Kendall Communicative Scale, or any other scale, checklist, etc. that will supplement your grammatical analyses of the language sample and assist you in reviewing how your student _uses_ language.

Additional Suggestions for Assessing Pragmatics

Roth and Spekman (1984) provide an excellent summary of information needed for assessing the pragmatic abilities of children and many methods for eliciting the type of information desired. They recommend evaluating communicative intentions, presupposition, and social organization of discourse. In addition to formal tests and/or observation of

---

*NOTE

Language develops on a continuum, usually following a sequence: pre-language skills, then one-word, two-word, and three-word utterances which eventually expand in both length and complexity. Different children develop these skills at different ages. Therefore, the only reason for referring to normative data would be to look at sequence—what type of language behavior precedes or follows another. Being aware of the sequence of language along the continuum will help you prevent the teaching of skills far beyond the ability level of the child. Also, following a developmental sequence will help prevent the "holes" and scatter so predominant in the language of hearing-impaired students.

Language Samples

ongoing classroom activities, they suggest specific activities that could be adapted for hearing-impaired students, as follows.

   Presupposition. One person is responsible for transmitting information to another so that the other person can draw or select a picture, build a structure, make a design, find a hidden object, and so forth.
1) Keep both students in view of each other so that both visual (sign, lipreading) and auditory cues will be available.
2) Have them take turns being the initiator and receiver.
3) Have one student sign/say descriptive information about one picture when three or four are available.
4) If possible, observe both the informant and the receiver and take data on how well one gives information and how well the other receives and understands the information.
5) Use any variation such as hiding a surprise and giving directions to find it.

   Discourse strategies. Have one person (adult or student) provide only partial information in carrying out a task. Observe if the second student can ask questions in order to "repair" the breakdown in the communication.

   Role play and group decision making are additional means to elicit communicative interactions, observe, and collect data.

Recording and Analyzing Spontaneous Language

Grammatical Recording and Analysis

There is no single "best" method for describing language skills in any detail. Although some prepackaged forms on which to record a child's grammatical utterances are available (e.g., Tyack & Gottsleben, 1974), it may be preferable for each teacher and speech-language pathologist to devise procedures that suit his or her own preferences and needs or to modify existing techniques and forms.

One method of evaluating the development of expressive verbal language in young children is the Mean Length of Utterance (MLU). This technique is appropriate to use until children are producing four to five words (Bloom & Lahey, 1978).

It has been identified as a reasonable way to compare the language development of one child to other children because many similar forms occur at the time a child reaches a certain MLU (Brown, 1973). The MLU, however, does not provide information about specific grammatical structures used by the child and therefore cannot account for difference in grammatical competence found in children who may have the same average utterance length (Cazden, 1968). This problem is certainly one that could apply to many hearing-impaired children, especially young ones whose number of utterances increases but whose use of appropriate grammatical constructions does not keep pace.

A variant of the Tyack and Gottsleben (1974) approach could be used for older children who are attempting to formulate complete structures. The following example of language (Table 18) is part of a language sample taken in a self-contained classroom for hearing-impaired students. The 10-year-old child was talking to a new student teacher about classroom, family, and home activities. Two columns are provided in order to identify the student's errors and the ages at which normally developing children would be expected to produce these forms. Although not complete, such a simple analysis could be done easily and quickly and at least provide the teacher and clinician with guidelines for developing be-ginning intervention objectives for grammatical structures. Information about some aspects of the student's use of language could be obtained informally; i.e., the teacher/clinician could keep track of turn-taking, topic maintenance, and appropriateness of responses. A quick scan of the sample shows that the student is using some variety in his communication such as informing and requesting information. He is also capable of changing the topic when the student teacher writes something he doesn't understand and then returning to the original topic when requested to do so. This information would be noted and used in the summary statement leading to beginning intervention plans.

Table 18

LANGUAGE SAMPLE AND ANALYSIS

Student's Language	Standard Form	Errors	Expected Ages
Alan			
1. I went to Port Angeles.	1. O.K.	1. none	1. O.K.
2. I ride two ferry boats.	2. I rode on two ferry boats.	2. irregular past – main verb (two-part verbs or particle)	2. 41-46 months
3. I open the present and I got necklace and bracelet.	3. I opened the present and I got a necklace and bracelet.	3. regular part – main verb; article	3. 41-46 months; 41-46 months
4. I went to Carla house.	4. I went to Carla's house.	4. possessive	4. 31-34 months
5. Larry and Peter and me learn how to sign.	5. Larry, Peter, and I are learning how to sign.	5. subject pronoun in compound subject; is verb-ing-first person plural	5. 46+ months
6. Do you ever play before?	6. Did you ever play before?	6. irregular past-auxiliary do	6. 47+ months
7. Miss Smith, you do this way?	7. Miss Smith, do you do it this way?	7. auxiliary do in interrogative reversal; object pronoun	7. 35-38 months
8. What that say?	8. What does that say?	8. irregular 3rd person singular-auxiliary do-interrogative reversal	8. 47+ months

Student's Language	Standard Form	Errors	Expected Ages
9. That supposed to be 14.	9. That is (that's) supposed to be 14.	9. contractable copula (to be)-3rd person singular	9. 41-46 months
10. Why you do that?	10. Why are you doing that?	10. present progressive—interrogative reversal	10. 35-40 months
11. Why you don't know how to sign yet?	11. Why don't you know how to sign yet?	11. interrogative reversal	11. 35-40 months
12. My brother went to play with his fire truck.	12. O.K.	12. none	12. O.K.
13. He get his fire truck for Christmas.	13. He got his fire truck for Christmas.	13. irregular past-main verb	13. 41-46 months
14. I get fire truck and light.	14. I got a fire truck and a flash light.	14. irregular past-main verb; article	14. 41-46 months; 41-46 months
15. He jumped down from the roof.	15. O.K.	15. none	15. O.K.
16. I went this way through the front.	16. O.K.	16. none	16. O.K.
17. He eleven and I'm ten.	17. He is (He's) eleven and I'm ten.	17. contractable copula (to be)-3rd person singular	17. 41-46 months

Language Samples

The Teacher Assessment of Grammatical Structures (TAGS)

(Moog & Kozak, 1983) provides an alternative to recording an entire sample of the child's language. Instead, the TAGS provides a checklist format that lists pre-sentences and simple and complex syntactic structures that follow a normal developmental sequence. Such a checklist would provide a relatively easy way for a teacher/clinician to look for a specific structure or structures in several different settings before checking that the child uses the structures 1) in imitation, 2) with a prompt, or 3) spontaneously. Because this is a checklist format for syntax, there is no place to record the student's utterances or social use of language. However, the teacher/clinician could develop an additional recording form that would include these other aspects of expressive language.

The test is described in detail in Section VI but a sample of the recording form for one portion of the Simple Sentence Level is provided in Table 19.

Language Samples

Table 19
TAGS RECORDING FORM

THREE-WORD COMBINATIONS

	C	I	P	S
NOUN-NOUN-NOUN boy ball chair				
NOUN-VERB-NOUN boy throw ball				
NOUN-NOUN-VERB boy girl throw				
NOUN-VERB-VERB boy run jump				
NOUN-PREPOSITION-NOUN ball on chair				
NOUN-COPULA-NOUN mom is doctor				
NOUN-COPULA-ADJECTIVE ball is red				

PRONOUNS IN THREE-WORD COMBINATIONS

	C	I	P	S
1st PERSON SUBJECTIVE I				
1st PERSON POSSESSIVE my, mine				
INDEFINITE everybody, everyone				
3rd PERSON SUBJECTIVE he, she				
1st PERSON PLURAL SUBJECTIVE we				
3rd PERSON PLURAL SUBJECTIVE they				
DEMONSTRATIVE this, that				

A very complete method for analyzing preschool language, The Bare Essentials in Assessing Really Little Kids (BEAR), was developed by Hasenstab and Laughton (1982). The technique described for analyzing syntactic, morphological, semantic, pragmatic, and phonological components of language includes charts describing a continuum of language from prelinguistic behaviors to complex transformations and a suggested form that provides space for recording the setting, stimulus, observed linguistic response, related behavior, and comments.

A method of evaluating expressive language that includes the semantic component is the Language Sample Analysis de-

Language Samples

veloped by Bloom and Lahey (1978), where the examiner classifies the child's utterances according to semantic categories. This method of evaluating spontaneous language progresses from single-word usage, to two- and three-word combinations showing syntactic-semantic relationships, to more complex sentences including modals, connectives, and relative clauses. The evaluation of grammatical morphemes is also included.

A very sophisticated approach to analyzing language samples has been developed by Kretschmer and Kretschmer (1978). This particular technique was developed in order "...to account for language differences as well as delays" (p. 184) and is appropriate to use when one is evaluating oral, written, pidgen sign, gesture, and fingerspelling (p. 192). The method of analysis includes techniques for identifying preverbal skills, communicative competence, and semantic and syntactic production, from simple to complex.

Miller and Chapman (1983) have developed a computerized method of analyzing expressive language called the Systematic Analysis of Language Transcripts (SALT). After the language sample is transcribed into the SALT format, all analyses are performed by the computer. These analyses include number of utterances by word and morpheme length, number of utterances per speaker turn, type-token ratio for words, MLU compared to age expectation, and so on. Using the program SEARCH, a teacher/clinician can specify exactly what parts of the student's language she wishes to analyze.

Recording forms. There are many variations of forms that could be used in order to record a language sample. Teachers or speech-language pathologists could develop forms for their own use or develop forms that would be used in one building or throughout their district. In order to develop forms, it is necessary to consider the following. It is essential to identify the context within which the sample is taken, and to provide space for recording (1) what the antecedent or stimulus event is, (2) what the response is, and (3) descriptions of the student's behaviors such as maintaining eye contact, etc. It is also critical to record exactly what the target student is producing. If it is not clear from the data recorded who is initiating and who is responding, be sure to identify who these people are. If desired, a key could be added that would identify T (teacher), S (student), P (peer), etc. as well as the mode of communication: gesture, vocalization, sign, and so forth. Table 20 provides an example of a recording form.

Table 20

LANGUAGE SAMPLE RECORDING FORM

Key: O = oral
      S = sign
      TC = Total Communication
      __ = Child's initial
      T = Teacher
      __ = Other

Student's Name _____
Date _____
C.A. _____

Context (describe)	Antecedent Event or Stimulus	Response	Other behavior/ Comments	Use

Language Samples

    The information from this form could be transferred to the forms that follow for analysis, or one could analyze the sample by using any one of the methods discussed above. The analysis forms that follow do not identify every structure that could occur at any given period, but they do include the most salient ones. They could easily be modified to meet the needs and/or requirements of the individual teacher/clinician, and can be added to as additional information about language development becomes available.

    Children normally develop new language structures while still using old (already learned) ones. Thus, although a child might begin to use two- and three-word utterances, he or she will continue to use one-word utterances as well. The same behavior can be observed in hearing-impaired children. For example, as the clinician and teacher analyze the language structure of a hearing-impaired student, they may find that the student is producing some language at Phase 2 and some at Phase 3 (see Tables 21-26 on the following pages). The caution here is that, although normal hearing children may be using some advanced structures, they usually have full command of the prerequisite structures. The same is not always true of the hearing-impaired child. Therefore, it is essential that the person(s) responsible for analyzing language in order to develop and monitor intervention plans be sure that those plans include teaching the prerequisite language structures so that the student does not have language gaps.

Table 21

LANGUAGE ANALYSIS FORM

Student's Name _____
Date _____
Age _____

Phase 1

STRUCTURE	EXAMPLES	COMMENTS

Communicative Intentions:
object request
action request
information request
greeting
transferring
showing off
acknowledging
answering
 	
Labeling:
  Nominals
    people
    animals
    objects
    food
    toys
    other		

STRUCTURE	EXAMPLES	COMMENTS

Non-Nominal
  gone
  that
  down
  there (completion of task)
  more
  pretty
  others
 	
Imitation
  simple motor; e.g.,
    pat-a-cake
    wave bye-bye
    peek-a-boo
    smile
  vocal/verbal; e.g.,
    animal sounds
    attempts to imitate sounds/
    words made by others
  turn-taking; e.g.,
    adult vocalizes, child vocalizes,
      etc. or
    adult claps, child claps, etc.		

Table 22

LANGUAGE ANALYSIS FORM

Phase 2

Student's Name _____
Date _____
Age _____

STRUCTURE	EXAMPLES	COMMENTS

Noun Phrase:
Proper nouns
    Mommy, Daddy, Aunt Susan, Rusty
 	
Count nouns
    human; e.g.,
        boy, baby
    non-human; e.g.,
        ball, truck
    mass nouns; e.g.,
        sugar, milk
 	
Modifiers:
color names—at first the actual color may not be correct; e.g., red truck, red ball—ball and truck may be green, blue, etc.
 	
big + N. Used without concept of big/little. May represent delayed imitation of adult input.		

STRUCTURE	EXAMPLES	COMMENTS
Sentences:		
Action-Object; e.g., throw ball / see puppy		
Action-Locative; e.g., sit chair / fall bed		
Agent-Object; e.g., mommy sandwich / boy ball		
Entity-Locative; e.g., sweater chair / boy bed		
Possessor-Possessed; e.g., puppy dish / daddy eye		
Entity-Attribute; e.g., truck red / girl pretty		
Experience-State; e.g., I (me) want, love, need		

STRUCTURE	EXAMPLES	COMMENTS
Dative-Receiver; e.g., give mommy bring teacher **Functional Relations** Existence: this, that, it, a; e.g., that cookie it a truck Recurrence: more, another, 'nother; e.g., more milk Non-existence no, all gone, away, no more; e.g., all gone juice Rejection: no, indicating opposition on part of the child; e.g., no sit no outside Denial; e.g., no push no break not gone		

STRUCTURE	EXAMPLES	COMMENTS
Simple Questions: 　yes/no; e.g., 　　new + point 　wh– ; e.g., 　　what + point 　　what do? 　　where go? 　　what this? or 　　what's this?		

Table 23

LANGUAGE ANALYSIS FORM

Phase 3

Student's Name _____
Date _____
Age _____

STRUCTURE	EXAMPLES	COMMENTS

Noun Phrase:
  Proper nouns
    siblings, playmates
 	
  Plurals
    regular; e.g.,
      trucks, balls
    irregular
      feet (may use feets, foots)
 	
  Determiners
    the, a; e.g.,
      the ball
      a doll
 	
  Pronouns
    me, I; e.g.,
      I want
 	
  Possessive marker; e.g.,
    mommy's dress		

STRUCTURE	EXAMPLES	COMMENTS

Possessives
    hers, his, mine, my; e.g.,
        That his teddy
 	
New modifiers
    some, a lot, two, hers, his,
    mine, colors
 	
Demonstrative pronouns
    this, that, there, those; e.g.,
        that a big truck
 	
Verb Phrase
Main verb
    Simple present
    Action:
        play, run; e.g.,
        baby sit here
    Process:
        want, need, love; e.g.,
        want more cookie		

STRUCTURE	EXAMPLES	COMMENTS
Present progressive: "be" omitted in beginning; e.g., me (I) going doggie running		
Regular past walked, talked (often overgeneralized to irregular verbs—runned); e.g., I walked I no spilled it I runned		
Occasional verb + participle; e.g., pick up, put on		
Regular third person singular; e.g., she/he plays		
Modals: can't, don't, Later: can + not do + not		

STRUCTURE	EXAMPLES	COMMENTS
Beginning auxiliary: gonna, hafta, wanna; e.g., I wanna go Contractable copula; e.g., Here's my coat. There's Johnny. Use of be + -ing; e.g., mommy going (to store). **Sentences** NP + VP + NP; e.g., Daddy throw ball. Tommy goes to school. Mary has a new coat. NP + (neg) + VP + NP; e.g., Doggie no bite you. Mommie not kiss me.		

STRUCTURE	EXAMPLES	COMMENTS
NP + (neg) + V; e.g., Tabby no bite. I can't go. Don't do that. He (he's) not big.		
NP + be (copula) + adj; e.g., I pretty. I'm pretty. The house is brown.		
Questions What + (N) + V; e.g., What you eat?		
Where + (N) + V; e.g., Where Daddy go? Eventually, appropriately inverted; e.g., Where is my sweater? Where did Daddy go? What did you eat? Rising intonation often continues to be used as yes/no question forms, e.g., Go now? We're going now?		

Table 24

LANGUAGE ANALYSIS FORM

Phase 4

Student's Name _____
Date _____
Age _____

STRUCTURE	EXAMPLES	COMMENTS
Noun Phrase All nouns singular and plural, regular and irregular; e.g., boxes, deer, children		
Predeterminer + definite article + plural; e.g., Some of the pencils are red.		
Predeterminer + possessive + Plural noun; e.g., All of my shirts are dirty.		
Predeterminer + possessive + mass noun; e.g., I drank all of my milk.		
Cardinal number + singular noun + plural noun; e.g., one time five marbles		

STRUCTURE	EXAMPLES	COMMENTS
Beginning noun derivations; e.g., hitter, painter, fisher		
Beginning comparatives; e.g., smaller		
Pronouns him, her, it, me, that's		
Verb Phrase		
Past regular; e.g., He walked. irregular; e.g., She came.		
Past modals could, would, should		
Past modals + negative – beginning uses couldn't, wouldn't, shouldn't		
Future We will (we'll) go shopping later. I am (I'm) going to John's party. Are we going to the park this afternoon?		

STRUCTURE	EXAMPLES	COMMENTS
Contractable auxiliary "be"; e.g., They're playing. I'm coming.		
Uncontractable "be" (copula); e.g., Are they the boys? Was that the right book?		
Uncontractable auxiliary "be"; e.g., Is he running?		
Irregular third person singular; e.g., He came. She ran.		
Contracted modals; e.g., He'll come.		
Contracted "be" + negative; e.g., He isn't nice. It's not hot.		
Contracted auxiliary "do" + negative; e.g., Don't go! He didn't come.		

STRUCTURE	EXAMPLES	COMMENTS
Sentences		
NP + VP + NP + (adv); e.g., John ran home fast.		
NP + VP + unmarked infinitive; e.g., She made him (to) come today. Help me (to) cut these flowers. Watch me (to) run.		
NP + be (copula) + adj. (contracted); e.g., The kitty's sick.		
NP + be (copula) + NP; e.g., That boy's name is John.		
Beginning passives; e.g., Jenny got hit. The dog got hurt.		
Beginning use of complement as object of verbs guess and think. May use different word order at first; e.g., I know what is that.		
Later, use of appropriate word order; e.g., I think (that) Mary is a good runner.		

STRUCTURE	EXAMPLES	COMMENTS

Questions
 yes/no – present, past; e.g.,
  Were you swimming?
 	
 With modals and "be"; e.g.,
  Can I talk to grandma?
  Is Rusty hungry?
 	
 With "do"; e.g.,
  Do you have a green sweater?
 	
 Wh– questions; e.g.,
  where, who, why, how many, how much
 	
 Conjunctions
 Daddy ate it and we didn't get any.
 We're going swimming 'cause it's hot.		

Table 25

LANGUAGE ANALYSIS FORM

Phase 5

Student's Name _____
Date _____
Age _____

STRUCTURE	EXAMPLES	COMMENTS
Noun Phrase All possessive pronouns; e.g., his, hers, ours Reflexive pronouns; e.g., myself, himself, herself Prenominalization to show old or known information; e.g., John gave Mary candy and she ate it. Comparatives; e.g., nicer, bigger Plural demonstratives; e.g., those, there Prepositions; e.g., until, along, among		

STRUCTURE	EXAMPLES	COMMENTS

Indefinite pronouns; e.g.,
     anyone, everything, everybody
 	
 Use of "the" and "a" to identify specific/ non-specific, old/new information; e.g.,
     the White House
     a white house on our block
 	
 Noun phrases expanded by use of adjectives, nouns used as adjectives, prepositional phrases; e.g.,
     the one at the top
     an exciting card game
 	
 Additional noun derivations; e.g.,
     pianist
 	
 Verb Phrase
   Past progressive; e.g.,
     I was running.
 	
   Past modal + have; e.g.,
     I could have gone.
 	
   Past modal + have + negative; e.g.,
     I couldn't have gone.		

STRUCTURE	EXAMPLES	COMMENTS
Auxiliary have + verb (present, perfect); e.g., I have (I've) read that book before. Auxiliary have + verb (present, perfect) + negative; e.g., I haven't been swimming this week. I haven't seen the puppy. Adverbial clauses; e.g., We'll go to recess after we finish math. Before we go, I want a drink. Adverb derivations; e.g., gently Modals and modal-like forms; e.g., have to, need to, ought to **Sentences** Earlier sentences plus: Relative clause in the final position; e.g., like the man that has the dog		

STRUCTURE	EXAMPLES	COMMENTS
All "do" support; e.g., I did go. He didn't go. Do you want to go? Don't you want to go? Did you have one?		
Conjunctions but, unless, or; e.g., We can't go skating unless it freezes. We can go to the movies or watch T.V. I'd like to go but my mom said "no."		
Verb reductions; e.g., I want the ball and (I want) the bat.		
Indirect questions; e.g., I don't know where to go. I don't know how to work that.		
"That" complement; e.g., I thought that she was nice.		
Ability to shift adverbial clause; e.g., I was happy when I went swimming. When I went swimming, I was happy.		

STRUCTURE	EXAMPLES	COMMENTS
When questions; e.g., When will we go? When are we going? Gerund as subject; e.g., Running is the hardest sport.		

Table 26

LANGUAGE ANALYSIS FORM

Phase 6

Student's Name _____
Date _____
Age _____

STRUCTURE	EXAMPLES	COMMENTS
Noun Phrase Replacement of the noun phrase with a noun clause; e.g., <u>What he said</u> was very interesting. Plural reflexive pronouns: ourselves, themselves Superlatives; nicest, darkest **Verb Phrase** Use of adverbs to show cause and effect; e.g., <u>Because he was tired</u>, he went to bed. Use of adverbs to express conditions; e.g., I'll finish my homework, <u>if</u> I have time. We'll go <u>even if</u> it rains.		

STRUCTURE	EXAMPLES	COMMENTS
Present perfect progressive; e.g., I have been learning going studying		
Addition of new prepositions: beyond, except		
Sentences		
Irreversible passive; e.g., That huge pizza was eaten by two boys.		
Indirect quotations; e.g., He said that he liked to swim.		
Tag questions; e.g., He can't have that, can he?		
Conjunctions; e.g., I can go only if I have written permission. Bill laughs whenever you sing.		
Gerund as object of verb; e.g., I like eating outside.		
Gerund as object of a preposition; e.g., Everyone was interested in flying.		

STRUCTURE	EXAMPLES	COMMENTS
If-then clauses; e.g., If you finish your work, then we can paint. Relative clause in medial position; e.g., The dog that chewed my shoe ran away.		

Language Samples

General Information to Consider Within the Language Sample
After recording the language sample, review the ways the student is using language. If you have carefully recorded context and what others have signed/spoken, this will not be difficult and will assist you in formulating impressions about the appropriateness of the student's interpersonal communication skills.

Vocabulary. Look for qualitative as well as quantitative use of vocabulary. Be sure the student is not using certain words over and over again when he or she should be learning to use new words that provide the same meaning, thus expanding his or her lexicon. Make sure the student is beginning to understand that a single word can have several meanings depending upon context thus finding "new" uses for "old" vocabulary.

Modifiers. Look for expanded use of adjectives, adverbs, and adverbial phrases such as:
John ate his dinner (quickly, fast).
John ate his hot dinner slowly.
John ate his very delicious dinner with gusto.

Expanded discourse. Look for expanded use of the various grammatical structures. Students must not continue to only make statements or comment. They must also ask questions, respond to others by informing, asking additional questions, providing directions, etc.

Social language. Look for turn-taking, "polite" language, topic maintenance, and repair. Although there are no developmental guidelines, these behaviors should increase as students acquire greater facility with using language. Once you begin to search for these characteristics, it is amazing how quickly you find occasions where the behaviors should have occurred but did not. Hearing-impaired students often do not use these language skills; e.g., they do not wait for a turn, do not recognize that it is their turn and their responsibility to carry on the conversation, and do not ask appropriate questions to repair a breakdown in communication.

Syntax. Because the building of a "simple sentence grammar" has long been identified as being important to teach to hearing-impaired children (Streng, 1972; Canaglia, Cole, Howard, Krohn, & Rice, 1973; Blackwell & Hamel, 1971; Heidinger, 1984; Blackwell, Engen, Fischgrund, & Zarcadoolas, 1978), the five basic sentence patterns and the semantic roles employed

Language Samples

within these patterns follow. The teacher/clinician could look for the various patterns as well as the different semantic relationships in the language of younger children. Sound knowledge and use of these basic sentence constructions are the "...basis upon which all subsequent development will take place" (Blackwell, Engen, Fischgrund, & Zarcadoolas, 1978, p. 68) and will assist hearing-impaired children in expanding their language skills to include more complex structures. The teacher/clinician needs to look for gradual and consistent use of different types of simple sentence structures which eventually expand to more complex structures and an increased variety of semantic relationships.

(1) <u>Semantic Roles of Nouns</u>

According to Heidinger (1984), nouns have the following semantic meanings.

Pattern #1   NP + V_i + (Adv)   mover - like agent - but doesn't affect another person or object; reflects action performed or indicated by the verb

patient - receives effect of action (The cup fell.) (The trees swayed.). The action is caused by something unknown (the wind) or some person.

experiencer - person or thing that experiences a change or has an internal experience (he died)

instrument - used by someone to do something (The knife cuts.)

entity - subject of stative verb; something or someone who exists without action being performed on it (or them) (She stayed.)

Language Samples

Pattern #2
$NP^1 + V + NP^2 + (Adv)$

agent – performs action that affects another or action on an object

patient – receiver of action or being (The man kicked <u>the door</u>.) (Lou has a <u>dog</u>.)

instrument – (Mary cut the cake with a <u>knife</u>.)

complement – comes into being as a result of some action or process (She sang <u>the song</u>. He painted a <u>picture</u>.)

beneficiary (recipient) – profits from action or process; <u>receive</u>, <u>accept</u>, <u>get</u> (Dad got the package for <u>mother</u>.)

possessor – (owner)
(<u>Lou</u> has a parrot.)

Pattern #3
$NP + V_L + Adj + (Adv)$

entity–stative–attribute
(The coffee is cold.)
(The coffee tastes good.)
(Her eyes became bigger.)

Pattern #4
$NP^1 + V_L + NP^1 + (Adv)$

entity–stative–equivalent
(John is a man.)
(The girls stayed good friends for years.)

Language Samples

Pattern #5
NP + V$_{be}$ + Adv + (Adv)   entity – stative – location
                                               time
                                               season
                                               beneficiary
                                               duration

    location –   The three little girls were <u>in the pool</u>.
    time –   Mary should have been home <u>sooner</u>.
    beneficiary –   The gloves are <u>for Mary</u>.

(2) <u>Semantic Classification of Verbs</u>

Verbs are usually categorized as action, process, or stative.* A particular verb cannot always be categorized as one type only, however, because its meaning may change within different contexts as its relationship to other grammatical elements within the sentence alters.

Action verbs: represent external activity or movement such as: pull, walk, talk, shave, sing, climb, etc.

Process verbs: represent internal activity of the mind such as thinking, a change in condition that can be observed, or other activities that occur internally. Examples are: want, feel, think, like, melt, daydream, die, digest, etc.

Stative verbs: describe a state of being or a change in state such as: be, seem, remain, look, appear, turn, turn into, change into, stay, etc.

*For a more detailed description of verbs such as process-stative and action-process, see Kretschmer and Kretschmer (1978).

It is important to look for earlier forms such as NP + V_i + (Adv), "Daddy go," gradually used in more sophisticated fashion, "The raccoons crept through the garden," as well as new sentence forms being added. The following list provides <u>examples</u> of the various sentence patterns and their corresponding semantic relationships.

<u>Sentence Pattern 1</u>: <u>NP + V_i + (Adv) + (Adv)</u>

This pattern obviously represents a direct outgrowth of early two-word utterances; "Daddy go," "Mommy come," "Bobby fall." The verb is intransitive, represented by V_i, and may therefore be used alone or followed by one or two adverbs. The simplest forms of Pattern 1 would be mastered in preschool (Blackwell, Engen, Fischgrund, & Zarcadoolas, 1978).

The ice cream melted.	Patient-process
The ice cream melted fast.	Patient-process-manner
Mary learns quickly.	Experiencer-process-manner
The raccoons crept through the yard.	Mover-action-location
The raccoons crept stealthily through the garden.	Mover-action-manner-location
The man swam every day for his health.	Mover-action-frequency-reason

<u>Sentence Pattern 2</u>: <u>NP + V + NP + (Adv)</u>

Pattern 2 is the most frequently used of the five basic sentence patterns and the one most likely to be overused by hearing-impaired children (Blackwell, Engen, Fischgrund & Zarcadoolas, 1978).

John hit Susie.	Agent-action-patient
John hit Susie hard.	Agent-action-patient-manner
John hit Susie with a stick.	Agent-action-patient-instrument
Andy grows corn.	Experiencer-process-complement
Andy grew corn last summer.	Experience-process-complement-time
Andy painted a beautiful picture.	Experiencer-process-complement

(Sentence Pattern 2, continued)

Andy wants some cake.	Experiencer-process-patient
Don gave Mary a ring.	Agent-action-receiver*-patient
Mary received a ring.	Receiver-action-patient
Don gave a ring to his fiancée.	
(Don gave a ring to fiancée.)	Agent-action-patient-receiver
(Don has a fiancée.)	Possessor-process-patient

*receiver or beneficiary

Sentence Pattern 3: NP + V_L + Adj. + (Adv)

In this pattern, the verb is a linking verb V_L that connects the modifier or attribute (Adj) to the noun phrase (NP). In traditional grammar, the adjective is referred to as a predicate adjective. It has been identified as being the most difficult of the initial five patterns for hearing-impaired children to learn (e.g., Blackwell, Engen, Fischgrund, & Zarcadoolas, 1978). The general semantic relationship expressed in Pattern 3 is entity-stative-attribute. The attribute may identify age, size, color, quality, shape or condition (Heidinger, 1984).

Mommy is pretty.	Entity-stative-condition
The man became ill on the street.	Entity-stative-condition-location
The kitten was very small.	Entity-stative-size
The window was red.	Entity-stative-color
She is twelve years old now.	Entity-stative-age-time
It is rectangular.	Entity-stative-shape
He became unhappy.	Entity-stative-condition
That circle should be rounder.	Entity-stative-shape
The answer seems appropriate.	Entity-stative-quality
The soup tastes good today.	Entity-stative-condition-time

Sentence Pattern 4: NP + V_L + NP + (Adv)

In this sentence pattern, the second noun phrase (NP) is equivalent to the first and is connected by the linking verb (V_1) which is usually the copular "be," especially in the language of young children. Other stative verbs that can be used in this pattern are: seem, remain, stay, become, appear, and a few particle verbs such as turn into, change into, and change to (Heidinger, 1984).

Daddy is a man.	Entity-stative-equivalent
The men remained friends for years.	Entity-stative-equivalent-duration
Joe will become a lawyer.	Entity-stative-equivalent
Cinderella turned into a princess.	Entity-stative-equivalent
The rain turned into hail.	Entity-stative-equivalent
That man may have been a bully at one time.	Entity-stative-equivalent-time

Sentence Pattern 5: NP + be + Adv + (Adv)

Pattern 5 always includes some form of the verb "be" and is always followed by an adverbial; a second adverbial may be added.

Everyone is here now.	Entity-stative-location-time
The principal could be outside.	Entity-stative-location
The spray is for sore throats.	Entity-stative-reason
He is never outside.	Entity-stative-frequency-location

Language Samples

Examples of Using Expressive Language
Recording and Analysis Forms

Two examples of language assessment follow; the first is that of an 11-1/2-year-old student, "Larry"; the second is that of a 3 year, 4-month-old girl, "Kate."

The language samples are not complete; that is, they are not the minimum 40 to 50 utterances discussed previously. However, when they were coupled with the results of formal testing, sufficient information was available in a very short amount of time and each teacher was able to develop intervention plans and short-term objectives for the beginning of the school year. Structures not observed at this time were either tested for or looked for later.

Larry

Larry is a student who is enrolled in a classroom for hearing-impaired students where total communication (both speech and sign) is used. He has a severe bilateral sensorineural hearing loss. Larry uses both speech and sign to communicate.

The teacher compiled a test battery that included formal assessment tools as well as the spontaneous language sample to measure both receptive and expressive language skills. The results of the formal testing complemented the findings from the language sample.

A review of Larry's language sample (see Tables 27 and 28) shows that Larry is using a variety of appropriate communicative signals such as informing, responding, commenting, requesting and, possibly, attention-getting. There are several instances of turntaking and one of repair where Larry requests clarification from the teacher about what they are going to do. Socially "polite" language is not apparent in that Larry asks to use the other student's eraser and returns it without using a "polite" language form such as "please" or "thank you." This information substantiated what the teacher had noticed previously and she decided to write one objective that would include work on social skills and "polite" language. It is obvious that Larry uses his language communicatively; students, teacher, and aide were all able to understand the intent of what Larry was communicating.

Reviewing the grammatical structures in the sample, the teacher observed that Larry was using structures primarily at the Phase 5 level, and most of these correctly. The one structure he used correctly one time and incorrectly another time was the indirect question form. The teacher felt that this was an emerging construction and added it to her list of intervention objectives for Larry. Other structures not found in the sample would be looked for later. One area that concerned Larry's teacher was that the sentences he was using were short and simple. There were several instances when he could have used either a conjoining or embedding process in order to develop more complex structures, but he did not. Therefore, work on complex structures was also added to the list of intervention objectives for Larry.

Results of formal testing of receptive language suggested that Larry exhibits problems with subject-verb agreement, future aspect "will," the derivational "-ist," and certain prepositions. Larry could have appropriately learned all of these structures earlier, and therefore the teacher decided to include them also in her list of intervention objectives. In expressive language, results derived from using formal tests suggested that Larry knew the generic identity of a number of items, but not the name of specific items or parts within a category; e.g., tool but not wrench, axe, or hammer. He also exhibited problems with comparatives and superlatives, subject-verb agreement, and opposites.

Table 27

LANGUAGE SAMPLE RECORDING FORM

Key: T = Teacher
      L = Larry
      P = Pat
      A = Aide

Note: All recording is in Total Communication

Student's Name: Larry
Date: 9/13/85
C.A.: 11 years, 6 months

Context (describe)	Antecedent Event or Stimulus	Response	Other behavior/ Comments	Use
At computer—correcting spelling errors in a letter with another student, Pat (P.)	L. I'm finished. I'm on my final draft.	P. So What!		informing
	L. Can I borrow your eraser?	P. Here (hands to Larry)	takes without looking or thanks L. returns eraser—no comment such as "thanks"	requesting
L. returns to computer—continues response to P.	P. Help me with this word.	L. Wait. I have to talk to Debbie for a minute. L. That's a tricky one (word P. was working on).	returned to help Pat with spelling a word	responding commenting
Classroom, getting ready for reading—L. talking to teacher	L. Are we starting to work in our workbooks?	T. In a minute	Looks at T.	requesting information

Context (describe)	Antecedent Event or Stimulus	Response	Other behavior/ Comments	Use
	L. I'm falling asleep.	No response	Looks at T.	informing
	L. I don't think well when I'm tired.	No response	Looks at T.	informing (getting attention?)
	L. I need to blow my nose.	T. The kleenex is on the window sill.		informing
Lunchtime: Larry talking to Pat (another student)	Pat drops some food	L. Don't be a pig. You dropped it on the table.	Pointed to food.	regulating
	Pat picks up pickle	L. That's your nose		commenting
	Pat points to pickle and says "your nose."	L. No it's not!		responding/ negating
Working at computer in classroom with Teacher	T. gives direction but it is not clear.	L. What are we going to do? I don't understand.	Looking at T.	requesting information— repairing communication
	T. We are going to try a new program.	L. Oh, I see. O.K. The other disk is missing. I found it. It was hiding.	Looks around— under	acknowledging information informing
The Speech-Language Therapist (CDS) enters room and signals L. to come with her.	CDS. Come on, Larry. Time to work with me.	L. I'm coming. I'm coming. I have to put my stupid stuff away. It takes an hour.	Looks at CDS. Puts things away and leaves room. Too many short choppy sentences?	responding acknowledging commenting

Context (describe)	Antecedent Event or Stimulus	Response	Other behavior/ Comments	Use
Talking to another student in class, Jan (J.)	L. Jan, do you know the weather report?	J. No.		questioning
	L. 80% chance of snow. I heard it's supposed to snow—maybe tonight—or Thursday or Friday! Maybe we'll stay home.			informing
Correcting spelling words	L. I don't know how to spell this one (points to a word).	J. I don't want to.		supposition
		T. I'll help you. How does it start?	good attending skills	statement—but really a request for assistance.
During reading, talking to class—	L. Everything's finished now.	A. Good, you can put your things away and get your library book.		
	L. When do we start the new book?	A. Tomorrow, I think.	Looks at aide	requesting information
	L. I thought we were going to start today.	A. No.		commenting
Getting ready to go to recess—talking to teacher	L. I hate these papers.	T. You need to take your time and work carefully.	Typical comment when he doesn't do his best work.	informing
	L. Yes, I could have done it right.			

Table 28

LANGUAGE ANALYSIS FORM

Phase 5

Student's Name **Larry**
Date **9/13/85**
Age **11 years, 6 months**

STRUCTURE	EXAMPLES	COMMENTS
Noun Phrase		
All possessive pronouns, e.g., his, hers, ours	our (workbooks), your (nose) (eraser) my (final draft)	
Reflexive pronouns; e.g., myself, himself, herself	none in sample	
Prenominalization to show old or known information; e.g., John gave Mary candy and she ate it.	You dropped it (food) on the table. I found it (disk).	pointed to food
Comparatives; e.g., nicer, bigger	none in sample	
Plural demonstratives; e.g., those, there	there (books)	
Prepositions; e.g., until, along, among	none in sample	

STRUCTURE	EXAMPLES	COMMENTS
Indefinite pronouns; e.g., anyone, everything, everybody	Everything's finished.	
Use of "the" and "a" to identify specific/non-specific, old/new information; e.g., the White House a white house on our block	none in sample	
Noun phrases expanded by use of adjectives, nouns used as adjectives, prepositional phrases; e.g., The one at the top. An exciting card game.	tricky one, final draft other disk, stupid stuff	
Additional noun derivations; e.g., pianist		
Verb Phrases		
Past progressive; e.g., I was running.	I was working on this yesterday.	
Past modal + have; e.g., I could have gone.	I could have done it right.	
Past modal + have + negative; e.g., I couldn't have gone.	none in sample	

STRUCTURE	EXAMPLES	COMMENTS
Auxiliary have + verb (present, perfect); e.g., I have (I've) read that book before.	none in sample	
Auxiliary have + verb (present, perfect) + negative; e.g., I haven't been swimming this week. I haven't seen the puppy.	none in sample	
Adverbial clauses; e.g., We'll go to recess after we finish math. Before we go, I want a drink.	When I'm tired . . . . for a minute	
Adverb derivations; e.g., gently		
Modals and modal-like forms; e.g., have to, need to, ought to	I need to blow my nose. Can I borrow your eraser? I have to talk to Debbie. I have to put my stupid stuff away.	

STRUCTURE	EXAMPLES	COMMENTS
Sentences Earlier sentences plus: Relative clause in final position; e.g., Like the man that has the dog.	none in sample	

All "do" support; e.g.,
    I did go. He didn't go.
    Do you want to go?
    Don't you want to go?
    Did you have one?
	Don't be a pig!
	I don't understand.
	I don't think well.	

Conjunctions but, unless, or; e.g.,
    We can't go skating unless it freezes.
    We can go to the movies or watch T.V.
    I'd like to go but my mom said "no."
	none in sample	

Verb reductions; e.g., I want the ball and (I want) the bat.	none in sample	

STRUCTURE	EXAMPLES	COMMENTS
Indirect questions; e.g., I don't know where to go. I don't know how to work that.	I don't know how to spell this one.	Used indirect question correctly here but not consistent; e.g., "Jan, do you know the weather report?" Maybe emerging.
"That" complement; e.g., I thought that she was nice.	I thought we were going to start today.	
Ability to shift adverbial clause; e.g., I was happy when I went swimming. When I went swimming, I was happy.	none in sample	
When questions; e.g., When will we go? When are we going?	When do we start the new book?	
Gerund as subject; e.g., Running is the hardest sport.	none in sample.	Have never observed this structure.

Language Samples

Kate

The second child, Kate, is 3 years, 4 months old, has a severe-to-profound bilateral sensorineural hearing loss, and has worn ear-level hearing aids since she was 17 months old. She is enrolled in a preschool classroom for hearing-impaired children. Informal observations and the Test of Auditory Comprehension of Language-Revised (TACL-R) were used to assess her receptive language ability.

Kate performed well on the TACL-R, missing only a few items such as one plural item, personal pronouns, and one interrogative. Although there are few items on the tests to check these language skills, informal observation and recording during class corroborated the more formal results. Kate's expressive language was evaluated as follows: a language sample was obtained at various times during the school day for a period of 4 days, and the SKI-HI Receptive Language Test was modified and used expressively. The language sample follows, in Table 29; analysis of the sample is found in Table 30.

Reviewing the data from receptive and expressive assessment which included ongoing observation of general behavior, the teacher came to the following conclusions. There are no major concerns about Kate's receptive language but Kate does need help in expanding her receptive vocabulary. Kate has the potential for developing good language but needs a great deal of help in language *use* as well as in improving expressive language skills; she often demands attention by using nonverbal tactics such as hitting and pulling.

As the teacher analyzed the language sample, it was evident that Kate did have turn-taking skills, could maintain a topic, and had some other pragmatic skills. Kate knows the names of classroom items and colors, and follows simple directions such as "Get the scissors," "Use your voice," "Go to the bathroom," etc. She is very inconsistent in responding appropriately to simple whquestions such as "What is your name?" "What do you want?" or yes/no questions such as "Do you want a cookie?" A major deficit appeared to be that she almost never initiated communicative interaction with either adults or peers, at least using language as a vehicle. Almost her entire expressive repertoire was in response to another person's (usually the teacher's) initiation; in a few instances she talked to herself spontaneously.

Kate is able to label objects but action words are practically non-existent. Many of her labels are incorrect. Of the utterances recorded in the language sample only four action verbs are used spontaneously. Other action words are present but always occur in structured situations or in situations in which Kate repeats part of a comment another person just expressed. Most of her expressive language is composed of one-word utterances. Two-word utterances appear to be emerging. In order to gather additional information about Kate's expressive language, the teacher used a receptive picture test—but used it expressively. Thus the teacher would point to a picture and either ask Kate to name it—e.g., cup; describe it—e.g., dirty; or tell what was happening—e.g., fall down. Kate was unable to name a number of foods, appliances, and tools and she was able to identify only one out of 15 actions (sit). Because Kate's understanding of language appears to exceed her expressive use of language, the teacher decided to emphasize work in the expressive area by helping Kate label and describe things that she sees and what is happening in the classroom. By focusing on increasing Kate's expressive language, the teacher hoped to help her manipulate her environment by increased use of verbal/signed communication and reduce her inappropriate physical contact with other children.

Table 29

LANGUAGE SAMPLE
RECORDING FORM

Student's Name Kate
Date 1/12/86
Age 3 years, 4 months

Key: T = Teacher
     B = Bill
     K = Kate
     S = Sally

Note: All recording is in Total Communication

Context	Antecedent Event or Stimulus	Response	Other Behaviors/ Comments	Use
K. pushed B.	K. saw T. watching her	K. "no push"	denying that she pushed B.	negation
Getting ready to go out	K. points to B.'s name by his coathook	K. "Bill" and points to name		informing
T. and K. looking at book	T. points to person in picture, "Who is that?"	K. "bear" and points	wrong label	labeling
T. and K. looking at a book	T. says "That's a bear?" "No, that's my girl."	K. "girl"		repeating
Free time - getting toys	picks up toy - not addressing anyone	K. "soft"		labeling
Children returning to group	T. tells K. to sit in "This chair" (a small one)	K. points to and moves toward big chair, says "big"	Does not want to sit in small chair; moves towards big chair; really wants to sit there.	informing/ rejection
Children returning to group	T. says "No, this is your chair (pats small one)	K. sits	Sort of pouty. Probably upset because she has to sit in little chair.	
"Language" group	T. points to K., says, "Are you here?"	K. "I am here."	This is a learned response; delayed repetition.	answering

Context	Antecedent Event or Stimulus	Response	Other Behaviors/ Comments	Use
"Language" group	T. "Are you a boy or a girl?"	K. "no"	incorrect answer	answering
"Language" group	T. "Who is here?"	K. "I am here."	learned response	answering
"Language" group	T. "Who else is here?"	K. says "Carol" and points	Points to picture of herself and Carol.	answering
"Language" group	T. says K. is not at school today	K. "tomorrow"	Points to floor.	informing
Language group is finished	T. tells K. to go to the bathroom	K. "me sit"		informing
Informal play with dolls, etc. in "home corner"	T. "How old are _you_?"	K. "two"	appropriate response – although wrong age	answering
Informal play with dolls, etc. in "home corner"	T. "No, you are three"	K. "three"		repeating
Informal play with dolls, etc. in "home corner"	T. holds up apple, "What is this?"	K. "orange" and point	incorrect answer but knows it is food	answering
Informal play with dolls, etc. in "home corner"	T. "Orange? No – apple"	K. "apple"		repeating
Informal play with dolls, etc. in "home corner"	K. holds up baby, says "baby"	T. "Yes, you have the baby."		informing
Informal play with dolls, etc. in "home corner"	T. asks K. to tell B. it's time to stop now.	K. "Bill, stop, stop"	goes to Bill	regulating when requested to do so

Context	Antecedent Event or Stimulus	Response	Other Behaviors/ Comments	Use
Informal play with dolls, etc. in "home corner"	K. "Bill stink"	NR		commenting/informing
Getting ready to go to bathroom	Trying to undo her overalls	K. "hard"	self-initiated to teacher	informing
Getting ready to go to bathroom	T. "Say – 'it is hard'"	K. "It is hard."		repeating
Children are drawing pictures	T. points to picture of another child, asks K., "What's that?"	K. Smiles and points		answering
Children are drawing pictures	T. "What is that?" pointing to picture of a bird	K. "fly fly"		answering
Children are drawing pictures	T, "Yes, it's a bird."	K. "bird"		repeating
Children are drawing pictures	K. is naming things she drew	K. "face" "sun" "green" "blue" "red"	talking to herself	informing
Children are drawing pictures	There is a doll "sitting" close to where K. is is drawing	K. "watch, watch" and points to doll	self-initiated command to doll	attention-getting; command
Children looking at calendar	T. says "The month is January"	K. "January"		repeating
Children looking at calendar	T. "The name of the month is January"	K. "month January"		repeating
Children looking at calendar	Picture of winter scene on wall next to calendar	K. "winter today"	self-initiated statement to teacher	informing

Context	Antecedent Event or Stimulus	Response	Other Behaviors/ Comments	Use
Children looking at calendar	K. goes to get the picture and T. says "Do not touch."	K. "not touch"		repeating
Finishing group - children getting up	K. turns to S.	K. "come"		requesting action

Table 30

LANGUAGE ANALYSIS FORM

Phase 1

Student's Name: Kate
Date: 1/12/86
Age: 3 yrs. 4 mo.

STRUCTURE	EXAMPLES	COMMENTS
Communicative Intentions:		
object request		
action request		
information request		
greeting		
transferring		
showing off		
acknowledging		
answering	no	correct response to yes/no question but not appropriate answer
negation		
Labeling:		
Nominals		
people	Carol	
	Larry	
	Girl	calling a picture of herself a bear
	bear	
animals		
objects	orange	
food	baby (doll)	wrong name but knew it was food
toys	face	
other	sun	

STRUCTURE	EXAMPLES	COMMENTS
Non-Nominals gone that down there (completion of task) more pretty others		
Imitation simple motor vocal/verbal	soft green big blue hard red two watch (verb) fly come name tomorrow three January apple month January it is hard bird "Who is that?" Bear "Are you here?" "I am here" "How old are you?" "Two"	
turn-taking	me sit	Kate takes turns consistently—when someone else takes the lead. This may be a problem, however, because she almost never initates a communication
Sentences Action-Object (throw ball, see puppy) Action-Locative (sit chair, fall bed) Agent-Object (mommy sandwich, boy ball) Entity-Locative (sweater chair) Agent-Action	Larry stop, stop; me sit	

Phase 2

STRUCTURE	EXAMPLES	COMMENTS
Functional Relations Existence (This, that, it, a; e.g., that cookie) Recurrence (more, another; e.g., more milk) Non-existence (no, allgone, away; e.g., allgone juice) Rejection (no milk) Denial (no push, no break) other Simple Questions What this? What do(ing)? Where go?	no push entity-time: winter today	

Summary

The above examples illustrate how two teachers combined information from both formal and informal methods of collecting receptive and expressive language data in order to establish initial intervention objectives. They were also able to identify some specific language structures to look for in the weeks to follow. By periodic assessment and ongoing monitoring of their students' language, these teachers are able to provide a systematic, developmentally sound intervention program. Because knowledge about language tests is one prerequisite to developing and using an appropriate test battery, descriptions of 36 tests follow.

SECTION VI:

TEST DESCRIPTIONS

Introduction

This section contains descriptions of 36 tests designed to assess receptive and/or expressive language or language related skills. Most were designed for use with hearing students, but are either being used to assess language skills of hearing-impaired students or could be used with them, with some adaptation. The remaining tests were intended to be used with hearing-impaired students. This section is organized in the following way:

1) Alphabetical list of tests covered in this book (Table 31).
2) Summary Chart by Test Characteristics (Table 32). On this chart, tests are listed in alphabetical order for quick reference. The following characteristics of each test are presented: target age group; norm group characteristics (hearing, hearing-impaired, etc.); communication mode tested (receptive, expressive, or both); language area tested (morphology, syntax, semantics, other); how test scores are reported or converted (age-equivalent, grade-equivalent, percentiles, other). This chart will help you evaluate and select tests appropriate for a particular category of students--for example, receptive tests of syntax for 6- to 9-year-old children.
3) Test Battery Summary Chart (Table 33). This chart is a duplicate of Table 12 found in Section III. It provides summary information about which test to use for given ages in order to assess the various areas of language.
4) Test Descriptions. Each test, presented in alphabetical order, is described and the following information is included: name, publisher, publisher's address, and approximate cost of test; a general description of the test; information on instructions

and test administration; norms and reliability and validity data; advantages and disadvantages of the test;and miscellaneous notes on the test, if applicable. All information included about norms, reliability, and validity is drawn from the test manuals, unless otherwise noted.

The purpose of this section is twofold: 1) To help you select tests to examine and buy for inclusion in your district's collection of language tests; and 2) To help you select tests from an existing collection for inclusion in a test battery for a particular student or group of students. It must be emphasized that there are no tests appropriate for use with all hearing-impaired students. Further, no single test is "perfect," and the comments about the disadvantages and advantages listed for each language test are subjective. They are, however, the result of input from the teachers of the deaf and speech-language pathologists who participated in the development of this book. In the end, the decision about which tests are included in a battery must be yours, and hinges on your asessment needs, the characteristics of a particular student, and your judgement of a test.

Test Descriptions

Table 31

ALPHABETICAL LIST OF TESTS

* designed for hearing-impaired students

1. Assessment of Children's Language Comprehension (ACLC)
2. Bankson Language Screening Test (BLST)
3. Bare Essentials in Assessing Really Little Kids - Concept Analysis Profile Summary (BEAR-CAPS)*
4. Boehm Test of Basic Concepts (BTBC)
5. Bracken Basic Concept Scale (BBCS)
6. Carolina Picture Vocabulary Test (CPVT)*
7. Carrow Elicited Language Inventory (CELI)
8. CID Scales of Early Communication Skills for Hearing-Impaired Children (SECS)*
9. Communicative Intention Inventory (CII)
10. Early Language Milestones (ELM)
11. Expressive One-Word Picture Vocabulary Test (EOWPVT)
12. Expressive One-Word Picture Vocabulatory Test - Upper Extension (EOWPVT-UE)
13. Grammatical Analysis of Elicited Language (GAEL)*
14. The Illinois Test of Psycholinguistic Abilities (ITPA)
15. Interpersonal Language Skills Assessment (ILSA)
16. Maryland Syntax Evaluation Instrument (MSEI)*
17. Miller-Yoder Language Comprehension Test
18. Northwestern Syntax Screening Test (NSST)
19. Peabody Picture Vocabulary Test-Revised (PPVT)
20. Preschool Language Assessment Instrument (PLAI)
21. Receptive One-Word Picture Vocabulary Test (ROWPVT)
22. Rhode Island Test of Language Structure (RITLS)*
23. Rockford Infant Developmental Evaluation Scales (RIDES)
24. Sequenced Inventory of Communication Development (SICD)
25. SKI-HI Receptive Language Test (SKI-HI RLT)*
26. SKI-HI Language Development Scale (SKI-HI LDS)*
27. Structured Photographic Expressive Language Test-II (SPELT-II)
28. Teacher Assessment of Grammatical Structures (TAGS)*
29. Test for Auditory Comprehension of Language-Revised (TACL-R)
30. Test for Examining Expressive Morphology (TEEM)
31. Test of Expressive Language Ability (TEXLA)*
32. Test of Receptive Language Ability (TERLA)*
33. Test of Syntactic Abilities (TSA)*
34. The Word Test (TWT)
35. Total Communication Receptive Vocabulary Test (TCRVT)*
36. Vane Evaluation of Language Scale (Vane-L)

Table 32

SUMMARY CHART BY TEST CHARACTERISTICS

TEST NAME	TARGET AGE GROUP	NORM GROUP	MODE REC.	MODE EXP.	Lexicon (VOC.)	MORPH.	SYNTAX	SEM. REL.	OTHER	AGE EQUIV.	GRADE EQUIV.	PERCENT-ILE
*=commonly used with hearing-impaired students												
Assessment of Children's Comprehension (ACLC)	3 to 6 years	365 hearing children, Fla. and Vermont areas, mixed SES	x		x			x				x
Bankson Language Screening Test (BLST)	4 to 8 years	637 hearing children middle SES, Wash., D.C. area	x	x		x	x	x	auditory/ visual perception	x		
Bare Essentials in Assessing Really Little Kids—Concept Analysis Profile Summary (BEAR-CAPS)	1-6 to 5-9 years	None	x		x			x	concepts			
Boehm Test of Basic Concepts (BTBC)	Grades K, 1, 2	9700+ hearing children, range of SES, across U.S.	x		x			x	concepts		x	
Bracken Basic Concept Scale (BBCS)	2-6 to 7-11 years	1109 hearing children across U.S. for diagnostic test; 879 hearing children across U.S. for screening test	x		x			x		x		x
Carolina Picture Vocabulary Test (CPVT)	4 to 11-6 years	767 hearing-impaired children in U.S. using manual communication	x		x					x		x

TEST NAME	TARGET AGE GROUP	NORM GROUP	MODE REC.	MODE EXP.	Lexicon (VOC.)	AREA TESTED MORPH.	AREA TESTED SYNTAX	AREA TESTED SEM. REL.	AREA TESTED OTHER	TEST RESULTS AGE EQUIV.	TEST RESULTS GRADE EQUIV.	TEST RESULTS PERCENTILE
*=commonly used with hearing-impaired students												
Carrow Elicited Language Inventory (CELI)	3 to 8 years	475 hearing children, middle SES		x		x	x					x
*CID Scales of Early Communication Skills for Hearing Impaired Children (SECS)	2 to 8 years	372 oral hearing-impaired children	x	x	x		x	x				x
Communicative Intention Inventory (CII)	8 to 24 months	none		x					use of language			
Early Language Milestone (ELM)	0 to 3 years	191 hearing children, New York Medical Center	x	x			x	x				x
Expressive One-Word Picture Vocabulary Test (EOWPVT)	2 to 12 years	1600 hearing children, San Francisco Bay area		x	x					x		x
Expressive One-Word Picture Vocabulary Test-Upper Extension (EOWPVT-UE)	12 to 15-11 years	465 hearing children, San Francisco Bay area		x	x					x		x
*Grammatical Analysis of Elicited Language (GAEL)	5 to 9 years	200 oral hearing-impaired children from 13 oral programs; 200 hearing children		x			x					x

Test	Age range	Sample							Scores
Illinois Test of Psycholinguistic Abilities (ITPA)	2-7 to 10 years	962 "normal" hearing children; middle SES	x	x				x	Psycholinguistic Age, "Psycholinguistic Quotient," and scaled scores
Interpersonal Language Skills Assessment (ILSA)	8 to 14 years	528 hearing children; 64 learning disabled children		x			use of social language skills		percentage
*Maryland Syntax Evaluation Assessment (ILSA)	6 to 12 years	220 hearing-impaired children		x		x			Computed syntax score and sentence ratio
Miller-Yoder Language Comprehension Test (M-Y)	4 to 8 years	172 hearing students, Madison, Wisconsin	x			x		x	
Northwestern Syntax Screening Test (NSST)	3 to 8 years	580+ hearing children	x	x		x			x
Peabody Picture Vocabulary Test (PPVT) - Revised	2 1/2 to 40 years	4200 hearing children and adolescents	x		x			x	x
Preschool Language Assessment Instrument (PLAI)	3 to 6 years	120 hearing children matched for age, sex, and SES	x	x			discourse skills	x	
Receptive One-Word Picture Vocabulary Test (ROWPVT)	2 to 12 years	1128 hearing children, San Francisco Bay area	x		x			x	Language Standard Score and Stanine

TEST NAME	TARGET AGE GROUP	NORM GROUP	MODE REC.	MODE EXP.	Lexicon (VOC.)	AREA TESTED MORPH.	AREA TESTED SYNTAX	SEM. REL.	OTHER	TEST RESULTS AGE EQUIV.	TEST RESULTS GRADE EQUIV.	TEST RESULTS PERCENT-ILE
*=commonly used with hearing-impaired students												
Rhode Island Test of Language Structure (RITLS)	5 to 17+ years	513 hearing-impaired children in east coast states; 304 hearing children, R.I.	X			X	X					X
Rockford Infant Developmental Evaluation Scales (RIDES)	0 to 4 years	None	X	X	X			X	Social/Fine Motor/Gross Motor	X		
Sequenced Inventory of Communication Development (SICD)	4 months to 4 years	252 hearing children; range of SES	X	X					Communication behaviors	X Communication Age		
*SKI-HI Receptive Language Test (SKI-HI RLT)	3 to 6 1/2 years	None	X		X			X				% correct
*SKI-HI Language Development Scale (SKI-HI LDS)	0 to 5 years	None	X	X					Communication behaviors	X		
Structured Photographic Expressive Language Test (SPELT-II)	4 to 9-5 years	1178 hearing children from North Central and Southern sections of U.S.		X		X	X			X		
*Teacher Assessment of Grammatical Structures (TAGS)	0 to 9+ years	None	X	X		X	X	X				

Test	Age	Sample								
Test for Auditory Comprehension of Language-Revised (TACL-R)	3 to 10	1003 hearing subjects in 20 states	x		x	x			x	x
Test for Examining Expressive Morphology (TEEM)	3 to 8 years	500 hearing children, Fresno, California		x	x		x		x	
*Test of Expressive Language Ability (TEXLA)	7 to 12 years	65 hearing-impaired children from Canadian Schools for the Deaf; 17 hearing children		x	x	x			x	x
*Test of Receptive Language Ability (TERLA)	7 to 12 years	92 hearing-impaired children from Canadian Schools for the Deaf; 17 hearing children	x		x	x			x	x
*Test of Syntactic Ability (TSA)	10 to 18-11 years	450 hearing-impaired children from 18 programs in U.S.	x			x			x	x
The Word Test (TWT)	7 to 12 years	467 hearing children; Milwaukee, Wisconsin		x	x			x	x	
*Total Communication Receptive Vocabulary Test (TCRVT)	3 to 12 years	77 hearing, 95 hard-of-hearing, 251 deaf children	x		x				x	
Vane Evaluation of Language Scale (VANE-L)	2-6 to 6 years	740 hearing children, New York	x	x	x	x		x	Auditory/ visual attention	x

Table 33

TEST BATTERY SUMMARY CHART

Communication Mode:
E = Expressive
R = Receptive
* = Designed for Hearing Impaired Children

Language Component

Age Groups

Morphology (Form)

0 to 5 Years

Test	R/E	Years
BLST	R/E	4 to 8
CELI	E	3 to 8
SPELT-II	E	4 to 9.5
TACL-R	R	3 to 10
*TAGS Pre-sentence	R/E	0 to 5
TEEM	E	3 to 8
VANE-L	R/E	2.6 to 6

6 to 12 Years

Test	R/E	Years
BLST	R/E	4 to 8
CELI	E	3 to 8
SPELT-II	E	4 to 9.5
TACL-R	R	3 to 10
*TAGS Simple Complex	R/E	5 to 9 9+
TEEM	E	3 to 8
*TERLA	E	3 to 8
*TEXLA	E	7 to 12
VANE-L	R/E	2.6 to 6

13 to 18 Years

Test	R/E	Years
*TAGS Complex	R/E	9+

Language Component

Age Groups

Lexicon/Vocabulary (Content)

0 to 5 Years

Test	R/E	Years
ACLC	R	3 to 6
BEAR-CAPS	R	1.6 to 5.9
BTBC	R	5 to 8
BBCS	R	2.6 to 8
CPVT	R	4 to 11.6
EOWPVT	E	2 to 12
PPVT-R	R	2.6 to 40
ROWPVT	R	2 to 12
*SECS	R/E	2 to 8
*SKI-HI RLT	R	3 to 6.6
TACL-R	R	3 to 10
*TCRVT	R	3 to 12
VANE-L	R/E	2.6 to 6

6 to 12 Years

Test	R/E	Years
ACLC	R	3 to 6
BTBC	R	5 to 8
BBCS	R	2.6 to 8
CPVT	R	4 to 11.6
EOWPVT	E	2 to 12
EOWPVT-UE	E	12 to 16
PPVT-R	R	2.6 to 40
ROWPVT	R	2 to 12
*SECS	R/E	2 to 8
*SKI-HI RLT	E	3 to 6.6
TACL-R	R	3 to 10
*TCRVT	R	3 to 12
TWT	E	7 to 12
VANE-L	R/E	2.6 to 6

13 to 18 Years

Test	R/E	Years
EOWPVT-UE	E	12 to 16
PPVT-R	R	2.6 to 40

Language Component

Age Groups

0 to 5 Years

Test	R/E	Years
ACLC	R	3 to 6
BLST	R/E	4 to 8
BEAR-CAPS	R	1.6 to 5.9
BTBC	R	5 to 8
BBCS	R	2.6 to 8
ELM	R/E	0 to 3
PLAI	R/E	3 to 6
*RITLS	E	5 to 17+
*SECS	R/R	2 to 8
*SKI-HI RLT	E	3 to 6.6
*TAGS Presentence	R/E	0 to 5
VANE-L	R/E	2.6 to 6

6 to 12 Years

Test	R/E	Years
ACLC	R	3 to 6
BLST	R/E	4 to 8
BTBC	R	5 to 8
BBCS	R	2.6 to 8
BLST	E	4 to 8
PLAI	R/E	3 to 6
*RITLS	R	5 to 17+
*SECS	R/E	2 to 8
*SKI-HI RLT	R	3 to 6.6
*TAGS Simple Complex	R/E	5 to 9 9+
TWT	E	7 to 12
VANE-L	R/E	2.6 to 6

13 to 18 Years

Test	R/E	Years
*RITLS	R	5 to 17+
*TAGS Complex	R/E	9+

Semantic Relationships/Semantic Knowledge (content)

Language Component

Age Groups

0 to 5 Years

Test	R/E	Years
CII	E	.7 to 2
PLAI	R/E	3 to 6
BLST	R/E	4 to 8
BEAR-CAPS	R	1.6 to 5.9
BTBC	R	5 to 8
ITPA	R/E	2.7 to 10
RIDES	R/E	0 to 4
SICD	R/E	.4 to 4
*SKI-HI LDS	R/E	0 to 5
VANE-L	R/E	2.6 to 6

6 to 12 Years

Test	R/E	Years
ILSA	E	8 to 14
PLAI	R/E	3 to 6
BLST	R/E	4 to 8
BTBC	R	5 to 8
ITPA	R/E	2.7 to 10
VANE-L	R/E	2.6 to 6

13 to 18 Years

Test	R/E	Years
ILSA	E	8 to 14

Pragmatics (Use)

Other

Language Component

Age Groups

0 to 5 Years

Test	R/E	Years
Syntax		
BLST	R/E	4 to 8
CELI	E	3 to 8
ELM	R/E	0 to 3
*GAEL	E	5 to 9
M-Y	R	4 to 8
NSST	R/E	3 to 8
*RITLS	R	5 to 17+
*SECS	R/E	2 to 8
SPELT-II	E	4 to 9.5
TACL-R	R	3 to 10
*TAGS Pre-sentence	R/E	0 to 5
VANE-L	R/E	2.6 to 6

6 to 12 Years

Test	R/E	Years
BLST	R/E	4 to 8
CELI	E	3 to 8
*GAEL	E	5 to 9
M-Y	R	4 to 8
*MSEI	E	6 to 12
NSST	R/E	3 to 8
*RITLS	R	5 to 17+
*SECS	R/E	2 to 8
SPELT-II	E	4 to 9.5
TACL-R	R	3 to 10
*TAGS Simple Complex	R/E	5 to 9 9+
*TERLA	R	7 to 12
*TEXLA	E	7 to 12
*TSA	R	10 to 19
VANE-L	R/E	2.6 to 6

13 to 18 Years

Test	R/E	Years
*RITLS	R	5 to 17+
*TAGS Complex	R/E	9+
*TSA	R	10 to 19

Test Descriptions

ASSESSMENT OF CHILDREN'S LANGUAGE COMPREHENSION (ACLC)

Hearing Norms
Ages 3-0 to 6-6 years
Receptive

Foster, R., Gidden, J.J., & Stark, J. (1972) <u>Assessment of Children's Language Comprehension</u>. Consulting Psychologists Press, Inc. 577 College Avenue, Palo Alto, CA 94306. Approximate cost: $19.75.

General Description
The <u>Assessment of Children's Language Comprehension</u> (ACLC) is a receptive test designed to measure children's comprehension of lexical items presented at different levels of difficulty. The first of the four subtests of the <u>ACLC</u> assesses children's comprehension of a single-word (one critical element) vocabulary; each subsequent subtest increases in the level of difficulty by one critical element up to four critical elements. The <u>ACLC</u> may be used to 1) identify the level at which a child is unable to process and remember lexical items in a syntactic structure and, more specifically, to 2) identify the nature of those lexical items. The test is designed for hearing children ages 3 to 6-1/2 years.

Instructions/Test Administration
The test stimuli are arranged on a series of 40 plates with each plate containing either four or five picture stimuli. The subject is required to "Point to" or "Show me" the picture which corresponds to the verbal stimulus presented by the examiner. The examiner records the child's response on a recording sheet as either correct or incorrect. The incorrect responses are marked according to which critical element is missed (e.g., first element, second element, both elements incorrect). The method for computing the child's score is outlined in the test manual. The test requires approximately 10 minutes to administer.

Test Descriptions

Norms

The ACLC was standardized on 365 Caucasian, Hispanic surname, Asian-American, and Black nursery school and school-age children. The mean scores for these subjects were collapsed because of the fact that no significant differences were found among the groups. The normative data for the four subtests are presented according to age (taken at 6-month intervals) and sex. Additional information regarding children diagnosed as neurologically or educationally handicapped is also presented.

Reliability

Odd-even reliability coefficients were computed for the first subtest (Part A: Vocabulary) alone and for Subtests B, C, and D combined, and are reported as .86 and .80, respectively.

Validity

No validity data are provided.

Advantages

1) The test is easy to administer and score in a short amount of time (approximately 15-20 minutes).
2) The recording sheet provides a Spanish translation.
3) The manual is easy to read.
4) The manual provides an introductory section on language development, as well as guidelines for application of the ACLC in a language training program.
5) Norms are grouped at 6-month intervals.
6) The same vocabulary is used throughout the entire test.
7) The test results identify the level at which the child is having difficulty understanding the syntactic structure.

Disadvantages

1) No data are given regarding the validity of the test and the data for reliability are limited.
2) The pictures are dated.
3) The test does not have sample items for all four subtests, only for the single element vocabulary subtest (Part A).
4) Pictures are small black and white line drawings. They may be difficult for some children to recognize.

BANKSON LANGUAGE SCREENING TEST (BLST)

Hearing Norms
Ages 4-0 to 8-0 years
Expressive/Receptive

Bankson, N.W. (1977). *Bankson Language Screening Test*. Pro Ed, 5341 Industrial Oaks Boulevard, Austin, TX 78735. Approximate Cost: $15.00.

General Description

The Bankson (BLST) is designed to screen expressive language skills in five general categories. These include both psycholinguistic skills (semantic knowledge, morphological rules, and syntactic rules) and perceptual skills (visual perception and auditory perception). Directions are also provided for screening receptive language skills for seven out of the eight subtests in the semantic knowledge category. Although a score is not derived for the receptive portion, the qualitative information obtained may be useful to the examiner. The BLST is a screening instrument designed to be used with children who may need further diagnostic language testing.

Instructions/Test Administration

For most of the 17 subtests, the test administrator reads aloud sentences with corresponding pictures depicting actions; the child fills in the appropriate word or phrase. For example: "This boy likes to run. In this picture he _____ (is running)." The test battery consists of 17 nine-item subtests (total = 153 items) organized into the five categories listed above.

Norms

The BLST was normed on 637 children between the ages of 4-1 and 8-0 years living in semi-rural counties adjacent to the Washington D.C. metropolitan area. The majority of these children came from a strictly middle-class population.

Reliability

Test-retest reliability was high (.96 overall reliability index).

Test Descriptions

Validity

Content validity – A review of preschool and primary grade academic curricula indicated that items in the BLST are representative of the kinds of tasks learned by 4- to 8-year-old children. In addition, correlations between selected subtests of the BLST and other language tests designed to measure similar skills were high. For example, the correlation between the Boehm Test of Basic Concepts and the BLST subtest of semantic knowledge was high (r=.89). These data support the validity of the BLST as a screening measure of skills assessed by other instruments in a diagnostic fashion.

Concurrent validity – BLST scores of 70 children were compared with their performances on three other language tests. Pearson Product-Moment Correlations were as follows: BLST and Peabody Picture Vocabulary Test (r = .54); BLST and Boehm Test of Basic Concepts (r = .62); and BLST and Test of Auditory Comprehension of Language (r = .64).

Advantages

1) The BLST identifies children in need of further in-depth analysis by diagnostic language tests; for example, children scoring at the 30th percentile and below on any subtest need further assessment.
2) Only about 25 minutes are required to administer the complete battery.
3) It assesses perceptual skills as well as psycholinguistic skills. (This is one of the few language tests available that also taps visual perception.)
4) The BLST is one of the few existing tests that assesses expressive language skills. Expressive items missed may be tested receptively.
5) It is sensitive to developmental differences at the lower end of the age spectrum.
6) Normative data are grouped by 6-month intervals.
7) The examiner can do a mini-screening using the "most discriminating" 38 items.
8) Instructions and items are easily adaptable for presentation to hearing-impaired students.
9) The auditory memory subtest may provide information that is useful: a) in writing auditory training objectives and b) before mainstreaming a hearing-impaired student because such a test will provide some

Test Descriptions

    information about how a student may function in a hearing classroom.

10) The **BLST** provides some information about a child's understanding of _categories_ and _functions_ which most other tests do not.

Disadvantages

1) No guidelines are given for choosing an "appropriate diagnostic test" for each subtest on the **BLST**, if needed.
2) The **BLST** was normed on hearing children.
3) The auditory memory subtest may be of use only with hard-of-hearing children, or when plans are being made to mainstream a child. See advantage 9 above.
4) Children often do not understand the required response to the stimulus phrase (e.g., Items #90, #104-107).

Test Descriptions

*BARE ESSENTIALS IN ASSESSING REALLY LITTLE KIDS - CONCEPT ANALYSIS PROFILE SUMMARY (BEAR-CAPS)

No Norms
1-6 to 5-9 years
Receptive

Hasenstab, M.S., & Laughton, J. (1982). Bare essentials in assessing really little kids: An approach. In M.S. Hasenstab, & J.S. Horner (Eds.), <u>Comprehensive intervention with hearing-impaired infants and preschool children</u> (pp. 204-209). Aspen Publications, Aspen Systems Corporation, 1600 Research Boulevard, Rockville, MD 20850. Approximate Cost: $32.50.

General Description

<u>Bare Essentials in Assessing Really Little Kids - Concept Analysis Profile Summary (BEAR-CAPS)</u> is designed to assess a child's conceptual understanding of relationships which appear in language development between the ages of 1-6 to 5-0 years. The concepts tested are divided into six categories: position/location, quantity, quality, size, pronouns, and body parts. <u>BEAR-CAPS</u> is a criterion-referenced tool; it yields information which is helpful for developing instructional objectives in a child's language program. It is based on the authors' idea that conceptual development is needed in order for the child to develop form, content, and use of language. Therefore, a language program based on concept development can be implemented.

Instructions/Test Administration

The <u>BEAR-CAPS</u> "kit" contains simple and attractive materials that are manipulated by the child in response to the examiner's instructions. The examiner instructs the child to perform the appropriate manipulation for a specific concept with simple and precise verbal instructions (e.g., "Put the button in the box."). The child is given three trials, and the directions for each trial become more simple. For example, (1) "Put the button in the box," (2) the examiner points to the button and says "put in," or (3) the examiner gives the button to the child and says "in." A score/summary sheet, which is arranged in developmental squence, is used to record the child's performance on each item.

Norms
BEAR-CAPS has not been normed. However, each item is given an age norm of comprehension for each concept. These age norms were taken from several sources.

Reliability
Not applicable.

Validity
Not applicable.

Advantages
1) BEAR-CAPS is designed for use with hearing-impaired children.
2) The information obtained regarding concept development may be integrated into a child's language program.
3) The test is designed for preschool-age children; other tests of concepts are designed for use with school-age children (e.g., Boehm).
4) The test can be used for any child (18 months - 5 years old) with suspected language problems or delay.

Disadvantages
1) The test does not assess conceptual development below the age of 18 months.
2) The test can not be purchased alone; it is found only in the book Comprehensive Intervention with Hearing-impaired Infants and Preschool Children.

Test Descriptions

BOEHM TEST OF BASIC CONCEPTS (BTBC)

Hearing Norms
Ages 5-0 to 7-11 years
Receptive

Boehm, A.E. (1967, 1969, 1970, 1971). Boehm Test of Basic Concepts. The Psychological Corporation, 757 3rd Avenue, New York, N.Y. 10017. Approximate Cost: $20.00.

General Description

The Boehm Test of Basic Concepts (BTBC) is designed to measure children's mastery of concepts considered necessary for achievement in the first years of school (kindergarten, first, and second grades). It may be used both to: 1) identify children with deficiencies in concepts representing four context categories (space, quantity, time, and miscellaneous), and 2) to identify individual concepts on which groups of children could profit from instruction. The BTBC is appropriate for use with hearing children in kindergarten, grade 1, and grade 2. It may be used with older hearing-impaired children as a criterion-referenced instrument.

Instructions/Test Administration

The test consists of two alternate forms, Form A and Form B. Each form consists of 50 groups of pictures arranged in approximate order of increasing difficulty and divided equally between two booklets, each containing 25 test questions. Both booklets of a given form are administered. Each item consists of a set of pictures; the examiner reads aloud statements about these pictures to the children (e.g., "Look at the boxes of eggs. Mark the box with the most eggs."). The children mark the picture illustrating the concept being tested. Each booklet requires 15 to 20 minutes to administer. Small groups of 8 to 12 children may be tested by one examiner. It should be used as a test for individual students when given to hearing-impaired children.

Norms

The standardization sample that served as the basis for the beginning-of-the-year norms consisted of 9737 children representing a range of socioeconomic backgrounds enrolled in kindergarten, grade 1, and grade 2 in each of 17 cities across the U.S. These children were tested in September and October of the 1969-70 school year. Data for midyear norms were obtained during the 1968-69 school year from testing conducted between mid-November and late February; this sample included 2647 children from schools in five cities.

Equivalence of scores on Forms A and B are demonstrated, as are equivalence of scores on corresponding items.

Norms are presented as percentage scores (percent of children passing each individual item, presented by grade and by socioeconomic level within each grade, for both beginning of the year and at midyear), and as percentile equivalents of raw scores by grade and socioeconomic level.

Reliability

Both split-half reliability coefficients and standard errors of measurement were computed for the midyear standardization sample and demonstrated as adequate. The former ranged from .68 to .90 for Form A and from .12 to .94 for Form B. (The reliability coefficient of .12 was obtained for the grade 2 high socioeconomic level students. The value of the BTBC for this group, therefore, lies only in the identification of children who are far below the group's average ability.)

Validity

Only content validity is discussed. Test items were selected from relevant curriculum materials and represent concepts basic to understanding directions and other "oral communications" from teachers at the preschool and primary-grade level.

Advantages
1) As mentioned above, the BTBC may be used both to identify children with deficiencies in specific concepts needed to achieve in school, and to identify individual concepts on which large numbers of children in a class could profit from instruction.
2) Items are arranged in order of increasing difficulty, so Part I and Part II could be administered at different times.

Test Descriptions

3) Administration of the test is simple, quick, and straightforward.
4) The BTBC may be used with hearing-impaired students of any age to determine whether the tested concepts have been mastered. For older children, key concepts may be fingerspelled.

Disadvantages
1) It was normed on hearing children (but see notes below).
2) Some items are not easily administered in simultaneous communication, i.e., some items may have no formal equivalent sign. Fingerspelling of items, however, may be inappropriate, unless the student uses this system on a regular basis.
3) The illustrations are sometimes ambiguous.

Notes:
1) Davis (1974)* administered the BTBC to 24 hearing-impaired children; 75% of the children scored at or below the 10th percentile when compared to norms for hearing children their age or younger. Item analysis of the responses indicated that their poorest performance was on time concepts, followed by quantity, miscellaneous, and space concepts, in that order.
2) The pictures in the BTBC can be cut up and presented individually to minimize visual confusion.
3) For some students you may wish to administer Form A with signs and Form B with fingerspelling, and compare results. Or administer one form orally for purposes of pre-mainstreaming assessment.
4) A Boehm Resource Guide for Basic Concept Teaching is available from The Psychological Corporation (address listed above).

* Davis, J. (1974). Performance of young hearing-impaired children on a test of basic concepts. Journal of Speech and Hearing Research, 17, 342-351.

BRACKEN BASIC CONCEPT SCALE (BBCS)

Hearing Norms
Ages 2-6 to 7-11 years
Receptive

Bracken, A. (1984). Bracken Basic Concept Scale. Charles E. Merrill Publishing Co., 1300 Alum Creek Drive, Columbus, OH 43216. Approximate Cost: $69.00.

General Description

The Bracken Basic Concept Scale (BBCS) was designed as a means of assessing conceptual knowledge of children with receptive language difficulties ages 2-6 to 8 years. The BBCS consists of two parts: a Diagnostic Scale to provide in-depth assessment and a Screening Test to identify children who may require further diagnostic assessment. The Screening Test is designed only for children ages 5-0 to 7-0 years.

The author states that a child must have an understanding of fundamental concepts in order to communicate effectively. In developing the BBCS, the author surveyed several psychological tests and tests addressing basic concepts, including the Boehm Test of Basic Concepts. Research in the study of concepts by several authors of these tests (Boehm, 1967; Kaufman, 1978; Cummings & Nelson, 1980)* cite the incidence of concept deficiencies among preschool and primary school-age children, thus emphasizing the need for a test such as the BBCS.

The BBCS consists of 11 subtests on the Diagnostic Scale. They include: Color, Letter Identification, Numbers/Counting, Comparisons, Shapes, Direction/Position, Social/Emotional, Size, Texture/Material, Quantity, and Time/Sequence. The Screening Test consists of 30 items which were selected from all of the subtests, except three: Colors, Numbers/Counting, and Letter Identification.

Instructions/Test Administration

The administration of both the Diagnostic Scale and the Screening Test is the same; the child is shown a plate with four stimulus pictures and is instructed to "Show me ____." or "Point to ____." A stimulus manual and separate record form are provided for the Diagnostic Scale, whereas the Screening Test consists of two alternate forms of the same stimuli onto which the examiner records the child's score directly. The BBCS is not a timed test. In addition, the Screening Test may be given in a group.

Diagnostic Scale. Each child begins with subtests I-V and continues through each subtest until he or she misses three consecutive items. A School Readiness Composite is established based on the child's score. The child's score obtained on the five subtests is used to estimate the child's success on subtests VI-XI. A basal and a ceiling are established on subtests VI-XI. (The basal is the number of items the child must answer correctly to continue taking the test.) Specific directions for recording the child's correct and incorrect responses and for deriving the child's score are provided in the manual.

Screening Test. The Screening Test is administered in the same manner as the Diagnostic Test. Two alternate forms of the Screening Test are provided: Form A or Form B. One scores the Screening Test by adding the number of items the child answered correctly and then deriving a standard score and corresponding percentile rank. This information is recorded on a Group Analysis Form in the Screening Test Directions booklist.

Norms

Diagnostic Scale. The Diagnostic Scale of the BBCS was standardized on 1109 children located in 44 sites across the U.S. The variables used in selecting children for the standardization sample were age, sex, ethnic group (Black, Caucasian, Hispanic, or other), geographic region, community size, and socioeconomic status. Children from various socioeconomic levels were selected.

Screening Test. The BBCS Screening Test was standardized on 559 kindergarteners and 320 first-grade children located in 17 geographic locations throughout the U.S. The test was administered in small groups. Half of the children completed Form A on the first day of testing and Form B on the second day; the other half completed the forms in reverse order. As with the Diagnostic Scale, the children were selected from various socioeconomic levels and ethnic groups.

Reliability

Diagnostic Scale. Internal consistency coefficients were calculated for each 1-year level for the School Readiness Composite (sum of scores for Subtest I-V), the remaining six subtests, and the total test. The reliability range is reported from .47 to .96 for the subtests and .94 to .98 for the total test. The median subtest and total test reliabilities are .85 and .97, respectively.

Screening Test. Alternate-forms reliability coefficients were calculated to demonstrate the correlation between the scores on Form A and scores on Form B. The coefficients are given in two age groups, 60 to 71 months and 72 to 83 months. A correlation coefficient of .77 (first age group) and .71 (second age group) was indicated for students taking Form A first. Students taking Form B first showed coefficients of .77 and .80 for the respective age groups.

Internal consistency reliability coefficients for ages 60 to 71 months were .80 for Form A and .79 for Form B. The coefficients for ages 72 to 83 months was .79 for Form A and .76 for Form B.

Validity

Diagnostic Scale. Content validity - The author determined content validity of the BBCS by analyzing frequently used test materials for the number of concepts in the test directions assumed to be understood by the child. The tests examined were the McCarthy Scales of Children's Abilities (MSCA), Standford-Binet, Weschler Preschool and Primary Scale of Intelligence (WPPSI), Kaufman Assessment Battery for Children (K-ABC), and the Woodcock-Johnson Psychoeducational Battery (W-J). Bracken (1984)* found that many concepts are assumed to be known by the children when they are taking these tests. Of the five tests examined, the K-ABC was the only test measure which was limited in its number of concepts used in the test directions.

Empirically derived validity - Because the BBCS is also a test of receptive language, high correlations between it and other receptive language tests would be expected. The results show a moderate to high degree with other concurrent measures (.68 to .88).

Test Descriptions

Screening Test. Content validity – Because the items on the Screening Test are derived from the Diagnostic Scale, the content validity need not be further examined.

Empirically derived validity – The difference in mean scores between Form A and Form B are greater than would be expected. This is partly because of the learning effect resulting from taking and benefitting from the previous form.

Bracken examined the effect of group administration of the Screening Test and concluded that the group administered screening tests correlate well with the individually administered Diagnostic Scale. However, it should be remembered that the Screening Test is designed to identify "at-risk" children rather than describe a performance level of low-functioning children.

Advantages

1) More concepts are included in the BBCS than on the Boehm Test of Basic Concepts: 258 vs. 50.
2) The Screening Test provided with the Diagnostic Scale allows for group administration and quick identification.
3) The normative sample was large: 1109 children for the Diagnostic Scale and 879 for the Screening Test.
4) Although the BBCS is normed on hearing children, a study by Bracken and Cato (1984) matched the scores from a group of deaf children to those of the BBCS standardization sample. The results showed that the deaf children scored aproximately 2 standard deviations below the mean.
5) Stimulus plates contain only four foils to a page; the pages are not cluttered.

Disadvantages

1) The information regarding normative data, reliability, and validity is difficult to understand in places.
2) The manual does not clearly state how many children represented specific age groups in the standardization sample or give information regarding what age intervals were sampled.

Test Descriptions

* Boehm, A.E. (1967). The development of comparative concepts in primary children. Unpublished doctoral dissertation, Columbia University.

Bracken, B.A., & Cato, L. (1984). Rate of conceptual development among deaf preschool and primary children as compared to a matched group of non-hearing-impaired children. (Manuscript in preparation.)

Cummings, J.A., & Nelson, B.R. (1980). Basic concepts in oral directions of group achievement tests. The Journal of Educational Research, 73, 159-163.

Kaufman, A.S. (1978). The importance of basic concepts in the individual assessment of preschool children. Journal of School Psychology, 16, 208-211.

Test Descriptions

*CAROLINA PICTURE VOCABULARY TEST (CPVT)

Norms for Hearing-
Impaired Children using
Total Communication
Ages 4-0 to 11-6 years
Receptive

Layton, T.L., & Holmes, D.W. (1985). *Carolina Picture Vocabulary Test*. Modern Education Corporation, P.O. Box 721, Tulsa, OK 74101. Approximate Cost: $68.50

General Description

The *Carolina Picture Vocabulary Test (CPVT)* is designed to assess the receptive sign vocabulary of deaf and hearing-impaired children ages 4-0 to 11-6 years.

Instructions/Test Administration

The *CPVT* requires approximately 15 minutes to administer. It consists of 130 plates; each plate contains four line drawings. The 130 test items were selected from vocabulary lists for deaf children (Silverman-Dresner & Guilfoyle, 1972)* and lists of sign words in *Signing Exact English* (Gustason, Pfetzing, & Zawolkow, 1972)*. In addition, a photographic stop-action picture is provided to demonstrate how to produce each sign. According to the manual, the sign may be either a common ASL or SEE sign.

When administering the *CPVT*, one obtains a basal and ceiling level. The raw score may be converted to scale scores, percentile ranks, and age equivalency scores.

Norms

The *CPVT* was standardized on 767 deaf and hearing-impaired children ranging in age from 2-6 to 16 years. The sample was obtained nationwide of children who attend day or residential school programs and who use manual communication as their primary means of communicating.

Reliability

Internal consistency – The split-half reliability method was used to estimate the internal consistency of the *CPVT*.

This was done according to age level, and the overall findings showed a total split-half reliability of .917.

Stability – Two studies were conducted to determine the test-retest reliability of the CPVT. In one study, 30 subjects were administered the CPVT 30 days after the initial testing. A correlation coefficient of .86 was computed for test-retest reliability. In the second study, 11 subjects were administered the CPVT 2 weeks after the initial testing. A correlation coefficient of .99 was obtained.

Standard Error of Measurement (SEM) – The SEM for the CPVT's raw scores was computed for each of eight age levels. The average SEM for the eight age levels was 4.39.

Validity

Content validity – The authors state that good content validity was met by their carefully selecting vocabulary items used by deaf children which are also adaptable for manual presentation.

Concurrent validity – The Test of Auditory Comprehension of Language (TACL) (Carrow, 1976) was used in a study to compare the language functions it measures with those of the CPVT. The results of the study indicated that the CPVT is a reliable test of language comprehension.

Construct validity – Age differentiation was used to measure the construct validity of the CPVT. Overall, the results suggested that a developmental trend in sign vocabulary could be found with children at the older age levels performing significantly better than the younger ones. However, significant differences were not found for adjoining ages. Based on these results, the authors suggest that although sign vocabulary scores improve with age, they do so after a 2-year period.

Advantages

1) The test was normed on deaf and hearing-impaired children who use manual signs as their primary means of communicating.

Test Descriptions

2) The CPVT contains more test items than are found in other vocabulary tests for the deaf and hearing-impaired child (e.g., Total Communication Receptive Vocabulary Test).

Disadvantages
1) The authors do not explain why the standardization sample included ages 2-6 to 16 years whereas the test includes only the age range of 4-0 to 11-6 years.
2) The vocabulary used in the CPVT was received only from academic programs which teach sign language in their curriculum.
3) The photographs of the signs are not all SEE signs or ASL signs. They appear to be a mixture of both. However, the author does list Signing Exact English in the reference section.
4) The signs in the photographs do not include endings such as -ing, -y, or -tion, or -man as in policeman.
5) In several examples, the same sign is used twice to refer to two words with similar meanings (e.g., handkerchief, #22, and tissue, #56).
6) Photographs are all black and white and many appear dark and difficult to interpret. Facial expressions are somewhat distracting.
7) Additional time may be required to verify signs used by students, or to clarify the production of signs from Signing Exact English.

* Gustason, G., Pfetzing, D., & Zawolkow, E. Signing Exact English. Rossmoor, CA: Modern Signs Press, 1972. (Revised edition, 1980, Modern Signs Press, Los Alamitos, CA.)

Silverman-Dresner, T., & Guilfoyle, G. Vocabulary Norms for Deaf Children. Washington, D.C.: Alexander Graham Bell Association for the Deaf, 1972.

CARROW ELICITED LANGUAGE INVENTORY (CELI)

Hearing Norms
Ages 3-0 to 7-11 years
Expressive

Carrow-Woolfolk, E. (1974). *Carrow Elicited Language Inventory*, DLM Teaching Resources, P.O. Box 4000, 1 DLM Park, Allen, TX 75002. Approximate Cost: $65.00.

General Description

The Carrow Elicited Language Inventory (CELI) is a diagnostic procedure designed to provide a reliable and efficient means of measuring a child's productive control of grammar. The test format employs elicited imitation of a sequence of sentences, which were systematically developed to include a comprehensive list of basic sentence constructions and specific grammatical morphemes. The test is designed for hearing children ages 3-0 to 7-11 years.

Instructions/Test Administration

The CELI consists of 52 stimuli (51 sentences and one phrase) which range in length from two to 10 words (average six words). The child's imitations of the stimulus sentences produced by the examiner are recorded during test administration. The child's responses are transcribed phonemically. The scoring procedure is fairly complicated and requires special training; errors are categorized by type (omissions, substitutions, transpositions, and reversals). Both total scores and subcategory scores (for performance on pronouns, adjectives, verbs, negatives, etc.) are obtained. Time required for testing is 45 minutes.

Norms

Norms were established on 475 Caucasian children, 3-0 to 7-11 years old, of middle socioeconomic status, none of whom had apparent speech or language disorders.

Reliability

Test-retest reliability was high (r = .98). The author obtained a measure of inter-examiner reliability by correla-

Test Descriptions

ting transcriptions and the scoring of two examiners; this was also high (.98).

Validity

Test scores improved with age in the norm sample, showing that the CELI does reflect developmental change. A study reported in the test manual showed that scores of children with language disorders differed significantly from scores of children with normal language. Also, correlations were high between scores on the CELI and Developmental Sentence Scoring obtained for 20 children with language disorders.

Advantages
1) The CELI is easy to administer; it does not require extensive training or knowledge of linguistics.
2) It permits identification of specific linguistic structures that are difficult for a particular child.
3) The CELI is adaptable for hearing-impaired children, if used with simultaneous communication. The tester could videotape the child's imitation of signed/spoken sentences and look at different aspects of his or her expressive performance (speech, signing, etc.).

Disadvantages
1) The CELI requires a long time to administer (45 minutes).
2) It requires training in scoring procedures (and possibly in using the International Phonetic Alphabet for transcribing responses).
3) The CELI was normed on hearing children.
4) Videotape equipment would be required to use the CELI effectively with hearing-impaired children.
5) Any articulation error necessitates scoring the response as an error; however, any modification of scoring techniques for use with hearing-impaired children invalidates the norms.

Notes:
1) The GAEL (see below) is similar and was developed for use with hearing-impaired students.
2) Refer to Section V of this book for cautions regarding use of elicited imitations to obtain an expressive language sample.

Test Descriptions

CENTRAL INSTITUTE FOR THE DEAF
*SCALES OF EARLY COMMUNICATION SKILLS FOR
HEARING-IMPAIRED CHILDREN (SECS)

Norms for hearing-
impaired children in
oral school programs
Ages 2-0 to 8-0
Expressive/Receptive

Moog, J.S., & Geers, A.V. (1975). CID Scales of Early Communication Skills for Hearing-Impaired Children. Central Institute for the Deaf, 818 South Euclid Avenue, St. Louis, MO 63110. Approximate Cost: $15.00

General Description

The CID Scales of Early Communication Skills for Hearing-Impaired Children (SECS) is designed to assess the receptive and expressive speech and language skills of hearing-impaired children ages 2-0 to 8-0 years. The test is divided into four scales: Receptive Language Skills, Expressive Language Skills, Nonverbal Receptive Skills, and Nonverbal Expressive Skills. Each scale contains test items which are arranged and numbered according to developmental level.

Instructions/Test Administration

The SECS is administered by the child's teacher rather than through a parent interview or a one-time structured testing session. The test items in each level of a scale are presented in two ways; "A" items are presented in a structured teaching situation, and "B" items in a natural spontaneous situation. All of the "A" items are scored together as are all of the "B" items.

When administering the test, the teacher rates each test item according to whether or not the child demonstrates that particular behavior. A (+) rating is given if the child demonstrates the skill consistently; a (±) is given if the behavior is only emerging but the child does demonstrate the behavior on occasion; or a (-) is given if the child does not demonstrate the behavior at any time. One obtains a raw score by assigning a value to the number of +, ±, and - ratings ob-

Test Descriptions

tained. From the raw score, a standard score and a percentile rank according to age group can be derived.

Norms

The SECS was normed on 372 hearing-impaired children who were enrolled in 14 different oral school programs across the U.S.

Reliability

Two teachers from CID rated 31 CID students between the ages of 4-0 and 8-0 years. The Spearman-Brown formula was used to calculate reliability coefficients for each scale. Overall, the coefficients were high; the mean for the two Receptive scales was .81 and .88 for the two Expressive Scales.

Validity

No data on validity were provided.

Advantages

1) The test is normed on hearing-impaired children.
2) The test assesses speech and language skills as low as the 2-year-old level.

Disadvantages

1) Although the test is normed on hearing-impaired children, normative data were obtained from oral school programs only; there is no allowance made for children using total communication.
2) The test language is often inappropriate and there are too few test items.

COMMUNICATIVE INTENTION INVENTORY (CII)

No Norms
8 months to 2-0 years
Expressive

Coggins, T.E., & Carpenter, R.L. (1981). The Communicative Intention Inventory: A system for observing and coding children's early intentional communication. Applied Psycholinguistics, 2, 235-251.

General Description

The Communicative Intention Inventory (CII) is an observational system designed to classify uses of language in developmentally young hearing children. It is intended to be used as a criterion-referenced measure of a child's intentional communication, where "intent" is defined as "... the deliberate pursuit of a goal by means of instrumental behaviors subordinated to that goal."

Instructions/Test Administration

The child interacts with his or her primary caretaker in a free-play situation for 45 minutes; this interaction is videotaped and then the examiner scores it, using criteria outlined in this article, as soon as possible. Eight categories of communicative behaviors are assessed: Comment on Action, Comment on Object, Request for Action, Request for Object, Request for Information, Answering, Acknowledging, and Protesting. Each of these categories is described in terms of 1) Gestural or Gestural-Vocal behaviors, and 2) Verbal behaviors that the examiner looks for in assessing the child's communicative intentions. These behaviors are thought to be necessary for the child's acquisiton of subsequent conversational skills. See Coggins & Carpenter (1981) for detailed instructions on administering, scoring, and interpreting results.

Norms

The Communicative Intention Inventory is a criterion-referenced measurement; therefore, no norms are provided. However, data on 16 children, all developing normally, are offered to provide the user with a perspective regarding the frequency of these behaviors in a group of 16- month-old children.

Reliability

Content reliability – Sixteen normally developing children consistently produced the eight communicative intentions of the *Inventory* with the same frequency, suggesting that the scale assesses similar behaviors across children.

Observer-scorer reliability – Ten graduate students trained in scoring the *CII* rated 33 behavioral sequences in specially constructed videotapes. The mean proportion of correct coding of the sequences was .91. This high degree of interscorer reliability suggests that the brief training procedure allows observers to recognize and accurately code intentional behaviors described in the *CII*.

Validity

Content validity – The authors selected the content of the *CII* by examining available literature on early communication and language development in children, including the authors' work on mother-child interactions. The test format attempts to reproduce a home-like setting in which the mother or other caretaker and the child interact in an unstructured play situation, thereby increasing the likelihood of obtaining a representative behavior sample.

Advantages

1) The *CII* assesses communication skills of very young children.
2) It does not rely on verbal behaviors and can easily be used with young hearing-impaired children.
3) Results may be used in planning intervention strategies for nonverbal cognitively delayed children, or for nonverbal children at a more advanced cognitive level. That is, behaviors shown to be poorly developed or lacking on the *CII* can become the target behaviors or objectives in an intervention program. (Examples are provided in the article.)

Disadvantages

1) Observer-scorers must be specially trained in coding techniques.
2) The caretaker-child pair must be videotaped for 45 minutes.
3) As the authors state, simply counting the number of specific communicative intents appearing in a sample may reveal little about a child's functional use of language.

Note: The *CII* is not a commercially available test. It may be found in the journal cited above.

Test Descriptions

EARLY LANGUAGE MILESTONE SCALE (ELM)

Hearing Norms
Ages 0 to 3-0 years
Receptive/Expressive

Coplan, J. (1983). *Early Language Milestone Scale*, Modern Education Corporation, P.O. Box 721, Tulsa, OK 74101. Approximate Cost: $55.00.

General Description

The ELM Scale was created to provide physicians and other professionals with a reliable method of screening young children, 0 to 3-0 years old, for potential communication and language problems. The format is similar to that of the Denver Developmental Profile: 41 items cover three divisions—Auditory Expressive, Auditory Receptive, and Visual Skills. Each behavior is developmentally sequenced and percentiles for each age are given for these behaviors.

Instructions/Test Administration

The administration of the test results in either a _pass_ or a _fail_. All 41 items are arranged in developmental order on a one-page graph. After determining the child's chronological age, the examiner asks questions of the parents or caregivers. Three consecutive behaviors below the CA must be passed to determine a basal. This procedure is repeated for all three sections. A ceiling is determined in two ways;
   a) The child achieves a basal without failing any behaviors at the 90th percentile.
   b) The child fails three consecutive items in any one of the three divisions.

Exceptions and limitations regarding the establishment of ceilings and basals are further illustrated in the manual. The child passes the ELM Scale only if he or she passes all three divisions. Included is a bag of objects containing a bell, crayon, cup, spoon, and block.

Norms

The normative group for the ELM Scale was drawn from patients of private practice pediatricians and outpatients of the New York Upstate Medical Center. A total of 191 children, 95 boys and 96 girls, were tested as part of routine well child care visits; 80% of the children were private practice patients and 20% were clinic children. Eighty percent of the children were Caucasian.

Reliability
    No reliability data are reported.

Validity
    The author reports that validation of the scale was achieved by administration of the scale to several groups of high-risk (cerebral palsied, mentally retarded) children. He and his colleagues contend that "the ELM Scale is able to discriminate between normal versus language delayed children in over 95% of cases."*

Advantages
    1) The ELM Scale uses a format familiar to most physicians and health care professionals.
    2) Both a manual and a training tape are included to familiarize the examiner with the scale.
    3) Samples of scoring technique are included.
    4) The scale generally takes only 3-4 minutes to administer.

Disadvantages
    1) Follow-up after a child fails the ELM Scale is not well covered.
    2) Items may be passed on parent report only, making the item dependent on the parent's powers of observation and reporting skills.
    3) Validity information is sketchy and no data are reported about reliability.
    4) The normative group included primarly Caucasian, private patients in upstate New York.

*Coplan, J., Gleason, J., Ryan, R., et al. (1982). Validation of An Early Language Milestone Scale in a high risk population. Pediatrics, 70, 677-683.

Test Descriptions

EXPRESSIVE ONE-WORD PICTURE VOCABULARY TEST (EOWPVT)

Hearing Norms
Ages 2-0 to 11-11 years
Expressive

Gardner, M.F. (1979, 1981). *Expressive One-Word Picture Vocabulary Test*. Academic Therapy Publications, 20 Commercial Boulevard, Novato, CA 94947. Approximate Cost: $47.00.

General Description

The *Expressive One-Word Picture Vocabulary Test (EOWPVT)* is designed to assess hearing children's verbal intelligence by means of their acquired one-word expressive picture vocabulary, i.e., the quality and quantity of a child's vocabulary based on what she or he has acquired from home and from formal education.

Instructions/Test Administration

The *EOWPVT* requires approximately 10-15 minutes to administer and is not a timed test. The child looks at a series of pictures, one per plate, and is asked to tell the examiner the "names of the things" in the pictures. As is the case with the *PPVT* (see below), a basal of eight consecutive successes is obtained, and the test ends when the child makes six consecutive incorrect responses.

Norms

The *EOWPVT* was standardized on 1,607 hearing children living in the San Francisco Bay area; ages ranged from 2 years through 11 years 11 months. An attempt was made to include appropriate proportions of minority groups and both sexes. Either the *PPVT* or the *Columbia Mental Maturity Scale* (*CMMS*) was administered concurrently.

Reliability

Split-half (odd-even) reliability was good, ranging from .87 to .96 for the different age groups.

Validity

Content validity - Items were selected to represent a common core of English words which could be illustrated without ambiguity. These words were selected to represent language typically learned and used by children in home and at school.

Criterion-related validity - Correlations of .29 and .59 were obtained between the EOWPVT and the PPVT and CMMS, respectively. The results were as expected because the PPVT taps receptive vocabulary and the CMMS taps general reasoning ability.

Advantages

1) Because the test plates present only one object per page, the child is not bombarded by stimuli or confused by several pictures on a page.
2) The EOWPVT is one of the few existing expressive tests of vocabulary.
3) No specific qualifications are required of the tester, other than familiarity with the test.
4) A mental age, IQ, and percentile score may be derived from a child's raw score.
5) The pictures are good with the exception of Plate #20, a picture of a train.

Disadvantages

1) Reliability and validity data are incomplete; for example, correlations with the PPVT are given for the younger age groups only.
2) Standard signs are not available for all pictures at upper age limits.

Note: It is unwise to use a test of vocabulary to determine an I.Q. The authors of this book recommend using the EOWPT only to review expressive vocabulary qualitatively and quantitatively.

Test Descriptions

EXPRESSIVE ONE-WORD PICTURE VOCABULARY TEST-UPPER EXTENSION (EOWPVT-UE)

Hearing Norms
Ages 12-0 to 15-11 years
Expressive

Gardner, M.F. (1983). <u>Expressive One-Word Picture Vocabulary Test-Upper Extension</u>. Academic Therapy Publications, 20 Commercial Boulevard, Novato, CA 94947. Approximate Cost: $46.00.

General Description

The <u>Upper Extension of the Expressive One-Word Picture Vocabulary Test (EOWPVT)</u> is a test which assesses the expressive vocabulary of hearing children ages 12-0 years to 15-11 years, yielding a basal estimate of a child's verbal intelligence. This basal estimate is based on the quality and quantity of a child's vocabulary derived from his or her home and formal education environment.

Instructions/Test Administration

The <u>EOWPVT-UE</u> is not a timed test; it takes approximately 10-15 minutes to administer and less than 5 minutes to score. It can be administered individually, requiring the child to give a verbal response, or in a group, where each child writes down his or her response. The child is required to look at a picture and tell or write down the name of the item(s) in the picture. There is one picture per plate with 70 plates total. A basal of eight consecutive correct responses is obtained, and the test is over when the child makes six consecutive errors.

Norms

The <u>EOWPVT-UE</u> was standardized on 465 children enrolled in public, private, and parochial schools in the San Francisco Bay area. Their ages ranged from 12 years to 15 years, 11 months. Analysis of data for sex and race showed that these dimensions did not contribute significantly to <u>EOWPVT-UE</u> scores.

Reliability
Split-half reliability was good, with reliability coefficients ranging from .89 to .94 with a median reliability of .92.

Validity
Content validity - The items in the final form were selected as representations of commonly known symbols, objects, and concepts that children ages 12 years and older are typically exposed to at home, school, and neighborhood environments.

Item validity - The items were selected on the basis of freedom from sexual bias, internal consistency, and as a representation of difficulty levels which assess a wide range of behaviors across the specified age range. The author also determined the relationship of item order to item difficulty. A correlation of -.99 was obtained, which indicated that the items are arranged in order of increasing difficulty.

Criterion-related validity - The raw scores from the PPVT-R and the WISC-R Vocabulary subtest were compared with the final form of the EOWPVT-UE. The correlations between the EOWPVT-UE and the PPVT-R were .69 to .80, and with the WISC-R vocabulary subtest were .74 to .84, both correlations considered to be good.

Validity of group administration - The performance of the standardization sample and a similar sample of students given the test as a group was compared and the performances indicated no significant difference between the two groups.

Advantages
1) Because the test plates present only one object per page, the child is not bombarded by stimuli or confused by several pictures on a page.
2) The EOWPVT-UE is one of the few existing tests of expressive vocabulary for older children.
3) No specific qualifications are required of the tester, other than familiarity with the test.
4) A mental age, IQ, and percentile score may be derived from a child's raw score.

Test Descriptions

Disadvantage
   1) Standard signs are not available for all pictures.

See **Note** above for **EOWPVT**.

*GRAMMATICAL ANALYSIS OF ELICITED LANGUAGE (GAEL)

Norms for oral hearing-impaired children
Ages 5-0 to 9-0 years
Expressive

Moog, J.S., & Geers, A.E. (1979). Grammatical Analysis of Elicited Language. Central Institute for the Deaf, 818 So. Euclid, St. Louis, MO 63110. Approximate Cost: $300.00.

General Description

The Grammatical Analysis of Elicited Language (GAEL) test (Simple Sentence Level and Complex Sentence Level) is designed to elicit and evaluate "important elements" of spoken language in young hearing-impaired children. It includes a set of toys and activities designed to elicit specific target sentences which constitute a sampling of sentence structures. The Simple Sentence Level samples structures which develop relatively early in the normal child, while the Complex Level samples more complex structures. Sixteen grammatical categories are assessed in both levels: articles, adjectives, quantifiers, possessives, demonstratives, conjunctions, pronouns, subject nouns, object nouns, Wh-questions, verbs, verb inflections, copula, the copula inflections, prepositions, and negation.

Instructions/Test Administration

The target sentences are constructed in the context of an activity. For example, the examiner will place the boy doll in the chair and state: "The boy is sitting in the chair." The examiner models specified sentence structures and the child is prompted to produce the same structured utterances. After the child has attempted the target sentence on his or her own, the examiner provides a spoken model to test the child's performance in imitation.

The number of correct responses in each of the 16 categories and for all categories combined is determined separately for prompted and imitated productions. One converts these correct scores into percentile ranks and standard scores by referring to normative tables for normal hearing 2-1/2- to 5-year-olds and hearing-impaired 5- to 9- year-olds.

Test Descriptions

Norms

Simple Sentence Level - The GAEL-S was standardized on 200 hearing-impaired children aged 5 years to 9 years (25 in each 6-month age category) and 200 normally hearing children aged 2-1/2 years to 5 years. The hearing-impaired children were enrolled in 13 oral programs across the country. Hearing levels (average speech frequency) were greater than 70 dB in the better ear. The children's hearing losses were acquired before age 2 years, and the children had no additional educationally significant handicaps.

Complex Level - The GAEL-C was standardized on 240 normally hearing children aged 3 years to 5-11 years, and 120 severely hearing-impaired children and 150 profoundly deaf children aged 8 years to 11-11 years. The hearing-impaired chidren were educated orally, were hearing-impaired before age 2 years, and had no additional educationally significant handicaps.

Reliability

Test-retest reliability was high: .96 for both the prompted and elicited portions of the test.

Validity

Mean language scores for most of the 16 grammatical categories increase with age; these results indicate that, for the most part, scores on the GAEL do reflect a developmental change in the child's ability to produce the structures sampled. Also, 15 normally hearing children diagnosed as being language-delayed scored at or below the 15th percentile for their age in both prompted and imitated productions.

Advantages

1) The GAEL is designed to avoid some of the problems encountered with spontaneous language samples and sentence imitation tasks, particularly with regard to hearing-impaired children. The test is composed of structured stimuli and an anticipated response. The child's response reflects what is considered to be his or her "best effort" at each particular structure of interest, rather than a collection of structures obtained by a more natural language sampling.

Test Descriptions

2) The <u>GAEL's</u> activities are designed to be appealing to children.
3) The manual is easy to read and complete, and includes helpful "Tips for Testers."
4) Norms are grouped in 6-month intervals.
5) Although it is a long test, it does provide an in-depth analysis of a child's expressive language for those items tested.
6) You can compare a child's scores with norms for either hearing or oral hearing-impaired children.
7) The test can be administered in simultaneous communication, but the examiner must be aware that it was normed on oral hearing-impaired children who were administered the test in oral communication only.
8) Emerging language can be identified.

Disadvantages

1) Transcribing and scoring procedures are complicated.
2) The test takes a long time to administer and score (approximately 2-1/2 hours).
3) The entire test must be tape-recorded (or videotaped if signed responses are obtained).
4) Only 25 children in each 6-month category were included in the norm group.
5) The <u>GAEL</u> was normed on hearing-impaired children in oral programs.
6) This is essentially an imitation test; see cautions listed in <u>Section V</u> of this book.
7) The test may actually be testing a child's auditory memory skills.
8) The test is very expensive.
9) As designed, this test does not evaluate a hearing-impaired child's <u>use</u> of daily language.
10) The activities and verbal precursors may become somewhat repetitious.

Test Descriptions

THE REVISED ILLINOIS TEST OF PSYCHOLINGUISTIC ABILITIES (ITPA)

Hearing Norms
Ages 2-7 to 10-1 years
Expressive/Receptive

Kirk, S.A., McCarthy, J.J., & Kirk, W.D. (1961, 1969). Illinois Test of Psycholinguistic Abilities. University of Illinois Press, Urbana, IL 61801. Approximate Cost: $58.00.

General Description

The revised edition of the Illinois Test of Psycholinguistic Abilities (ITPA) is a revision of the Experimental Edition published in 1961 and includes 10 basic subtests plus two supplementary tests for children ages 2-7 years to 10-1 years. Based upon Osgood's (1959) model of the Communication Process, the test was designed to provide diagnostic information about "various facets of cognitive ability" which will assist in planning intervention for those students who have learning problems. Terminology has been changed to make it more easily understood and some new items have been added.

Instructions/Test Administration

The ITPA consists of 10 discrete subtests and two supplementary tests considered "educationally relevant." The subtests evaluate receptive, expressive, and mediating processes of language at both the automatic and representational levels. Performance on specific subtests should help to pinpoint specific psycholinguistic abilities and disabilities. The entire battery may be administered in about 1 hour by an experienced examiner. Subtests may be administered according to need; the whole battery does not need to be given. Below is an outline of the 12 ITPA subtests.

Functions at the Representational Level

A. The Receptive Process (Decoding)
   Test 1: Auditory Reception - deriving meaning from verbally presented material. A nod or shake of the head is a sufficient response.

Test 2: Visual Reception - measures a child's ability to gain meaning from visual symbols. There are 40 picture items. The child needs only to point to the correct picture.
B. The Organizing Process (Association)
Test 3: Auditory-Vocal Association - The child must relate concepts presented orally. These concepts are presented as analogies such as: "I cut with a saw," "I pound with a ____."
Test 4: Visual-Motor Association - The child must relate concepts presented visually. The child must point to one of four pictures that "goes with" the target picture.
C. The Expressive Process (Encoding)
Test 5: Verbal Expression - expressing concepts vocally. The child must talk about or describe objects he is shown.
Test 6: Manual Expression - expressing ideas manually. The child pantomimes the use of various articles such as a telephone or guitar.

Functions at the Automatic Level

These subtests measure the child's ability to perform automatic, nonsymbolic tasks. They are neither receptive nor expressive.
A. Closure (filling in missing parts; integrating discrete units into a whole)
Test 7: Grammatic Closure - making use of what is known in our grammatical system in order to "fill in" when certain elements are missing. The ability to "fill in" or close assists in handling syntax and grammatic inflections (e.g., one dog, two dogs).
Test 8: Supp. Test 1: Auditory Closure - test of the organizing process at the automatic level. The child must fill in missing parts of words, such as "airp____."
Test 9: Supp. Test 2: Sound Blending - another means of assessing the organizing process at the auditory-vocal channel. Sounds of a word are spoken singly at half-second intervals. The child must be able to put the sounds together mentally, in order to form the correct word.
Test 10: Visual Closure - identifying a common object from an incomplete visual presentation. A specified object is hidden in various places within the picture and the child must find the object.

Test Descriptions

B. Sequential Memory (reproducing a sequence of auditory or visual stimuli)
Test 11: Auditory Sequential Memory - reproducing from memory sequences of digits increasing in length from two to eight digits.
Test 12: Visual Sequential Memory - reproducing sequences of non-meaningful figures from memory.

Norms

The norm sample comprised 962 normally hearing children in Illinois and Wisconsin, half of whom were male and half female. They were 2 years to 10 years old and were from five communities of middle socioeconomic level. The normative data are presented in 6-month intervals.

One may obtain several scores in analyzing ITPA test performance: 1) a raw score on each subtest (including a composite raw score on all 10 main sub-tests); 2) psycholinguistic age (PLA) (an age equivalent of a particular raw score); 3) psycholinguistic quotient (PLQ) (a global score indicating the child's rate of psycholinguistic development); and 4) scaled scores (linear transformations of raw scores).

A lengthy section in the test manual describes the use of ITPA scores in evaluating inter- and intra-individual differences.

Reliability

Extensive data are presented on internal consistency, stability, reliability of difference scores, and standard errors of measurement, as well as on interscorer reliability for the Verbal Expression Subtest.

Data are also given on the relationship of ITPA performance and various cognitive and demographic characteristics: chronological age, sex, social class, position among siblings, number of siblings, and intelligence.

Validity

The content validity of each subtest is discussed in the test manual (Ch. 3: "Construction of the ITPA Subtests"). Correlations of various subtests with external measures are not provided.

Advantages
1) The ITPA taps a variety of psycholinguistic skills not usually tested, e.g., manual expression, auditory association, and visual association, and can therefore provide a more complete picture of a child's strengths and weaknesses. For those familiar enough with various subtests, combinations of results may yield useful information relevant to educational planning.
2) The ITPA has two tests that tap expressive skills.
3) Normative data are presented for 6-month age intervals.
4) Although the ITPA is not normed on hearing-impaired children, some subtests may provide relevant information regarding mainstreaming of particular hearing-impaired children. If a child is to be mainstreamed into an oral program, this information might contribute to predicting how successful the child's performance might be in the oral program.

Disadvantages
1) Precisely because of the ITPA's complexity, the examiner must make a considerable effort to become thoroughly familiar with and skilled in administration and interpretation of all the subtests.
2) Some subtests (e.g., Auditory Reception) may not be useful for many hearing-impaired children.
3) Some subtests (e.g., Verbal Expression) have complicated scoring procedures.
4) Data on the validity of the ITPA subtests are incomplete.

Test Descriptions

INTERPERSONAL LANGUAGE SKILLS ASSESSMENT (ILSA)

Hearing norms
Ages 8-0 to 14-0 years
Expressive

Blagden, C.M., & McConnell, N.L. (1985). <u>Interpersonal Language Skills Assessment</u> (ILSA). LinguiSystems, Inc. 716 17th Street, Moline, IL 61265. Approximate Cost: $42.00.

General Description

The <u>Interpersonal Language Skills Assessment</u> (<u>ILSA</u>) provides a system for the structured observation and analysis of social language behaviors for hearing children ages 8 to 14 years.

Instructions/Test Administration

The <u>ILSA</u> consists of a Transcript Form and a test manual. The examiner obtains an expressive language sample while observing 3-4 students playing a table game for approximately 15-30 minutes and codes the child's language according to the type of utterance such as command, question, etc. The sample is recorded on audio tape; notes regarding non-verbal behavior should be taken during the test session. The student's comments are transcribed onto the <u>ILSA</u> Transcript Form. There are 16 pragmatic categories which are used to classify the student's comments. They are as follows:

Accusing	Informing
Advising-Future	Justifying
Advising-Past	Off-Task
Anticipating	Prompting
Commanding	Requesting Information
Commenting	Requesting Repetition
Depreciating-Other	Supporting Other
Depreciating-Self	Supporting Self

In addition to being classified by category, each comment is coded for Subject (the player who makes the comment), Negation (use of), an Inadequate comment, and a Circle Check (indicating that a more complex comment was made). Definitions and examples of each of the 16 categories as well as all codes are provided in the test manual.

Norms

Normative data were collected on 528 normal hearing students aged 8 to 13 years and 64 learning disabled children. Norm tables are arranged in three age categories: 8-0 to 9-11, 10-0 to 11-11, and 12-0 to 13-11 years. Mean scores and percents are presented for all categories tested by the ILSA, as well as a rank order of categories by frequency of occurrence. Data include standardized scores, percentile ranks, and standard deviations.

Reliability

No reliability information is provided.

Validity

No validity information is provided.

Advantages:

1) Few other assessments attempt to measure social language in an organized fashion.
2) The table game format is appealing to most students in the target population.
3) The social skills of language within the test are those often not identified but are ones that should be in hearing-impaired students.
4) Teachers could select one or two social/language behaviors from the test to measure and teach to hearing-impaired students.

Disadvantages

1) If the entire test is used, transcription and analysis are time-consuming.
2) A videotape of the game would very likely be required to use this tool with hearing-impaired students in a total communication environment.

Test Descriptions

*MARYLAND SYNTAX EVALUATION INSTRUMENT (MSEI)

Normed on hearing-impaired
students
attending residential schools
Ages 6-0 to 11-11 years
Expressive

White, A.H. (1981). <u>Maryland Syntax Evaluation Instrument</u>.
Support Systems for the Deaf, Box 428, Sanger, TX 76266.
Approximate Cost: $65.00.

General Description

The Maryland Syntax Evaluation Instrument (MSEI) is an expressive (written) test designed to provide educators of the deaf with a "meaningful way to evaluate and diagnose the language of their hearing-impaired students."

Instructions/Test Administration

The MSEI consists of a color filmstrip with 10 pretest and 10 posttest pictures used to elicit a written language sample of 10 sentences (one sentence per picture). The pictures are designed to elicit a variety of sentence types. Children too young to write may respond using speech or signs.

The child's language sample is recorded and scored on an evaluation form. Scoring consists of a complicated analysis of each word-string. (The scoring section of the manual is 14 pages long and instruction in scoring procedures requires several hours.) Instead of scoring errors, the examiner gives credit for what the child knows about English syntax.

Norms

The MSEI was standardized on 220 hearing-impaired children at three different residential schools for the deaf, each with a different methodological philosophy: total communication, oral, and the Rochester Method. Of these subjects, 84% had hearing losses of 90 dB HL or greater in the better ear.

Reliability

Reliability between Form A and Form B was .88. Interscorer reliability was high; a Pearson Product-Moment correlation coefficient was .74 for 25 language samples.

Predictive Validity

Teachers' rankings of 30 subjects' language samples correlated highly (r = .94) with MSEI computed syntax scores for those samples.

Advantages

1) The MSEI was designed for use with hearing-impaired children who attend residential schools.
2) It may be administered individually or in groups.
3) The MSEI may yield information relevant to diagnosis and evaluation.
4) The pictures are good and most students tend to like them.

Disadvantages

1) The MSEI takes a long time to administer and score.
2) The complicated scoring system requires several hours of training. The author's definitions of terms used in scoring and sentence types differ from currently accepted linguistic use.
3) The MSEI tests only *written* expressive language.
4) Appropriate equipment is needed, e.g., tape recorder and/or videotape equipment, for recording responses when MSEI is administered in simultaneous communication.
5) Norms are based on written responses only.
6) Within the norm group, numbers in age categories vary greatly (e.g., 15 in the 6-0 to 6-11 age category, 85 in the 9-0 to 9-11 group).
7) It would be useful to have norms for a hearing sample as well (i.e., how does a hearing child with syntactic competence perform?), which MSEI lacks.
8) As the author points out, norm subjects may not be representative of hearing-impaired children in all programs (subjects were from residential schools only).

Test Descriptions

MILLER-YODER LANGUAGE COMPREHENSION TEST (M-Y)
(Clinical Edition)

Hearing Norms
Ages 4-0 to 8-0 years
Receptive

Miller, J.F., & Yoder, D.E. (1984). <u>The Miller-Yoder Test of Grammatical Comprehension: Clinical Edition</u>. Pro Ed, 5341 Industrial Oaks Boulevard, Austin, TX 78735. Approximate Cost: $49.95.

General Description
The <u>Miller-Yoder Test</u> is a picture selection test for measuring hearing children's grammatical comprehension. The Clinical Edition replaces an earlier Experimental Edition published in 1975.

Instructions/Test Administration
The <u>M-Y</u> consists of 84 sentences forming 42 sentence pairs with 10 basic grammatical forms tested (e.g., preposition, possessive, verb inflections, passive reversible, reflexivization). The sentence pairs differ only in the particular grammatical feature being tested (e.g., "Spot is barking at <u>her</u>," vs. "Spot is barking at <u>him</u>."). Each sentence is represented by a drawing. There are 42 plates with four pictures appearing on each plate (two are tested, two are distractors). The test administrator reads the test sentence out loud, and the child selects the corresponding picture. The <u>Miller-Yoder</u> takes about 20 minutes to administer. Two practice plates are provided. The new format of the <u>M-Y</u> allows the examiner to administer the entire test or portions of the test, which are arranged according to developmental age level. Analysis of the data provides 1) a total score (TS) whereby the examiner can compare the test child's score with those of others his age or find out which age level he is closest to, 2) a developmental age level which provides the examiner with age levels at which 60% or 90% of the population passed, and 3) an error analysis which permits the examiner to compare the test child's incorrect sentences with what would be expected according to the difficulty of the sentence.

Norms

Owings (1972)* and Carlson (1977)* both developed normative data for the M-Y. A total of 172 subjects from the Madison, Wisconsin area participated in the studies. All subjects were from middle socioeconomic groups and had no handicapping conditions. All were from monolingual homes. Age norms and the developmental sequence of the test were developed from the combined studies.

Reliability

Owings' (1972) study demonstrated that the M-Y was reliable (.93 Hoyt Reliability Index). During the development of the Clinical Edition the original data from the Owings study were re-examined for internal consistency. An internal consistency reliability coefficient of .92733 was obtained.

Validity

Content validity is based on data obtained in Owings' (1972) work. This study was limited to 3- to 6-year-old children only. Concurrent validity is reported in the manual as demonstrated through 10 years' use of the earlier edition of the M-Y as a routine clinical procedure at the University of Wisconsin Speech and Language Center in combination with formal and informal assessment procedures.

Advantages

1) The test is quick and easy to administer.
2) It can be adapted for use with hearing-impaired children.
3) A variety of grammatical constructions, ranging from simple to more complex, is tested.
4) The score sheet shows at a glance areas of strengths and weaknesses. Individual error analysis is possible.
5) It is possible to give the entire test, or any portion the examiner wishes.
6) Norms are now available for ages 4 to 8 years.

Disadvantages

1) Test validity information is based on 3- to 6-year-old children only, from the 1972 study by Owings.
2) Considerable practice is necessary before one can perform the new scoring technique quickly and accurately.

Test Descriptions

* Carlson, K. (1977). Miller-Yoder Test of Grammatical Comprehension: Norms for three through eight year olds. Unpublished paper. Madison: University of Wisconsin-Madison.

Owings, N.O. (1972). Internal reliability and item analysis of the Miller-Yoder Test of Grammatical Comprehension. Unpublished Master's thesis. Madison: University of Wisconsin-Madison.

Test Descriptions

NORTHWESTERN SYNTAX SCREENING TEST (NSST)

Hearing Norms
Ages 3-0 to 7-11 years
Receptive/Expressive

Lee, L.L. (1971). Northwestern Syntax Screening Test. Northwestern University Press. 1831 Hinman Ave., Evanston, IL 60201. Approximate Cost: $10.00.

General Description
The NSST is intended to screen receptive and expressive use of syntactic forms by children aged 3 to 8 years.

Instructions/Test Administration
The NSST consists of 40 sentence pairs (20 receptive pairs, 20 expressive pairs) with accompanying pictures. Each sentence pair tests a specific syntactic form. Sentences are arranged in approximate order of increasing difficulty.

For the receptive items, the examiner reads a sentence and the child points to the appropriate picture, given a choice of two or four pictures. For the expressive items, the child produces a sentence for two pictures after the examiner first produces the sentence (delayed imitation). The picture to be referred to first has an asterisk beside it. For example: The boy is sitting.* The boy is not sitting. The examiner says: "Show me 'The boy is sitting.'" The examiner scores the expressive portion of the test by determining whether a response is correct. If a child changes the response but uses the same test item and maintains correct grammar and meaning, the sentence is still considered correct. For instance, this would occur if the examiner says: "The baby is not sleeping," and the child states: "He is not sleeping," where the pronoun does not affect the test item "not" nor the correctness of the sentence. A score of 1 is given for each correct response. A perfect score would be 40 on each of the two parts of the test, receptive and expressive. Either the receptive or expressive portion may be administered and scored separately.

Time required for testing is approximately 15 minutes. A shorter version of the NSST may be administered if large numbers of children must be screened.

Test Descriptions

Norms

As of 1971, data were collected on 344 public school children between the ages of 3-0 and 7-11 with no known language disorders. More recent data were collected on 242 children from middle- and upper-income homes where Standard American dialect was spoken. Percentile rankings and standard deviations are provided for each 1-year age interval for the receptive and expressive subtests. Children scoring lower than 2 standard deviations below the mean on either portion of the test require further testing. Guidelines for interpretation of test scores are provided.

Reliability

No reliability data are provided.

Validity

No validity data are provided.

Advantages

1) The NSST is a short and easy screening test to administer (although scoring the expressive items is somewhat complicated). It is convenient for screening large numbers of children.
2) The examiner can give the test using total communication.
3) The NSST would be appropriate for older hearing-impaired students, especially those with low English skills.
4) Pictures are clear and simple.
5) Items are arranged in approximate order of increasing difficulty.

Disadvantages

1) No information is provided regarding reliability and validity of the NSST.
2) The expressive portion of the test is essentially an imitation task.
3) Some grammatically correct sentences may be scored as incorrect.
4) Memory span is not considered in the test design, but may affect student responses.

Test Descriptions

PEABODY PICTURE VOCABULARY TEST - REVISED (PPVT)

Hearing Norms
Ages 2-6 to 40-0 years
Receptive

Dunn, L.M., & Dunn, L.M. (1981). Peabody Picture Vocabulary Test - Revised. American Guidance Service, Publisher's Building, Circle Pines, MN 55014. Approximate Cost: $49.00 (regular edition), $65.00 (special edition).

General Description

The Peabody Picture Vocabulary Test - Revised (PPVT) is an individually administered, norm-referenced test of receptive vocabulary designed for people aged 2-6 to 40 years of age.

Instructions/Test Administration

Two parallel forms, L and M, are provided. Each form contains five training items followed by 175 test items arranged in order of increasing difficulty. Each item has four simple black and white illustrations arranged on one page in a multiple-choice format. The subject's task is to select the picture which best illustrates the meaning of the stimulus word presented by the examiner. The test requires 10 to 20 minutes to administer.

Norms

The PPVT was standardized on 5,028 hearing subjects (4,200 children and adolescents, and 828 adults). Norm subjects represent 6-month age intervals from ages 2-5 to 6-5, and 1-year intervals beyond. Males and females are represented equally (100 of each sex at each age level); also represented are a range of geographic locations, occupations, ethnic groups, and community size. Raw scores convert to age-referenced norms. (Grade-referenced derived scores are available from the publisher on request.) Three types of norms are reported: standard score equivalent, percentile ranks, and stanines. Also reported are developmental-type age norms: age-equivalent scores.

Exhaustive data are presented in the revised version of the PPVT regarding test construction, standardization, and norms development.

Test Descriptions

Reliability
Exhaustive data are provided regarding standard error of measurement, alternate forms, and internal consistency.

Validity
Exhaustive data are provided regarding content validity, construct validity, and criterion-related validity.

Advantages
1) The test is brief and easily administered (i.e., instructions are easy for children to understand).
2) The PPVT has been shown to be adaptable for use with hearing-impaired children as a test of either signed or written vocabulary reception (see Notes below).
3) Test administration can be learned in a short time.
4) Pictures are clear and easy to understand.

Disadvantages
1) It is often difficult to reach a ceiling with hearing-impaired children. Therefore, test administration may be prolonged.
2) Test items may be represented by more than one sign, or may not be easily represented by a sign at all. Therefore, the tester may want to fingerspell test items to older students. In this case, results may be affected by the student's ability to understand fingerspelling.

Notes:
1) Forde (1977)* presented the PPVT stimuli in printed form to 196 deaf and hard-of-hearing children in year 7 of their educational program. PPVT scores correlated with SAT scores for word meaning, paragraph meaning, and language (ranging from .61 to .67). These correlations may be spuriously inflated, however, because reading is involved in both tests. These data are based on the old version of the PPVT.
2) The Total Communication Receptive Vocabulary Test, which was normed on hearing-impaired students, may be a preferable test at least for younger hearing-impaired students.

* Forde, J. (1977). Data on the Peabody Picture Vocabulary Test. _American Annals of the Deaf_, _122_, 38-43.

PRESCHOOL LANGUAGE ASSESSMENT INSTRUMENT (PLAI)

Hearing norms
Ages 3-0 to 6-0 years
Receptive/Expressive

Blank, M., Rose, S.A., & Berlin, L.J. (1978). Preschool Language Assessment Instrument. Grune and Stratton, Inc., 6277 Sea Harbor Drive, Orlando, FL 32831. Approximate Cost: $74.00.

General Description

The PLAI is an experimental test designed to assess the 3- to 6-year-old hearing child's ability to meet the language demands of a verbally based instructional situation. In other words, the PLAI assesses the preschool child's discourse skills; the examiner places demands on the child which require comprehension and use of language at various levels of abstraction. The 60 test items are divided into four main groupings:

I. Matching Perception - e.g., "What things do you see on the table?"
II. Selective Analysis of Perception - e.g., "What shape is the bowl?"
III. Reordering Perception - e.g., "Show me the part of the egg we don't eat."
IV. Reasoning about Perception - e.g., "What will happen to the cookies when we put them in the oven?"

Instructions/Test Administration

The test contains a manual, a related textbook, The Language of Learning: The Preschool Years, by the test authors, and picture plates for the 60 test items. The test requires approximately 20 minutes to administer. The examiner shows the child one test plate at a time and asks questions related to the picture stimulus. The majority of the test items require a verbal response from the child; however, for 10 test items the child is required to point to one picture from a selection of several on a page. The answers are recorded completely on the score form.

Analysis of each answer is possible both quantitatively and qualitatively. A numerical score of 0-3, with 3 being "Fully Adequate" and 0 being "Inadequate," is given for each test item. A mean score is obtained for a child's performance in each of the four groupings. These scores reflect the child's ability to comprehend complex language, as well as his or her cognitive skills. For example, pointing to a stack of four spools, the examiner asks "What would happen to the pile if I took this one [point to the bottom one] away?" The examiner derives a percentile ranking from the numerical scores in order to compare a child's performance to that of others of similar age and socioeconomic background.

A second, qualitative, analysis yields information regarding the quality of a child's expressive language. This form of scoring is optional. The child's response is coded in one of seven categories: Fully Adequate, Acceptable, Ambiguous, Inadequate-Invalid, Inadequate-Irrelevant, Inadequate-Don't Know, or Inadequate-No Response. The test booklet defines the code to be assigned to the child's response. The scores for each category are then summed and a percentage of the child's responses in each category is calculated. The information provided assists a teacher in knowing whether a child processes and understands complex information and, separately, how well he is able to respond--in a single word or complete sentence.

Norms

One hundred and twenty children aged 3-0 to 5-11 years were matched for age, sex, and socioeconomic background. Normative data are reported at half-year intervals by skill group and socioeconomic level.

Reliability

Inter-rater reliability was judged to be from 92-94 percent among four raters evaluated.

Split-half reliability was assessed for the total sample. Skill group scores are I=.64, II=.80; III=.83; and IV=.86. The scores reflect a high degree of internal consistency.

The developers assessed test-retest reliability using 34 subjects. Scores for each skill group were I=.73; II=.83; III=.86; and IV=.88.

Test Descriptions

Validity

Content validity - The developers demonstrated content validity by having five psychologists and special education teachers categorize the 60 test items after reading selected chapters in the textbook. Agreement between the five raters was reached on 75% of the items; 95% agreement on the items was reached by at least four of the five raters.

Discriminative validity - The PLAI was administered to a group of 14 preschool language-impaired children. They all scored below the 25th percentile. The authors concluded that the PLAI will discriminate among children according to their language ability.

Construct validity - Two measures of construct validity are reported by the authors. First, test performance increases with age; and second, the individual skill groups reflect increasing difficulty. (Group II is more difficult than Group I, etc.) The authors additionally report a difference in overall test scores between children from middle and lower socioeconomic groups.

Advantages

1) The test helps determine whether the child _understands_ complex as well as simple language constructions.
2) The student receives credit for comprehending the information which is reflected in a simple one-word answer, but may receive additonal credit for a complete, grammatically correct sentence.
3) The test is brief, which is appropriate for preschool-aged children.
4) It attempts to assess a child's language for instructional purposes, using discourse commonly used in teaching environments.
5) The sentences used to elicit answers can easily be signed.
6) It is one of the few tests designed to evaluate more than vocabulary, word endings, and syntax.

Disadvantage

1) Some pictures are small and contain too many objects on one page.

RECEPTIVE ONE-WORD PICTURE VOCABULARY TEST (ROWPVT)

Hearing Norms
Ages 2-0 to 11-11 years
Receptive

Gardner, M.F. (1985). <u>Receptive One-Word Picture Vocabulary Test.</u> Academic Therapy Publications, 20 Commercial Boulevard, Novato, CA 94947. Approximate Cost: $36.00.

General Description

The <u>Receptive One-Word Picture Vocabulary Test (ROWPVT)</u> is designed to assess hearing children's receptive single-word vocabulary. The <u>ROWPVT</u> evaluates only a child's receptive vocabulary skills whereas its expressive counterpart, the <u>Expressive One-Word Picture Vocabulary Test (EOWPVT)</u>, assesses a child's expressive single-word vocabulary. The author states that, by using both the ROWPVT and the EOWPVT, one can compare results to show differences in a child's receptive and expressive language skills.

Instructions/Test Administration

The <u>ROWPVT</u> requires approximately 10-15 minutes to administer and it is not a timed test. The examiner provides a stimulus word which depicts one of four pictures the child sees on a page. The child is required to identify the picture which illustrates the stimulus word. The items are administered within a critical range. One determines this range by first establishing a basal of eight consecutive correct responses, and then ends it when a ceiling of six incorrect responses out of eight consecutive items has been obtained. The child's raw score, the number of correct responses, is used to compute four types of derived scores: (1) language age, (2) language standard score, (3) stanine, and (4) percentile rank.

Norms

The <u>ROWPVT</u> was standardized on 1,128 children ages 2-0 years through 11-11 years who resided in the San Francisco Bay area. The <u>EOWPVT</u> was administered concurrently and used for correlations with the scores obtained from the <u>ROWPVT</u>. The

Test Descriptions

vocabulary subtest of the Weschler Preschool and Primary Scale of Intelligence (WPPSI) or the Weschler Intelligence Scale for Children-Revised (WISC-R) was administered to 935 children in order to obtain validity information.

Correlation of the raw scores between the ROWPVT and the EOWPVT was high: .89.

Reliability

Cronbach's Alpha, an average of all possible split-half reliabilities, was employed to estimate reliability for the ROWPVT. Reliability was high; coefficients ranged from .81 to .93 with a median value of .90.

The Standard Error of Measurement (SEM) was calculated to determine how much the obtained scores would vary if the ROWPVT were administered several times to the same individual. The median SEM was found for raw scores to be 3.33, and for language scores, 4.50.

The Standard Error of Difference, which compares the standard scores of one test to another, ranged from 5.61 to 8.08 with a median of 6.09. Additionally, the 85 percent confidence limit ranged from 8.08 to 11.63 with a median of 8.77.

Validity

Content validity was established during the ROWPVT's development. Teachers from grades K-6 evaluated the pictures and verbal descriptions for their appropriateness.

Developers established item validity by retaining only those items which yielded a greater percent passing as chronological age increased.

They established criterion-related validity by comparing the raw scores from the ROWPVT with the raw scores from the WPPSI and the WISC-R. The median coefficient value was low: $r = .41$. However, this may have been because of a lower raw score range for both the WPPSI and the WISC-R. Therefore, because of the high correlation between the raw scores of the EOWPVT and ROWPVT ($r = .89$), additional criterion-related validity can be inferred from the EOWPVT.

Advantages
1) The pictures are good; they are simple line drawings presented across the page.

2) The ROWPVT requires little time to administer and score.
3) It provides a receptive counterpart to the <u>EOWPVT</u>.

<u>Disadvantage</u>
1) Standard signs may not be available for all pictures.

Test Descriptions

*RHODE ISLAND TEST OF LANGUAGE STRUCTURE (RITLS)

Norms for hearing-impaired
children and youth
Ages 5-0 to 17+ years
Receptive

Engen, E., & Engen, T. (1983). Rhode Island Test of Language Structure. Pro Ed, 5341 Industrial Oaks Boulevard, Austin, TX 78735. Approximate Cost: $49.95.

General Description

The RITLS is designed to assess hearing-impaired children's level of language development and to provide sufficient assessment data for planning intervention. The RITLS provides information about the child's comprehension of language structure through presentation of simple to complex sentence structures of the language. In other words, it tests children's syntactic and semantic processing of sentences. The test is designed for use with hearing-impaired children ages 5-0 to 17+ years. Although the test is designed primarily for use with the hearing impaired, normative data are given for hearing children ages 3-6 to 6-0 years. The authors point out that these are the years when a hearing child is developing his or her comprehension of simple and complex sentence structures; however, hearing-impaired children may have delays in these areas throughout their school-age years. The test manual does provide suggestions for using the RITLS with language-delayed hearing children.

Instructions/Test Administration

The RITLS consists of a test manual, a test booklet with 100 picture test items, and a score sheet. There are 50 simple sentences and 50 complex sentences. The examiner reads a sentence to the child while showing a page with three different pictures on it, and the child selects the picture which describes the sentence the examiner read. The manual includes verbal instructions to give to the child as well as instructions about how to give the test. The child's responses are recorded on a response sheet and then entered on the analysis sheet, which classifies the correct and incorrect responses for each sentence category. After obtaining a raw score, examiners can determine percentile and standard score according to age.

Norms

The RITLS was normed on 513 hearing-impaired children ages 5-0 to 17+ years and 304 hearing children ages 3-6 to 6-0 years. In addition, a pilot study included 69 hearing-impaired children ages 5 to 16 years and 91 5-year-old hearing children. The hearing children were from the Rhode Island area and the hearing-impaired children were from several east coast states.

Because by age 7 the hearing children were able to complete the test with few errors, normative data are presented for hearing children only up to age 6.

Reliability

The Kuder-Richardson formula 20 was used to evalute reliability for the two groups of children in the pilot study. The results showed good reliability: .72 for the 91 hearing subjects and .88 for the 69 hearing-impaired subjects.

Validity

The authors discuss content validity and construct validity in the test manual, and present information to support the validity of the items used on the RITLS.

Rank order of difficulty of the sentence types was determined for the normative and pilot study groups. The Spearman rank order correlation coefficient for the hearing-impaired group was .94, and for the hearing group it was .85.

Advantages

1) The test was normed on hearing-impaired subjects and also provides normative information on hearing children.
2) For the most part, the pictures are good; the actions in the pictures are easy to understand.
3) The manual provides much information on the research which went into devising the test as well as language problems encountered by school-age hearing-impaired children.

Test Descriptions

4) The test is easy to score.

<u>Disadvantage</u>
1) The manual, although informative, is difficult to read, particularly when one is preparing to give the test. For example, information about test administration is at the end of the manual, whereas normative data are scattered throughout the beginning section. The examiner <u>must</u> read and prepare carefully.

ROCKFORD INFANT DEVELOPMENTAL EVALUATION SCALES (RIDES)

No Norms
Ages 0 to 4-0 years
Receptive/Expressive

Developed by staff from Project RHISE, Children's Development Center, Rockford, IL (1979). Scholastic Testing Service, Inc., 480 Meyer Road, Bensenville, IL 60106. Approximate cost: $33.56.

General Description

The Rockford Infant Developmental Evaluation Scales (RIDES) is designed to assess a young child's developmental functioning level in five major skill areas: (1) Personal-Social/Self-Help, (2) Fine Motor/Adaptive, (3) Receptive Language, (4) Expressive Language; and, (5) Gross Motor. The items in each skill area are developmentally sequenced and arranged at 3- to 6-month intervals.

Instructions/Test Administration

The RIDES is a checklist consisting of 308 developmental behaviors ranging from birth to 4-0 years. It is designed for use as an informal assessment tool.

The RIDES is not a timed test, and may be administered in several sessions in order to obtain the best results. The RIDES can be administered in three ways:
(1) by asking the parent(s) for information and scoring an item on the basis of their report,
(2) by observing the child for spontaneous actions and behaviors; and
(3) by presenting to the child a specific task in order to elicit the desired response.

The administration of the RIDES requires age-appropriate materials for each child being evaluated. The RIDES manual provides a complete description of all materials needed for administration. The administration of the RIDES begins in the age range immediately preceding the child's chronological age. Each item is scored on a 0-1-2-3 scale. A score of 0 indicates the child was unable to perform the appropriate response; 1 indicates a particular behavior is emerging; 2 indicates a particular behavior is performed on occasion; and 3 indicates the child can perform a particular behavior consistently on several occasions. The manual includes a complete description of the scoring scale.

After scoring each skill area, the examiner records scores on the Individual Child Progress Graph. The graph provides a visual display of the child's functional level in each skill area.

Norms

The RIDES is not a standardized test; therefore, no normative data are provided.

Reliability

Not applicable.

Validity

Not applicable.

Field Evaluation

The RIDES was field-tested during its development. In all, 32 manuals, checklists, and evaluation forms were distributed to 14 agencies in seven states that served young children. Thirty-two professionals reviewed the RIDES manual and in some cases administered it. The RIDES was administered to children by the early intervention team developing the RIDES as well as by the 32 professionals in other agencies.

Advantages

1) The manual is well written with clear, concise directions for administration and scoring.
2) The manual is well organized; it is divided into the five skill areas and includes descriptions of each test item.
3) The test items are arranged developmentally in 3-6 month age intervals.
4) The RIDES assesses a wide range of developmental functions for 0-4 years.
5) The RIDES is easy to administer and score.
6) The RIDES can be adminstered at various age intervals to show the child's progress.

Disadvantages

1) Several items under Receptive Language at 3-6 months and 9-12 months are not appropriate for hearing-impaired children; to pass, the child must have good auditory skills (e.g., stops activity when name is called; listens to and understands new words).
2) The <u>RIDES</u> does not include a cognitive skill area.

Test Descriptions

SEQUENCED INVENTORY OF COMMUNICATION DEVELOPMENT (SICD-R)

Hearing Norms
Ages 4 months to 4-0 years
Receptive/Expressive

Hedrick, D., Prather, E., & Tobin, A. (1975; Revised edition, 1984). Sequenced Inventory of Communication Development. University of Washington Press, 4045 Brooklyn Avenue, N.E., Seattle, WA 98105. Approximate Cost: $250.00.

General Description

The SICD-R is designed to evaluate the receptive and expressive communication skills of normal and retarded children who are functioning between 4 months and 4 years of age. According to the authors it has also been used successfully with visually impaired and hearing-impaired children. Its primary usefulness is in screening the communicative behaviors of children and identifying areas that might require further, in-depth assessment. Although actual test items have not been revised, new data and a Spanish translation have been added. The Instruction Manual has been separated from the Test Manual and the Receptive and Expressive profiles have been updated to include cognitive and pragmatic aspects of communication.

Instructions/Test Administration

The SICD-R has two major sections: receptive and expressive. The receptive section includes behavioral items (some parental response items) that test sound and speech awareness, discrimination, and understanding. The expressive section includes three types of expressive behaviors which are elicited—imitating, initiating, and responding—as well as a sample of the child's spontaneous language. This language sample is evaluated for length and grammatic and syntactic structures of verbal output. A person experienced in using the SICD can complete the test in 30 to 60 minutes. The SICD-R includes a Spanish translation which has been used in the Miami, Florida area since 1978, with periodic revisions being made as necessary.

Norms

The original SICD was standardized on 252 Caucasian children, 21 at each of 12 age levels between 4 and 48 months. Equal numbers of children were drawn from high, middle, and low socioeconomic groups, based on parental education and occupation. Language development was judged normal by the child's parents, and hearing was normal. Age groups of subjects passing receptive and expressive items at four percentage levels are given in the manual. Also shown are means and standard deviations for both the receptive and expressive "communication age." In addition, the revised edition includes new field data on 333 normal Caucasian children and 276 normal Black children from Detroit. A discussion of these data is included.

Reliability

Interexaminer reliability, test-retest reliability, and scoring reliability all exceeded .90.

Validity

No validity data are provided.

Advantages

1) The test may be administered in total communication.
2) The SICD-R assesses a range of communicative and linguistic behaviors for a young age group.
3) Parental responses are used; this can be an advantage because parents are often very familiar with their children's behavior.
4) The imitation and auditory discrimination items may be appropriate for some hearing-impaired children, especially those who have mild to moderate hearing losses.
5) The SICD-R contains items testing understanding of functions, e.g., "What do you cook with?"

Disadvantages

1) Items involving sound discrimination and auditory responses are not appropriate for all hearing-impaired children and should not always be included in the total scores.

Test Descriptions

2) Some expressive areas are assessed by only three or four items; therefore, results must be interpreted cautiously.
3) No validity data are provided.
4) Much practice is required to administer the SICD efficiently and effectively.

*SKI-HI RECEPTIVE LANGUAGE TEST (SKI-HI RLT)

>No normative data but designed to be
>used with hearing-impaired children
>Ages 3-0 to 6-6 years
>Receptive

Longhurst, T.M., Briery, D., & Emery, M. (1975). SKI-HI Receptive Language Test. Project SKI-HI, Dept. of Communication Disorders, Utah State University, Logan, UT 84322. Approximate Cost: $56.00.

General Description

The SKI-HI Receptive Language Test (RLT) was developed to be used with hearing-impaired children and is similar to the Assessment of Children's Language Comprehension Test (ACLC), which was developed to determine how many word classes in different combinations of length and complexity a child comprehends. It probes the hearing-impaired child's ability to understand single-word utterances, as well as two-, three-, and four-critical element utterances. These "critical elements" consist of agents, actions, attributes, relations, and objects, such as dirty cup, big happy clown, etc.

Instructions/Test Administration

In the SKI-HI RLT, the child is required to point to the picture corresponding to the word, phrase, or sentence read by the examiner. The child must correctly identify 50 common vocabulary items before continuing with the remainder of the test. There are 20 plates with five test items per plate at the single element level. In Parts B and C (two and three critical elements), there are 10 plates with four pictures per plate. In Part D (four critical elements), there are 10 plates with five pictures per plate.

Norms

The SKI-HI RLT is not a standardized test; therefore, no normative data are provided.

Reliability

No reliability data are provided.

Test Descriptions

Validity
No validity data are provided.

Advantages
1) The pictures are colored and are much bigger and clearer than those in the ACLC, and are therefore more appropriate for use with young children.
2) Like the ACLC, the test a) is developmentally sequenced, b) is one of the few tests of semantic relationships, and c) requires a pointing response only.
3) It gives practical information about the length of utterance the child can comprehend.
4) It tests vocabulary items first, so the examiner knows that later errors are not made because the child is unfamiliar with words used in the phrases.

Disadvantages
1) Some of the pictures (e.g., for prepositions) are confusing, or are laid out in a confusing manner on the page.
2) No norms or reliability and validity data are provided.
3) There is only one training picture.
4) The large recording sheet is hard to manipulate (but can be re-typed on standard size paper).

Test Descriptions

*THE SKI-HI LANGUAGE DEVELOPMENT SCALE (SKI-HI LDS)

No normative data
Ages 0 to 5-0 years
Receptive/Expressive

Tonelson, S., & Watkins, S. (1979). The SKI-HI Language Development Scale. Project SKI-HI, Dept. of Communication Disorders, Utah State University, Logan, UT 84322. Approximate Cost: $1.25 (manual); $.34 (each test form).

General Description
　　The SKI-HI Language Development Scale (LDS) lists expressive and receptive language skills that children from 0 to 5 years old would "normally demonstrate." It is designed to be administered by parents of hearing-impaired children but is an excellent tool for coordinated use by preschool teachers in nursery programs and parents, as well as parents and home visitors in early childhood programs.

Instructions/Test Administration
　　The LDS is developmentally ordered and contains a list of communication and language skills in varying intervals for different ages (2-month intervals for infants 0 to 2 years old; 6-month intervals for children 4 and 5 years old). Each age interval is represented by enough observable receptive and expressive language skills to obtain a good profile of a child's language ability.
　　The scale may be explained to parents and left with them for 1 week, during which time they observe and check (with plus or minus marks) the child's receptive and expressive language behaviors. It may also be used by the teacher in the classroom in the same way. Parent and teacher can, if they wish, compare results and together develop plans for language goals. One determines a child's developmental language profile by noting the highest unit in which 50% or more skills are observed.

Norms
　　The SKI-HI LDS is not a standardized test; therefore, no normative data are provided.

Test Descriptions

Reliability

Inter-rater reliability estimates were high for all units: mean percentage of agreement among raters for the expressive language scale was 68%. Test-retest rater reliability indicated good reliability for both receptive and expressive units. Internal consistency of both scales was high.

Validity

Concurrent validity - Concurrent validity was good; LDS scores correlated highly with scores on the Bzoch-League Receptive-Expressive Emergent Language Scale (REEL).

Construct validity - "Coefficients of reproducibility" as determined by the Guttman Scaling technique were uniformly high for both units and for items within units, indicating good construct validity.

Advantages

1) The LDS was developed for use with hearing-impaired infants and children and includes few auditory skills (i.e., language skills are evaluated independently of hearing).
2) A wide range of skills are assessed from 0 to 5 years.
3) When the test is administered by parents, observations are more likely to be made over a wider time range and therefore may be more valid than those made during one session by an independent observer.
4) Units are not labeled by age intervals, which may enhance objectivity of parental reports, but age intervals are available and may be used if desired.
5) The form can be left with parents to complete at their leisure, used in the classroom, or used jointly.
6) The age level sheet is helpful for assigning a language age to a unit and discussing the child's delay(s) with the parents.

STRUCTURED PHOTOGRAPHIC EXPRESSIVE LANGUAGE TEST - II (SPELT-II)

Hearing Norms
Ages 4-0 to 9-5 years
Expressive

Werner, E. O'H., & Kresheck, J. (1983). <u>Structured Photographic Expressive Language Test-II</u>. Janelle Publications, Inc.; P.O. Box 12, Sandwich, IL 60548. Approximate Cost: $50.00.

General Description

The SPELT-II, a revision of the SPLT (1974), is a method of assessing a child's production of expressive morphology and syntax. Revisions were made to the SPLT, including the addition of the word "expressive" to the title, and thus the instrument became the SPELT-II in 1983.

The SPELT-II is designed to measure hearing children's production of specific morphological and syntactical structures. Responses are elicited through structured visual and auditory stimuli. The visual stimuli are colored photographs of children, adults, and animals interacting in everyday situations and activities. The auditory stimuli are brief statements or questions the examiner says while showing the picture. The visual and auditory stimuli provide a contextual framework to which a child can relate and form meaningful responses.

The SPELT-II analyzes a child's ability to use several common grammatical forms, and to perform rule-governed changes in sentence structures. The grammatical forms and types of sentences generated are listed in the manual.

Instructions/Test Administration

The materials needed to administer the SPELT-II are the packet of photographs and a response form. It takes approximately 25 minutes to administer the SPELT-II. The directions for test administration and the verbal instructions for the examiner to give to the child are simple; all that is required is that the examiner show one photograph at a time to the child while saying the eliciting statement. Elicitation statements (e.g., "Tell me about this picture," "What do you see?") are clearly written out on the response form. The examiner writes the child's responses on the response form.

After the test has been administered, the child's responses are scored. If a target structure or form is produced correctly, a check mark is placed in the blank space next to the item number. An X is used to indicate an incorrect response. NR is placed to mean the child did not respond. The manual explains how to determine whether a response is correct or not. Examples of scoring responses are provided in the manual. In addition, examples of scoring responses for Black English are also given.

Norms

The SPELT-II was standardized on 1178 Caucasian monolingual children between the ages of 4-0 and 9-5. They were randomly selected from preschools and public schools from the North Central and Southern sections of the country. The children were from either urban or rural communities and primarily middle class socioeconomic status.

Raw scores and means were calculated at each 6-month interval for the normative sample. No significant difference in male versus female performance was found. In addition, no significant difference between scores of children from different geographic areas was noted.

Reliability

Three types of reliability were calculated on the SPELT-II; test-retest, internal consistency, and interscorer reliability.

Test-retest - Test-retest reliability was high, resulting in a coefficient of .91. The test-retest method was tested a second time with a group of 23 language-delayed children between the ages of 4-0 and 8-0. A coefficient of .87 was indicated.

Internal consistency - A split-half reliability measure on the odd numbered items vs. the even numbered items was used to measure internal consistency; 500 tests were selected from the total number of 1178, 50 tests selected from each 6-month interval. The split-half reliability coefficient was a value of .70. On the whole, internal consistency was adequate for the age group studied.

Interscorer reliability – A correlation of .99 indicated that examiners using the scoring guide in the manual are consistent in scoring the SPELT-II.

Validity

The SPELT-II developers measured validity in three ways: content validity, construct validity, and concurrent validity.

Content validity – Each morphological structure used in the SPELT-II was scored for its content validity. Content validity was good for the following items: regular noun plurals, singular noun possessives, verb forms (present, past, future, and copula), prepositions, pronouns, and for the various syntactic structures used.

Concurrent validity – The developers assessed concurrent validity by comparing SPELT-II with other standardized measures of syntactic development, namely the Test of Language Development (TOLD) and the Developmental Sentence Scoring (DSS) method.

SPELT-II/TOLD: The two tests were administered to 20 normal children between the ages of 4-7 and 5-11. All children scored within their age range on both tests. The results showed an 86% agreement between the two tests.

SPELT-II/DSS: The SPELT-II was administered to 30 language-delayed children between the ages of 4-3 and 9-0. Examiners obtained a spontaneous language sample for each child and analyzed these by the DSS method according to the directions provided by Lee (1974). The correlation between the scores on the SPELT-II and the DSS method was .82.

Construct validity – Because the SPELT-II is a developmental test, an increase in score should be observed with an increase in age. Indeed mean scores do increase with age; a correlation of .97 was found between age and score.

Validity of the SPELT-II is also demonstrated by the finding that the data obtained follow the patterns of normal language development.

Advantages

1) The content of the SPELT-II is geared to the developmental level of the child and is arranged in developmental sequence.
2) The test is easy to give and requires little time to administer.

Test Descriptions

3) The elicitation statements could easily be signed.
4) The pictures are exceptionally good; they are actually color photographs.
5) The manual is clearly written and the directions are explicit.
6) The manual provides samples of scoring techniques and possible responses.
7) The test was normed on a large sample of children, 1178.
8) The reliability and validity of the test are good.
9) The norms are arranged at 6-month intervals.
10) The <u>SPELT II</u> addresses problems of language delayed children.

*TEACHER ASSESSMENT OF GRAMMATICAL STRUCTURES (TAGS)

> No normative data but designed to be used with hearing-impaired children
> Ages 0 to 9-0+ years
> Receptive/Expressive

Moog, J.S., & Kozak, V.J. (1983). <u>Teacher Assessment of Grammatical Structures</u>. Central Institute for the Deaf, 818 So. Euclid, St. Louis, MO 63110. Approximate Cost: $16.50.

General Description

The <u>Teacher Assessment of Grammatical Structures (TAGS)</u> is a series of checklists which have been developed to evaluate a child's <u>understanding</u> and <u>use</u> of the grammatical structures (especially syntax) of English and to suggest a sequence for teaching these structures. The checklists were designed particularly for use with hearing-impaired children who use spoken and/or signed English, and are meant to be used as an alternative to language sampling.

Instructions/Test Administration

The structures listed on the three <u>TAGS</u> checklists are organized into three levels, allowing the examiner to evaluate a child's syntactic development from the use of single words, phrases, and two- and three-word sentences (Pre-sentence Level), through simple sentences of four or more words (Simple Sentence Level), to more complex sentences (Complex Sentence Level). Although choice of checklist is based on a child's level of syntactic development, the authors suggest the following age ranges for each level: TAGS-P (Pre-Sentence Level): 5 years old and under; <u>TAGS-S</u> (Simple Sentence Level): 5 to 9 years old; and <u>TAGS-C</u> (Complex Sentence Level): 9+ years old.

On each checklist the grammatical structures are listed in expected order of development. A checklist is completed over a period of days or weeks for each child by his or her teacher. It serves as a tool for helping the teacher record

Test Descriptions

observations of each child in an organized manner, and monitors a child's progress through four levels of competence: comprehension, imitated production, prompted production, and spontaneous production. Teachers may need to contrive situations where structures can be produced in order to evaluate a child's level of competence for some structures.

Norms

TAGS is a criterion-referenced measurement tool, not a norm-referenced one; therefore, no norms are necessary.

The order of development of grammatical structures is based on 1) the authors' experience in teaching hearing-impaired children, 2) their experience with standardized language tests, and 3) their knowledge about language development of normally hearing children.

Reliability

TAGS is not a standardized test; therefore, no reliability data are given.

Validity

The authors state that evaluation in which these checklists are used is valid because: 1) the teacher, through firsthand experience, knows the child's skills well; and 2) the ratings are based on observations over a period of time, in a variety of situations, including teaching situations. No other data are provided.

Advantages

1) The TAGS was designed for use by teachers of the hearing impaired.
2) It is useful in planning language instruction, measuring and recording progress, and reporting to parents.
3) Grammatical structures are listed in expected order of development (but see caution listed below).
4) The manual is easy to read and use.
5) The checklists are color-coded and correspond to colored sections of the manual.
6) Criteria for accepting a spoken or signed word as "recognizable" are included.

Disadvantages

1) The checklists are complex. A teacher would need some time to become thoroughly familiar with and skilled in using these forms.
2) The authors do not provide the theoretical basis and language development research for the developmental order of grammatical structures they describe.

TEST FOR AUDITORY COMPREHENSION OF LANGUAGE-REVISED (TACL-R)

Hearing Norms
Ages 3-0 to 9-11 years
Receptive

Carrow-Woolfolk, E. (1985). Test for Auditory Comprehension of Language-Revised. DLM Teaching Resources, P.O. Box 4000, 1 DLM Park, Allen, TX 75002. Approximate Cost: $95.00

General Description

The Test for Auditory Comprehension of Language-Revised (TACL-R) is a revised version of the TACL (1973). The TACL-R, as does the TACL, measures auditory comprehension of lexical, morphological, and syntactic structures of language without requiring language expression from the child. The TACL-R is designed to be used with normal hearing children ages 3-0 to 9-11 years. It may be used as a diagnostic tool: performance on specific items and groups of items allows the examiner to determine a child's areas of linguistic difficulty.

Instructions/Test Administration

The TACL-R items are organized into three sections: word classes and relations, grammatical morphemes, and elaborated sentences. The 120 test items are arranged according to level of difficulty.

Each plate consists of line drawings, three per plate, one representing the referent for the linguistic form being tested, the others representing contrasting linguistic forms and/or a decoy. (See sample response form for specific form classes, function words, morphological constructions, grammatical categories, and syntactic structures tested.)

The test is administered individually and requires about 10 minutes. The child points to the correct picture in the test booklet in response to the examiner's verbal stimuli. Basal and ceiling levels are obtained. The raw score may be converted to an age equivalent score, percentile rank by age group, and to standard scores. The child's performance on specific classes of items may also be examined.

Norms

The TACL-R was normed on 1003 hearing subjects ages 3-0 to 9-11 years in 20 states across the U.S. Within each age level, the sample was distributed according to family occupation, ethnic origin, age, sex, community size, and geographical location.

Reliability

Standard Error of Measurement - The Standard Error of Measurement (SEM) was found to be small relative to the mean scores, which suggests that the TACL-R is a reliable measure of the child's ability.

Split-Half Reliability - The test developer assigned two groups for calculating the split-half correlations for the TACL-R: all odd-numbered and all even-numbered items. Correlation coefficients were calculated for age and grade levels for the total sample. A correlation coefficient of .96 was found for all ages combined.

Test-Retest Reliability - 100 subjects in the norming sample and 29 subjects with speech and language disorders were retested 3-4 weeks following the initial administration. The test-retest reliabilities ranged from .89 to .95.

Validity

Content Validity - The manual provides extensive information regarding the analysis and research that went into the development of the TACL-R, which the author believes establishes content validity.

Construct Validity - The TACL-R was found to show that test performance does increase with age. For each TACL-R score the correlation with age was found to be above .97.

A comparison was also made between the norming sample performance and that of a group of subjects with speech and language disorders. The results showed that the group of subjects with speech and language disorders performed significantly below their age level. Subjects with only articulation disorders did not differ from the norming sample.

Criterion-Related Validity - The scores on the TACL-R were compared to those of the original TACL. A correlation coefficient of .71 was found.

Test Descriptions

Advantages
1) The TACL-R requires only a pointing response.
2) The TACL-R provides information on specific language structures in the lexical, morphological, and syntactic areas; these resutls may be used in educational planning.
3) The examiner can administer the test using total communication.
4) The line drawings are clear.
5) The test items have been arranged according to developmental level; the lack of such an arrangement was a problem in the orignial TACL.

TEST FOR EXAMINING EXPRESSIVE MORPHOLOGY (TEEM)

Hearing Norms
Ages 3-0 to 8-0 years
Receptive

Shipley, K.G., Stone, T.A., & Sue, M.B. (1983). Test for Examining Expressive Morphology. Communication Skill Builders, 3130 N. Dodge Blvd., P.O. Box 42050, Tucson, AZ 85733. Approximate cost: $19.95.

General Description

The Test for Examining Expressive Morphology (TEEM) is designed to assess the expressive morpheme development of hearing children ages 3 to 8 years.

Instructions/Test Administration

The TEEM requires approximately 10 minutes to administer, and it is not a timed test. It consists of a test manual, score form, and a test book. The TEEM is designed as a sentence-completion test in which the examiner shows the child a picture(s) and provides partial information about it. The child is then required to complete a sentence about the picture(s). For example, "Here is a boat. Here are two ____." The child's responses are recorded and transferred to the "Analysis of Results" section of the score form. A raw score is obtained and used to derive an age level equivalent.

Norms

The TEEM was standardized on 500 hearing children ages 3 to 8 years who live in Fresno, CA. Prestandardization testing was completed on 40 hearing children ages 3 to 7 years from Reno, Nevada. The purpose of the prestandardization was to establish test reliability and validity.

Reliability

Using the prestandardization sample of 40 hearing children, developers administered the TEEM to 12 randomly selected subjects on two different occasions at 7- to 14-day intervals. Reliability was good; an r of .94 was found between the test scores from the two test administrations.

To evaluate inter-tester reliability, a speech-language pathologist administered the TEEM to 12 randomly selected subjects. An r of .95 was found for the test scores obtained by different examiners.

Validity

Content validity was presumed within the test construction because, according to the authors, (1) it uses a sentence-completion model; (2) items were selected from six major morpheme types; and (3) the allomorphic and morphological structures chosen are developed between 2 years and 8 to 10 years of age.

Developers established construct validity by comparing the 40 TEEM scores with chronological age. A Pearson r of .87 between age and TEEM scores was obtained.

They evaluated concurrent validity by comparing the 40 subjects' TEEM scores wih the results of a language measure using the Peabody Picture Vocabulary Test (PPVT) (Dunn, 1965).* A Pearson r of .84 was found between the two language measures.

Advantages

1) The test can be administered quickly and easily.
2) The line drawings are clear.
3) The TEEM is one of the few tests of expressive morphology.
4) There are approximately three to five items testing each allomorph within the six morpheme groups, 54 items in all.
5) The score form provides information regarding the age in which 75% and 90% of children responded correctly to each test item.
6) The examiner can administer the test in total communication.

Disadvantages

1) Test items are sequenced randomly and not by level of difficulty; therefore, the entire test must be administered in order to utilize normative data.
2) Test reliability and validity were evaluated from the prestandardization sample; there is not information provided about the standardization sample of 500 subjects.

* Dunn, L. (1965). Peabody Picture Vocabulary Test. Circle Pines, MN: American Guidance Service, Inc.

*TEST OF EXPRESSIVE LANGUAGE ABILITY (TEXLA)

>Norms are available
>for hearing-impaired
>students from residen-
>tial settings in Canada
>Ages 7-0 to 12-0 years
>Expressive

Bunch, G.O. (1981). Test of Expressive Language Ability.
G.B. Services, 10 Pinehill Crescent, Toronto, Ontario
M6M 2B6, Canada. Approximate Cost: $25.00.

General Description
   The TEXLA assesses the hearing-impaired child's expressive (written) control of 13 basic grammatical principles
(e.g., plural nouns, prepositions, future tense, etc.). It
omits singular nouns from the TERLA (see below), and adds "to
be" and "to have."

Instructions/Test Administration
   An illustration is presented with one or two written sentences describing it. One sentence is incomplete. The child
must read the printed sentences, examine the illustrations,
and then complete the sentence by writing an appropriate response. There are 90 items (60 items for TEXLA SHORT). All
correct items receive a score of one; thus a perfect score is
90 (60 for TEXLA SHORT). Spelling errors do not normally make
an item incorrect. Subscores may be obtained for each of the
13 grammatical principles tested. The full test requires
about 30 minutes to administer.
   Information on interpreting test results and planning educational intervention is provided.

Norms
   The TEXLA was normed on 65 prelingual hearing-impaired
children aged 7 to 12 years, drawn from two major Canadian
residential schools for the deaf. (Numbers of children ranged
from 7 in the 7-year-old age category to 14 in the 9-year-old
age category.) Vocabulary included in the test was considered
by a panel of teachers to be a part of the language used as

Test Descriptions

soon as the hearing-impaired child enters school. The majority of the hearing-impaired subjects (62 of 65) had severe or profound hearing losses. The TEXLA was also administered to 17 normally hearing first-graders at the end of the school year. Mean scores and standard deviations are presented for 1-year age intervals. Raw scores may also be converted to percentile ranks and standard scores.

Reliability

Reliability coefficients of .99 and .98 for TEXLA and TEXLA SHORT respectively indicate adequate levels of internal consistency. Coefficients for the 13 basic grammatical principles range from .96 (plural nouns) to .71 ("to have"). No test - retest data are provided.

Validity

Content validity - A panel of experienced teachers of the deaf agreed unanimously that all principles tested were used receptively within the first 2 to 3 years of primary school. All words included in the test items were judged to be among those which hearing-impaired children are exposed to soon after school entry, and therefore were appropriate for the older children to use expressively.

Concurrent validity - Correlation coefficients between the TEXLA and the PPVT were calculated for 31 hearing-impaired students aged 11-5 to 13-11 years. Coefficients were .64 (Form A) and .74 (Form B); these are acceptable levels for demonstrating concurrent validity. In addition, the TEXLA, TEXLA SHORT, TERLA, and TERLA SHORT correlated highly with each other, indicating that the tests assess closely associated abilities. (No information is provided, however, on the number of subjects included in this study.) Finally, TEXLA scores showed improvement of language skills with age, thus reflecting a validly developed test.

Advantages

1) Total scores and subscores may be compared to norms for either first-grade hearing children or hearing-impaired children aged 7 to 12.
2) The TEXLA SHORT form correlated at the .98 level with the TEXLA, indicating that it may be used effectively for screening purposes.

Test Descriptions

3) Diagnostic information may be obtained (e.g., on whether a child is using a deviant rule or is responding randomly) for specific grammatical principles.
4) One can compare receptive and expressive abilities by also administering the TERLA.
5) Diagnostic information from the TERLA and TEXLA leads directly to teaching objectives (details in the Manual).
6) Teachers of hearing-impaired students assisted in he development of the TEXLA.

Disadvantages

1) Scoring is somewhat subjective and time-consuming (no data regarding inter-tester reliability are provided). Judgments must be made as to whether each response is acceptable (e.g., some misspellings are acceptable, some not).
2) Norms involve small numbers of subjects (an average of 11 subjects per 1-year age interval). Not all norm subjects who were administered the TERLA were also given the TEXLA.
3) Authors developed norms by using hearing-impaired children from residential schools located in Canada. These groups may not be the same as public school hearing-impaired students in the U.S.
4) Some hearing-impaired children have difficulty understanding what they are expected to say/sign in order to respond correctly. They often have problems "clozing" on or filling in the missing item.
5) The test questions must be read and the answers written in order to conform to norms.

*TEST OF RECEPTIVE LANGUAGE ABILITY (TERLA)

Norms are available
for hearing-impaired
students from residential settings in
Canada.
Ages 7-0 to 12-0 years
Receptive

Bunch, G.O. (1981). Test of Receptive Language Ability.
G.B. Services, 10 Pinehill Crescent, Toronto, Ontario
M6M 2B6, Canada. Approximate Cost: $25.00.

General Description
The TERLA assesses the hearing-impaired child's receptive control of 12 basic grammatical grinciples (e.g., singular nouns, comparative adjectives, prepositions, verb tenses). It may be used as both a norm-referenced and criterion-referenced test.

Instructions/Test Administration
The test administrator reads a single printed word or verb phrase for each item (total = 90 items for the long version, 58 items for the short version). Each item is accompanied by the written word or phrase and three illustrations (two for "comparatives"). The child selects the illustration that best represents the printed word or phrase. All correct items receive a score of one; thus, a perfect score is 90 (58 for TERLA SHORT). Subscores may be obtained for each of the 12 grammatical principles tested. The TERLA requires approximately 10 to 15 minutes to administer.

Information on interpreting test results and planning educational intervention is provided.

Norms
The TERLA was normed on 92 prelingual hearing-impaired children aged 7 to 12 years, drawn from two major Canadian residential schools for the deaf. (Numbers of children ranged from 11 in the 12-year-old age category to 20 in the 9-year-old age category.) The majority of these subjects (87 of 92)

had severe or profound hearing losses. The TERLA was also administered to 27 normally hearing first-graders at the end of the school year. Mean scores and standard deviations are presented for 1-year age intervals. Raw scores may also be converted to percentile ranks and standard scores.

Reliability

Reliability coefficients of .96 and .92 for TERLA and TERLA SHORT respectively indicate adequate levels of internal consistency. Reliability coefficients for each of the 12 grammatical principles ranged from .92 (plural nouns) to .54 (for both comparative adjectives and present progressive plural). Coefficients for the TERLA SHORT ranged from .86 to .16. No test-retest data are provided.

Validity

Content validity - A panel of experienced teachers of the deaf agreed unanimously that all principles tested were used receptively within the first 2 years of primary school. All words included in the test items were judged to be among those which hearing-impaired children are exposed to soon after school entry.

Concurrent validity - The Peabody Picture Vocabulary Test (PPVT), Forms A and B, was the criterion measure in a study involving 31 hearing-impaired subjects 11-5 to 13-11 years old. Correlation coefficients between TERLA and the PPVT were fair: .71 (Form B) and .67 (Form A). Also, the TEXLA, TEXLA SHORT, TERLA, and TERLA SHORT scores correlated highly with each other, indicating that the tests assess closely associated abilities. No information, however, is provided regarding the number of subjects involved in this study. Within the norm group TERLA scores improved with age, reflecting developmental differences.

Advantages

1) Children's total scores and subscores may be compared to norms for either first-grade hearing children or hearing-impaired children aged 7 to 12.
2) The test can be administered quickly and easily. The only response required is pointing

Test Descriptions

3) Diagnostic information on a child's receptive grasp of specific grammatical principles may be obtained. For example, the tester can determine whether a child consistently uses a deviant rule for a certain principle, or whether the child responds in a random fashion, indicating total lack of competence.
4) Diagnostic information from the TERLA leads directly to teaching objectives.
5) It may be administered to children taught in either communication mode, i.e., oral or total communication.
6) Classroom teachers of hearing-impaired children assisted in developing the test. No special training is required to administer it.

Disadvantages

1) Numbers of norm subjects for each age level are small, ranging from 11 children at age 12 to 20 children at age 9.
2) Some picture choices are confusing, especially for verb tenses, comparatives (older, happier), and some prepositions.
3) The norm group may be different from hearing-impaired students attending public schools in the U.S.

*TEST OF SYNTACTIC ABILITIES (TSA)

> Normative data were collected on hearing-impaired students from 18 programs in the United States
> Ages 10-0 to 18-11 years
> Receptive

Quigley, S.P., Steinkamp, M.W., Power, D.J., & Jones, B. (1978). Test of Syntactic Abilities. Dormac, Inc., P.O. Box 752, Beaverton, OR 97005. Approximate Cost: $95.00.

General Description

The Test of Syntactic Abilities (TSA) provides diagnostic information regarding deaf students' ability to comprehend and use the syntactic structures of standard (written) English. It consists of two parts: 1) TSA - Screening Test (120 items) provides a relatively quick (1 hour) assessment of students' general knowledge of syntactic structures. 2) TSA - Diagnostic Battery (20 individual test of 70 items each, 20 to 30 minutes per test) provides in-depth diagnostic information on several syntactic structures. Nine basic syntactic structures are assessed: Negation, Verb Processes, Pronominalization, Relativization, Complementation, Conjunction, Determiners, Question Formation, and Nominalization.

Instructions/Test Administration

The TSA test items are written in a multiple-choice format; the student marks his or her choice in a test booklet. Test instructions may be communicated in any manner; however, in giving instructions, the tester may not read or sign any actual test items to students. The TSA may be administered to groups or to individuals.

Two types of items are included: recognition items and comprehension items. In the former, the student chooses the correct (grammatical) sentence from a choice of four. In the latter, the student must understand the meaning (syntactic structure) of a stimulus sentence or sentences in order to choose the correct alternative from among four response choices. For comprehension items, the student selects from four alternatives the word or phrase that best fills the blank in a stimulus sentence.

The student receives nine scores on the screening test, one score for each of the nine structures listed above.

Norms

The TSA is the result of 10 years' extensive research, pilot testing, and standardization. The revised TSA was standardized on about 450 students in 18 educational programs for the deaf in the U.S. (both residential and day programs represented). Students represented nine age levels from 10 to 19 years, had profound prelingual hearing losses, IQs of at least 80 on a performance test, and no other apparent disabilities. Test scores convert to percentile and age equivalency scores.

Reliability

Reliability coefficients for internal consistency are exceptionally high for all tests (.93 or better). High test-retest reliability coefficients show stability over time for the sample retested (N=54). Also reported are data for Standard Error of Measurement and intercorrelations among test scores.

Validity

Content validity - The authors established the content validity of the TSA "...by showing that the linguistic structures examined by the test were systematically chosen from the domain of English syntax as described by transformational generative grammar." Developers validated syntactic deviancies incorporated in the TSA battery through extensive study of deaf children's responses to the research version of the TSA and the written language samples obtained concurrently. The test items were designed to be neither too difficult nor too easy, and according to the authors the reading level of the test (elementary level) is within easy comprehension of the deaf children taking it.

Concurrent validity - Substantial correlations were found between relevant subtests of achievement test scores (e.g., the Standard Achievement Test) for the norm subjects and various subtests of the TSA, establishing concurrent validity of the TSA.

Advantages
1) Test administration and scoring are simple and require no special training. However, the examiner **must** be knowledgeable about linguistic terms.
2) Conversion tables are provided for interpretation of test scores.
3) Specific diagnostic tests are provided as follow-up to the screening test.
4) Detailed instructions and suggestions are given regarding classroom implementation of programs based on test results and designing of individualized language remediation programs.
5) Students may be tested in groups.
6) Information is provided on deviant response patterns commonly used by hearing-impaired children such as the tendency to impose a subject-verb-object pattern on a sentence whether appropriate or not.
7) TSA workbooks are available to teach these syntactic structures.

Disadvantages
1) The TSA assesses reading of specific syntactic structures, not conversational use of language.
2) The screening test takes a long time to administer (1 hour). However, this disadvantage is balanced by the fact that students may be tested in groups. Each diagnostic subtest requires approximately an hour to administer, as well.
3) Reading levels are reportedly too difficult for many 10- and 11- year old hearing-impaired children.
4) Some students find it confusing to transfer their answers to the response sheet.
5) The test items are in small print, which is difficult for some students to read.

Note:
The TSA is also available on Apple II diskettes.

Test Descriptions

THE WORD TEST (TWT)

Hearing Norms
Ages 7-0 to 12-0 years
Expressive

Jorgensen, C., Barrett, M., Huisingh, R., & Zackman, L. (1981). *The Word Test*. LinguiSystems, Inc., Suite, 806, 1630 Fifth Avenue, Moline, IL 61265. Approximate Cost: $36.00.

General Description

The Word Test (TWT) is a test of expressive vocabulary and semantics. It assesses the hearing child's strengths and weaknesses in categorizing, defining, verbal reasoning, and choosing appropriate words.

Instructions/Test Administration

TWT consists of an examiner's manual and score forms. Each of the six subtests is administered orally. A sample "script" is contained in the manual for each subtest section. A raw score is obtained for each subtest, as well as a total test score. A subtest is terminated after three consecutive failures. The test requires approximately 20-30 minutes to administer.

Norms

Developers selected 476 subjects aged 7-0 to 11-11 years for the standardization study. Students with learning disabilities, mental disability, or hearing loss were excluded from the sample. Developers attempted to represent minorities in the sample. No other restrictions were applied. All students were from the greater Milwaukee, WI area. Normative data are reported at half-year age levels.

Reliability

A split-half reliability coefficient for each subtest and age level is provided as well as Kuder-Richardson (KR20) coefficients for each subtest by age.

Validity

The authors demonstrated content validity by conducting an extensive review of tests in the areas of vocabulary and semantics combined with a review of the literature to aid item selection. The empirical validity of <u>TWT</u> was established by the method of internal consistency. All items on <u>TWT</u> were selected to show: 1) steady age progression in percent of subjects passing, and 2) significant discrimination as reflected in the Chi Squared Test. Extensive validity data by subtest and age level are reported in the manual.

Advantages
1) The test requires a minimum amount of time to administer, score, and interpret.
2) The test content includes skills not found in other language tests.
3) Normative data and reliability and validity information are excellent.
4) Sample questions are provided for each subtest.

Disadvantage
1) Some examiner discretion is required in determining acceptable answers. This could lead to inter-examiner variation, resulting in different test scores.

Test Descriptions

*TOTAL COMMUNICATION RECEPTIVE VOCABULARY TEST (TCRVT)

> Normative data are
> available for deaf and
> hard-of-hearing children
> Ages 3-0 to 12-0 years
> Receptive

Scherer, P. (1981). *Total Communication Receptive Vocabulary Test*. Mental Health & Deafness Resources, Inc., P.O. Box 1083, Northbrook, IL 60062. Approximate Cost: $25.00.

General Description

The *Total Communication Receptive Vocabulary Test* (TCRVT) assesses the hearing-impaired child's skill in identifying individual words presented in simultaneously signed and spoken language.

Instructions/Test Administration

This test consists of 75 test plates (four pictures per plate). The student indicates the correct picture after being given the directions, "Show me ___," and is given a score of 1 or 0 for each item. Test items are presented in order of difficulty. The test is terminated when the child has missed five words consecutively.

The test requires about 20 minutes to administer.

Norms

This test was standardized on 423 children aged 3 to 12: 77 hearing (ages 3 to 5 years), 95 hard of hearing (ages 4 to 11 years), and 251 deaf (ages 3 to 12 years). The children had no additional handicaps, learning disabilities, behavior problems, or atypical (e.g., bilingual) language environments in the home. The hearing-impaired children were prelingually deaf and had been exposed to total communication for at least 2 years, except in the case of the youngest preschoolers. Subjects represented a cross-section of residential and day programs, and city and suburban areas.

Normative data are presented in 1-year age levels. Numbers of norm subjects within each hearing/age category range from eight children in the hard-of-hearing 7-year-old age level to 42 children in the deaf 7-year-old age level. One can convert raw scores to an "age level" by consulting tables representing degree of hearing loss: hearing (no loss); hard of hearing, 35-58 dB loss; or deaf, 85 dB and above loss. Also, comparative age conversions may be made for deaf children with one parent who has good to excellent signing skills, as compared to those with one parent with poor to fair signing skills.

Reliability
No reliability data are presented.

Validity
Test items represented words that most deaf children are exposed to in their education during the preschool and primary years. Also, all words were among the 500 most common words in the English language and were words that could be signed easily.

Advantages
1) The test was normed on hearing-impaired children and was designed to be administered in simultaneous communication. Therefore all words have sign equivalents.
2) Age conversions are available for both deaf and hard-of-hearing children
3) Age conversions are available for children with hearing parents who use total communication and for those children whose parents do not.
4) Items are arranged in order of increasing difficulty, so the entire test does not have to be given.

Disadvantages
1) As the author points out, this test appears to be more useful for children aged 3 to 10 years; scores tend to ceiling out beyond this age range.
2) Reliability data are not provided and validity data are inadequate.
3) Some normative age levels contain few subjects, e.g., eight children in the hard-of-hearing 7-year-old category.

Test Descriptions

4) Pictures for some items are not clear and/or are confusing (e.g., see the following items: #10 girl, #25 snow, #28 night, #49 smell, #59 bashful).

VANE EVALUATION OF LANGUAGE SCALE (VANE-L)

Hearing Norms
Ages 2-6 to 6-0 years
Receptive/Expressive

Vane, J.R. (1975). <u>Vane Evaluation of Language Scale</u> (VANE-L). Clinical Psychology Publishing Co., Inc., 4 Conant Square, Brandon, VT 05733. Approximate Cost: $15.00.

Generalization Description

The <u>Vane-L</u> is designed to measure language acquisition of young children ages 2-6 to 6-0 years. It assesses receptive and expressive language skills, as well as handedness and attention. The section evaluating receptive language includes body parts, simple directions, and basic concepts. The expressive language section assesses the child's ability to express himself or herself by answering questions, repeating sentences, and defining words. There is an item within the expressive language section which assesses auditory motor ability.

The <u>Vane-L Scale</u> is primarily designed to be used as a screening instrument rather than a diagnostic tool.

Instructions/Test Administration

The <u>Vane-L Scale</u> is an individually administered test. The directions are simple and administration time is approximately 10 minutes. A test kit containing bottles, beans, blocks, and toy cars is used for assessing the basic concepts. The scoring is also simple; one point is given for each correct answer. The scores are totaled and entered onto the front page of the score form. The scores are then converted to percentile ranks.

Norms

The <u>Vane-L Scale</u> was standardized on 740 children from New York, New Jersey, and Vermont. The characteristics of the standardization sample were drawn from the U.S. Census data (1970) with respect to age, sex, race, occupation of parent, and urban-rural residence.

Test Descriptions

Reliability
No data on reliability are provided.

Validity
No data on validity are provided.

Advantages
1) The <u>Vane-L</u> is a quick assessment of some basic language acquisition skills which can provide information regarding the need for further diagnostic testing.
2) It tests a young population, 2-6 to 6-0 years old.

Disadvantages
1) The standardization sample was confined to the northeastern part of the U.S.
2) The auditory motor section requires the child to imitate a series of tappings. This is not appropriate for young hearing-impaired children because it actually tests their auditory motor/memory abilities and may not be related to language development.

Note:
The manual provides data on the pattern of language scores for each age group and sex.

REFERENCES

Baker, H.J., & Leland, B. (1967). *Detroit Tests of Learning Aptitude*. Indianapolis, IN: Bobbs-Merrill Co.

Bates, E. (1976). *Language in context: The acquisition of pragmatics*. New York: Academic Press.

Berko Gleason, J. (1985). Studying language development. In J. Berko Gleason (Ed.), *The development of language* (pp. 1-35). Columbus, OH: Charles E. Merrill.

Berry, S.R. (1981). *Written Language Syntax Test*. Washington, D.C.: Gallaudet College.

Blackwell, P., Engen, E., Fischgrund, J.E., & Zarcadoolas, C. (1978). *Sentences and other systems: A language learning curriculum for hearing-impaired children*. Washington, D.C.: A.G. Bell Association for the Deaf.

Blackwell, P., & Hamel, C. (1971). *The language curriculum*. Providence, RI: Rhode Island School for the Deaf.

Bloom, L. (Ed.). (1978). *Readings in language development*. New York: John Wiley & Sons.

Bloom, L., & Lahey, M. (1978). *Language development and language disorders*. New York: John Wiley & Sons.

Boehm, A.E. (1967). The development of comparative concepts in primary children. Unpublished doctoral dissertation. New York: Columbia University.

Bracken, B.A., & Cato, L. (1984). Rate of conceptual development among deaf preschool and primary children as compared to a matched group of non-hearing-impaired children. (Manuscript in preparation.)

Brooks, P. H. (1978). Some speculations concerning deafness and learning to read. In L. Liben (Ed.), *Deaf children: Development perspectives* (pp. 87-101). New York: Academic Press.

Brown, R. (1973). *A first language: The early stages*. Cambridge, MA: Harvard University Press.

Canaglia, J., Cole, N., Howard, W., Krohn, E., & Rice, M. (1973). *Apple Tree, A developmental language program*. Beaverton, Oregon: Dormac, Inc.

References

Carlson, K. (1977). Miller-Yoder Test of Grammatical Comprehension: Norms for three through eight year olds. Unpublished paper. Madison, WI: University of Wisconsin-Madison.

Cazden, C. (1968). The acquisition of noun and verb inflections. Child Development, 39, 433-438.

Cazden, C. (1970). The situation: A neglected source of social class differences in language use. Journal of Social Issues, 26, 35-60.

Clark, H.H., & Clark, E.V. (1977). Psychology and language: An introduction to psycholinguistics. New York: Harcourt, Brace Jovanovich.

Coggins, T.E., & Carpenter, R.L. (1981). The Communicative Intention Inventory: A system for observing and coding children's early intentional communication. Applied Psycholinguistics, 2, 235-251.

Conrad, R. (1977). The reading ability of deaf school leavers. British Journal of Educational Psychology, 47, 138-148.

Cooper, R. L. (1967). The ability of deaf and hearing children to apply morphophonological rules. Journal of Speech and Hearing Research, 10, 77-85.

Coplan, J., Gleason, J., Ryan, R., et al. (1982). Validation of An Early Language Milestone Scale in a high risk population. Pediatrics, 70, 677-683.

Cummings, J.A., & Nelson, B.R. (1980). Basic concepts in oral directions of group achievement tests. The Journal of Educational Research, 73, 159-163.

Curtis, S., Prutting, C., & Lowell, E. (1979). Pragmatic and semantic development in young children with impaired hearing. Journal of Speech and Hearing Research, 22:3, 534-552.

Davis, J. (1974). Performance of young hearing-impaired children on a test of basic concepts. Journal of Speech and Hearing Research, 17, 342-351.

Dore, J. (1975). Holophrases, speech acts and language universals. Journal of Child Language, 2, 21-40.

Dore, J. (1976). "Oh Them Sheriff": A pragmatic analysis of children's responses to questions. In S. Errin-Tripp & C. Mitchell-Kernon (Eds.), Child discourse (pp. 348-350). New York: Academic Press.

References

Forde, J. (1977). Data on the Peabody Picture Vocabulary Test. *American Annals of the Deaf*, 122, 38-43.

Furth, H. (1966). *Thinking without language*. New York: Free Press.

Gallagher, T. (1983). Preassessment: A procedure for accommodating language use variability. In T. Gallagher & C. Prutting, (Eds.), *Pragmatic assessment and intervention issues in language* (pp. 2-28). San Diego, CA: College-Hill Press, Inc.

Guilford, J.P. (1956). *Fundamental statistics in psychology and education*. New York: McGraw-Hill.

Gustason, G., Pfetzing, D., & Zawolkow, E. (1972). *Signing exact English*. Rossmoor, CA: Modern Signs Press. (Revised edition, 1980, Modern Signs Press, Los Alamitos, CA).

Halliday, M. A. K. (1975). *Learning how to mean - Explorations in development of language*. London: Edward Arnold.

Hammermeister, F. (1971). Reading achievement in deaf adults. *American Annals of the Deaf*, 116, 25-28.

Harkins, J. (Ed.) (Winter, 1985). Hearing-impaired children and youth: A demographic and academic profile. *Newsletter, Gallaudet Research Institute* (R. Trybus, Director), 1-4.

Hasenstab, M. S. (1983). Child language studies: Impact on habilitation of hearing-impaired infants and preschool children. In R. Truax & J. Shultz (Eds.), *Learning to communicate: Implications for the hearing impaired. The Volta Review*, 85:5, 88-100.

Hasenstab, S., & Horner, J. (1982). *Comprehensive intervention with hearing-impaired infants and preschool children*. Rockville, MD: Aspen Systems Corp.

Heidinger, V. A. (1984). *Analyzing syntax and semantics*. Washington, D.C.: Gallaudet College Press.

Kaufman, A. S. (1978). The importance of basic concepts in the individual assessment of preschool children. *Journal of School Psychology*, 16, 208-211.

Kazden, A. E. (1980). *Research design in clinical psychology*. New York: Harper and Row.

Kerlinger, F. (1973). *Foundations of behavioral research* (2nd Ed.) New York: Holt, Rinehart and Winston.

Klee, T. (1985). Clinical language sampling: Analysing the analysis. *Child Language Teaching and Therapy*, 1:2, 182-198.

References

Kolzak, J. (1983). The impact of child language studies on mainstreaming decisions. In R. Truax & J. Shultz (Eds.), _Learning to communicate: Implications for the hearing impaired._ The Volta Review, 85:5, 129-137.

Kramer, P. E. (1977). Young children's free responses to anomolous commands. _Journal of Experimental Psychology,_ 24, 219-234.

Kretschmer, R., & Kretschmer, L. (1978). _Language development and intervention with the hearing impaired._ Baltimore, MD: University Park Press.

Lakoff, R. (1977). What can you do with words: Politeness, pragmatics, and performatives. In A. Rogers, B. Wall, & J. Murphy (Eds.) Proceedings of the Texas Conference on Performatives, Presuppositions and Implications. Arlington, VA: Center for Applied Linguistics.

Launer, P., & Lahey, M. (1981). Passages: From the fifties to the eighties in language assessment. _Topics in Language Disorders,_ 1:3, 11-29.

Lee, L. (1974). _Developmental sentence analysis._ Evanston, IL: Northwestern University Press.

Limber, J. (1973). The genesis of complex sentences. In T. Moore (Ed.), _Cognitive development and the acquisition of language_ (pp. 169-185). New York, NY: Academic Press.

Ling, D. (1976). _Speech and the hearing-impaired child: Theory and practice._ Washington, DC: The Alexander Graham Bell Society.

Longhurst, T., & Grubb, J. (1974). A comparison of language samples collected in four situations. _Language, Speech and Hearing Services in the Schools,_ 5:2, 71-78.

Lucas, E. (1980). _Semantic and pragmatic language disorders._ Rockville, MD: Aspen Systems Corp.

Luetke-Stahlman, B. (1982). A philosophy for assessing the language proficiency of hearing-impaired students to promote English literacy. _American Annals of the Deaf,_ 127:7, 844-851.

McDade, H. L., Simpson, M., & Lamb, D. E. (1982). The use of elicited imitation as a measure of expressive grammar: A question of validity. _Journal of Speech and Hearing Disorders,_ 47, 19-24.

References

McGinnis, M. (1985). Social language: Toward fluency and flexibility. In R. Truax & J. Shultz (Eds.), <u>Learning to communicate: Implications for the hearing impaired</u>. <u>The Volta Review</u>, 85;5, 101-115.

Meadow, K. P. (1978). The "natural history" of a research project. In L. Liben (Ed.), <u>Deaf children: Developmental perspectives</u> (pp. 21-40). New York: Academic Press.

Menyuk, P. (1969). <u>Sentences children use</u>. Cambridge, MA: The MIT Press.

Miller, J. F. (1981). <u>Assessing language production in children: Experimental procedures</u>. Baltimore, MD: University Park Press.

Miller, J. (1973). Sentence imitation in preschool children. <u>Language, Speech and Hearing Services in the Schools</u>, 16, 1-14.

Miller, J., & Chapman, R. (1975). Length variables in sentence imitation. <u>Language, Speech and Hearing</u>, 16, 1-14.

Miller, J., & Chapman, R. (1983). <u>SALT: Systematic analysis of language transcripts</u>. Madison, WI: Language Analysis Laboratory, Waisman Center, University of Wisconsin.

Muma, J. (1978). <u>Language handbook: Concepts, assessments, intervention</u>. Englewood Cliffs, NJ: Prentice-Hall, Inc.

Nelson, K. (1973). Structure and strategy in learning to talk. <u>Monographs of the Society for Research in Child Development</u>, 38 (Serial No. 149).

Ouellette, S. (1985). Cited in article, "Most deaf students leave college without receiving bachelor degrees." <u>Report on Education Research</u>, 17: sample issue, 4.

Owens, R. E. (1984). Language test content: A comparative study. <u>Language, Speech and Hearing Services in the Schools</u>, 14, 7-21.

Owings, N. O. (1972). Internal reliability and item analysis of the Miller-Yoder Test of Grammatical Comprehension. Unpublished Master's Thesis. Madison, WI: University of Wisconsin-Madison.

Popham, J. W. (1981). <u>Modern educational measurement</u>. Englewood Cliffs, N.J.: Prentice-Hall, Inc.

Power, D., & Quigley, S. (1973). Deaf children's acquisition of passive voice. <u>Journal of Speech and Hearing Research</u>, 16, 5-11.

References

Prutting, C., Gallagher, T., & Mulac, A. (1975). The expressive portion of the N.S.S.T. compared to a spontaneous language sample. *Journal of Speech and Hearing Disorders*, 40, 40-49.

Quigley, S. P., & Paul, P. V. (1984). *Language and deafness*. San Diego, CA: College-Hill Press.

Quigley, S. P., Smith N. L., & Wilbur, R. B. (1974). Comprehension of relativized sentences by deaf students. *Journal of Speech and Hearing Research*, 17, 325-342.

Quigley, S. P., Wilbur, R. B., Power, D. J., Montanelli, D. S., & Steinkamp, M. W. (1976). *Syntactic structures in the language of deaf children*. Urbana, IL: University of Illinois, Urbana-Champaign. Final Report, Project No. 232175, U. S. Department of Health, Education, and Welfare, National Institute of Education. ERIC Document #119447, available through ERIC Document Reproduction Services: paper (247 pages) and microfiche.

Roth, F. P., & Spekman, M. J. (1984). Assessing the pragmatic abilities of children: part I. Organizational framework and assessment parameters. *Journal of Speech and Hearing Disorders*, 49, 2-11.

Schirmer, B. (1985). An analysis of the language of young hearing-impaired children in terms of syntax, semantics and use. *American Annals of the Deaf*, 103:1, 15-19.

Schlesinger, I. M. (1971). Production of utterances and language acquisition. In D. I. Slobin (Ed.), *The otogenesis of grammar*. New York: Academic Press.

Silverman-Dresner, T., & Guilfoyle, G. (1972). *Vocabulary norms for deaf children*. Washington, DC: The Alexander Graham Bell Society.

Simon, C. S. (1981). *Communicative competence: A functional-pragmatic approach to language therapy* (Revised Edition). Tucson, Arizona: Communication Skill Builders, Inc.

Siple, P. (1978). *Understanding language through sign language research*. New York: Academic Press.

Slobin, D. I., & Welsh, C. A. (1973). Elicited imitation as a research tool in developmental psycholinguistics. In C. A. Ferguson and D. I. Slobin (Eds.), *Studies of child language development* (pp. 485-497). New York: Holt, Rinehart, and Winston.

References

Snow, C. (1977). The development of conversation between mothers and babies. Journal of Child Language, 4, 1-22.

Sowell, E. J., & Casey, R. J. (1982). Research methods in education. Belmont, CA: Wadsworth Pub. Co.

Streng, A. (1972). Syntax, speech and hearing. New York: Grune and Stratton.

Swisher, L. (1976). The language performance of the oral deaf. In H. Whitaker & H. A. Whitaker (Eds.), Studies in Neurolinguistics, 2, 59-93.

Swisher, M. V., & Thompson, M. (1985). Mothers learning simultaneous communication: The dimensions of the task. American Annals of the Deaf, 130:3, 212-217.

Taylor, L. (1984). Assessment of exceptional students: Educational and psychological procedures. Englewood Cliffs, NJ: Prentice-Hall, Inc.

Turnure, J., Buium, N. & Thurlow, M. (1976). The effectiveness of interrogatives for promoting verbal elaboration productively in young children. Child Development, 47, 851-855.

Tyack, D., & Gottsleben, R. (1974). Language sampling, analysis and training: A handbook for teachers and clinicians. Palo Alto, CA: Consulting Psychological Press.

deVilliers, J.G., & deVilliers, P.A. (1973). A cross-sectional study of the acquisition of grammatical morphemes. Journal of Psycholinguistic Research, 2, 267-278.

deVilliers, J.G., & deVilliers, P.A. (1978). Language acquisition. Cambridge, MA: Harvard University Press.

Wiig, E., & Semel, E. (1980). Language assessment and intervention. Columbus, OH: Charles E. Merrill.

White, B. L. (1975). The first three years of life. Englewood Cliffs, NJ: Prentice-Hall, Inc.

Williams, F. (1979). Reasoning with statistics. (2nd ed.) New York: Holt, Rinehart and Winston.

TESTS DESCRIBED IN SECTION VI, LISTED ALPHABETICALLY BY AUTHOS(S)

Bankson, N. W. (1977). *Bankson Language Screening Test*. Austin, TX: Pro Ed.

Blagden, C. M., & McConnell, N. L. (1983). *Interpersonal Language Skills Assessment*. Moline, IL: LinguiSystems, Inc.

Blank, M., Rose, S. A., & Berlin, L. J. (1978). *Preschool Language Assessment Instrument*. New York: Grune and Stratton.

Boehm, A. E. (1967, 1969, 1970, 1971). *Boehm Test of Basic Concepts*. New York: The Psychological Corporation.

Bracken, A. (1984). *Bracken Basic Concept Scale*. Columbus, OH: Charles E. Merrill.

Bunch, G. O. (1981). *Test of Expressive Language Ability*. Toronto: G. B. Services.

Bunch, G. O. (1981). *Test of Receptive Language Ability*. Toronto: G. B. Services.

Carrow-Woolfolk, E. (1974). *Carrow Elicited Language Inventory*. Allen, TX: DLM Teaching Resources.

Carrow-Woolfolk, E. (1985). *Test for Auditory Comprehension of Language - Revised*. Allen, TX: DLM Teaching Resources.

Coggins, T. E., & Carpenter, R. L. (1981). The Communicative Intention Inventory: A system for observing and coding children's early intentional communication. *Applied Psycholinguistics, 2*, 235-251.

Coplan, J. (1983). *Early Language Milestone Scale*. Tulsa, OK: Modern Education Corp.

Dunn, L. M., & Dunn, L. M. (1981). *Peabody Picture Vocabulary Test - Revised*. Circle Pines, MN: American Guidance Service.

Engen, E., & Engen, T. (1983). *Rhode Island Test of Language Structure*. Austin, TX: Pro Ed.

Foster, R., Gidden, J. J., & Stark, J. (1972). *Assessment of Children's Language Comprehension*. Palo Alto, CA: Consulting Psychologists Press.

Gardner, M. F. (1979, 1981). *Expressive One-Word Picture Vocabulary Test*. Novato, CA: Academic Therapy Publications.

Gardner, M. F. (1983). *Expressive One-Word Picture Vocabulary Test - Upper Extension*. Novato, CA: Academic Therapy Publications.

Gardner, M. F. (1985). *Receptive One-Word Picture Vocabulary Test*. Novato, CA: Academic Therapy Publications.

Hasenstab, M.S., & Laughton, J. (1982). Bare Essentials in Assessing Really Little Kids: An approach. In M.S. Hasenstab, & J. S. Horner (Eds.), *Comprehensive intervention with hearing-impaired infants and preschool children* (pp. 204-209). Rockville, MD: Aspen Publications.

Hedrick, D., Prather, E., & Tobin, A. (1975; revised ed., 1984). *Sequenced Inventory of Communication Development*. Seattle: University of Washington Press.

Jorgenson, C., Barrett, M., Huisingh, R., & Zackman, L. (1981). *The Word Test*. Moline, IL: LinguiSystems, Inc.

Kirk, S. A., McCarthy, J. J., & Kirk, W. D. (1961, 1969). *Illinois Test of Psycholinguistic Abilities*. Urbana, IL: University of Illinois Press.

Layton, T. L., & Holmes, D. W. (1985). *Carolina Picture Vocabulary Test*. Tulsa, OK: Modern Education Corporation.

Lee, L. L. (1971). *Northwestern Syntax Screening Test*. Evanston, IL: Northwestern University Press.

Longhurst, T. M., Briery, D., & Emery, M. (1975). *SKI-HI Receptive Language Test*. Logan, UT: Project SKI-HI, Utah State University.

Miller, J. F., & Yoder, D. E. (1984). *The Miller-Yoder Test of Grammatical Comprehension: Clinical Edition*. Austin, TX: Pro Ed.

Moog, J. S., & Geers, A. E. (1975). *CID Scales of Early Communication Skills for Hearing-Impaired Children*. St. Louis, MO: Central Institute for the Deaf.

Moog, J. S., & Geers, A. E. (1979). *Grammatical Analysis of Elicited Language*. St. Louis, MO: Central Institute for the Deaf.

Moog, J. S., & Kozak, V. J. (1983). *Teacher Assessment of Grammatical Structures*. St. Louis, MO: Central Institute for the Deaf.

Project RHISE (1979). *Rockford Infant Developmental Evaluation Scales*. Bensenville, IL: Scholastic Testing Service, Inc.

Tests

Quigley, S. P., Steinkamp, M. W., Power, D. J., & Jones, B. (1978). *Test of Syntactic Abilities*. Beaverton, OR: Dormac, Inc.

Scherer, P. (1981). *Total Communication Receptive Vocabulary Test*. Northbrook, IL: Mental Health & Deafness Resources, Inc.

Shipley, K. G., Stone, T. A., & Sue, M. B. (1983). *Test for Examining Expressive Morphology*. Tucson, AZ: Communication Skill Builders.

Tonelson, S., & Watkins, S. (1979). *The SKI-HI Language Development Scale*. Logan, UT: Project SKI-HI, Utah State University.

Vane, J. R. (1975). *Vane Evaluation of Language Scale*. Brandon, VT: Clinical Psychology Publishing Co., Inc.

Warner, E. O'H., & Kresheck, J. (1983). *Structured Photographic Expressive Language Test - II*. Sandwich, IL: Janelle Publications, Inc.

White, A. H. (1981). *Maryland Syntax Evaluation Instrument*. Sanger, TX: Support Systems for the Deaf.

GLOSSARY

<u>AMERICAN SIGN LANGUAGE (ASL)</u> - is a gestural/visual language created and used by the deaf community in the United States. American Sign Language is also known as ASL, Sign, or Ameslan, and is now recognized as a separate, distinct language from English. It is a language in which arbitrary but rule-governed combinations of handshapes, positions, orientations, and movements are the meaningful units that are comparable to morphemes in spoken language. Use of space and movement, along with facial expression and body posturing, also serve roles in its syntax and semantics.

<u>CORRELATION COEFFICIENT</u> - is a descriptive statistic which summarizes the strength of the relationship between two variables. Most correlation coefficients are symbolized by r, R, or the Greek p. A high correlation indicates that the variables "go together," have common elements, etc., whereas a low correlation suggests that the variables are relatively independent of one another.

<u>CRITERION-REFERENCED MEASUREMENT</u> - is a type of measurement concerned with whether or not a particular performance measure stops at, falls below, or exceeds a predetermined point.

<u>EXPRESSIVE LANGUAGE</u> - is the process of forming ideas or thoughts, finding words or signs to express them, formulating sentences to provide structure to the words, and producing the combined product in a spoken or signed form.

<u>FREQUENCY DISTRIBUTION</u> - is a tabulation of the frequency of occurrence of each value or interval of values for a particular variable.

<u>MEAN</u> - is the sum of a set of observations divided by the number of observations. It is the "center of gravity" of the observations, for which the deviations from the mean on the "high side" are balanced by the deviations from the mean on the "low side." Mean = average.

MEDIAN – is a point on a scale from a set of observations which has as many observations above it as there are below it. It is a point which divides the frequency distribution in half, and corresponds therefore to the 50th percentile. It is the measure of "central tendency."

MLU – Mean length of utterance: A method of evaluating the expressive language of young children using a set of rules whereby the utterances or morphemes of the children are counted and averaged.

MODE – is that observation in a set of data which occurs more often than any other observation.

M – Modifier: A word that expands upon the meaning of other words such as an adjective or adverb, or, in some instances, another noun; e.g., doll, baby doll.

MORPHEME – is the smallest unit of meaning in a language. Morphemes can be classified as either free or bound morphemes, depending upon whether or not they can occur in isolation or as a word in a sentence.

MORPHOLOGY – is the set of rules for forming words out of morphemes, the smallest meaningful units in our language.

N – Noun: A word that identifies people, places, objects (sweater, mother, home). Can, by different *use* in sentences, change to another form; e.g., a run (noun) in a stocking changes to a verb in "Run to the store!"

NORMS – are devices for interpreting scores on standardized tests. An individual's raw score is compared with the distribution of raw scores obtained by some well defined group of individuals (the "norm" group).

NP – Noun phrase: A group of words formed by combining nouns and modifiers that can act as the subject, direct object, or indirect object in a sentence; e.g., the beautiful brown dog.

Glossary

PRAGMATICS - is the use of language; the reasons people speak or use language and the influence of context on how people choose the form of language to use in order to reach their communicative goals.

RECEPTIVE LANGUAGE - refers to the ability of a person within a given community to understand the incoming language from those around him. The language input may be signed or spoken or both. The person receives and processes the spoken or signed messages composed of words, phrases, clauses, and sentences and is able to demonstrate an understanding of this information.

SEMANTICS - is the study of the relationships between words and grammatical forms in a language and their underlying meaning. The semantic component of language is concerned with the meanings of single words and word combinations, with multiple word meanings, with figurative language, and the effect of structure and context on the nature of meaning.

SIMULTANEOUS COMMUNICATION - involves the concurrent use of signs and fingerspelling with speech.

STANDARD DEVIATION - is one of the most precise measures of the degree of dispersion ("spread") of a frequency distribution. In a very rough sense it is a measure of how far the "typical" observation deviates from the mean of the observations. A distribution which has a large standard deviation has a big spread of scores around the mean; a distribution which has a small (near zero) standard deviation has very little spread.

SYNTAX - is a set of rules for stringing words, phrases, and clauses together in an acceptabale pattern which will be understood by people with whom you communicate. For example, in English, "The boy went home with his mother" is acceptable word order;* "The home boy with mother went" is not.

TOTAL COMMUNICATION - is a method of education which incorporates use of appropriate aural, oral, manual, tactile, and visual modes of communication to ensure effective communication with and among hearing-impaired persons.

Glossary

<u>TRANSFORMATION</u> - is a process by which rules are used in order to add to, delete, or reorder basic sentences in order to produce variations in the surface structure; e.g., adding "do" and reordering as in "Do you want to go?" or deleting "that" as in "I want something (that) you have".

<u>V</u> - verb: A word that expresses existence, action, occurrence, or feelings.

V_I - Intransitive verb: A verb that is used in such a way that it does <u>not</u> require a direct object; e.g., "The boy <u>ran</u>."

V_T - Transitive verb: A verb used in such a way that it requires a direct object such as "The boy <u>hit</u> ____" (the ball, the other boy, etc.).

<u>VP</u> - Verb phrase: A group of words formed by using verbs in all their forms, auxiliary verbs, adverbs, and prepositional phrases; e.g., ____ jumped over the fence.

INDEX

American Sign Language (ASL), 21, 88
   assessment of, 94
Attention span, 87
Chronological age, 67, 75, 86-87
"cloze," 86
Cognition development, 77
Communication modes, 69, 88
Communicative intentions, 8
Conductive hearing loss, 87
Content, 18
   as test battery consideration, 18
   semantics, 18
Corrected age, 67
Correlation, 36-37
Criterion-Referenced, 33-34
Developmental age (DA), (See Functional age)
Developmental Sentence Analysis, 99-100
Developmental Sentence Score (DSS), 99
Diagnostic test, 38-39
Discourse, 106, 139
"Discourse mechanism," 10
Expressive language, 7, 53
   assessment of, 28, 55, 77, 85, 101, 106-107, 111-114, 146-147, 157
Form, of language, 14, 16
   as test battery consideration, 68
   phonology, 14
   morphology, 14
   syntax, 14, 16

Formal testing, 40, 53
   administration, 85
   test battery consideration, 68
Functional age (FA), 52, 67, 75, 86-87
Functors, 22
Health, 87
Hearing aids, 87
Informal testing, 54
   examples of, 54
   test battery consideration, 68
Intervention Plan, 77-78, 107
Language
   assessment, 27-28, 52
   components, 8-10, 14, 16, 18
   definition of, 7
   development in hearing-impaired children, 21-23, 25-26
   tests, (See Language tests)
Language component, 69
Language sample, 85, 96-107, 110-114, 139-147, 157, 165
   elicited, 97-98
   examples of, 146-147, 157
   formal, 98-100
   informal, 100-105
   recording, 106-107, 110-114
   spontaneous, 98
   written, 97
Language Sample Analysis, 111-112
Language tests
   evaluation components, 31-41

language sample, 85,
  96-107, 110-114, 139-147,
  157, 165
  obtaining, 31
  reasons for testing, 29
  review, 29
  test battery, 52-55,
  65-69, 75, 77-78, 84-91,
  93-95
Lexicon (See Vocabulary)
Lighting, 87
Mean Length of Utterance (MLU),
  21, 87-88, 106-107
Modifiers, 139
Morphology, 14
Norm group, 32-33
Norm-referenced, 33
Passive Voice, 9
Phonology, 14
Pragmatics, 8-10
  as test battery
  consideration, 68
  assessment of, 55
  communicative intentions, 8
  "discourse mechanisms," 10
  hearing-impaired
  population, 23, 25
  major aspects of, 8-10
  "social-signaling," 10
  spontaneous language
  sample, 98-102, 105-106
Presupposition, 9, 106
Receptive language, 7, 53
  assessment of, 28, 52, 77,
  84-85, 147, 157
Reinforcement, 89
Reliability, of test, 37-39
  screening vs. diagnostic
  test, 38
  Kuder-Richardson (K-R), 38
  parallel forms, 37

split-half, 38
test-retest, 37
Resource personnel, 93-95
Scales,
  Language/Communication,
  54-55
Screening tests, 38-39
  as part of test battery, 68
Semantics, 18, 140-145
"social signaling," 10
Sensorineural hearing loss, 87
Simultaneous communication, 5,
  88-89
  assessment of, 94
Social Language, 139
Syntax, 14, 16, 102, 139-140
Systematic Analysis of Language
  Transcripts (SALT), 112
Test battery, 52-55
  administration, 84-91, 93-95
  development, 65-69
  examples, 69
  for hearing-impaired child,
  75, 77-78
  language sample, 85,
  96-107, 110-114, 139-147,
  157, 165
  modifications, 82-83
Test Environment, 87, 87, 91
Test Modification, 82-83
Test Reliability, (See
  Reliability)
Test Validity, (See Validity)
Tests, (Also see Language
  tests)
  descriptions, (See Section
  VI: Test Descriptions)
  teacher/clinician made, 54
Total Communication, 89
Turn-taking, 101

Use of language (See
    Pragmatics)
Validity of test, 34
    construct validity, 34, 36
    content validity, 34-35
    criterion-related
    validity, 34, 36
    face validity, 34-35
Verbs, 142-145
Videotaping, 95, 104
Vocabulary, 18
    assessment of, 77, 86, 139